INTERPRETING POLICEWORK

INTERPRETING POLICEWORK

Policy and Practice in Forms of Beat Policing

ROGER GRIMSHAW

and

TONY JEFFERSON

University of Sheffield

London
ALLEN & UNWIN
Boston   Sydney   Wellington

**Allen & Unwin, the academic imprint of
Unwin Hyman Ltd**

PO Box 18, Park Lane, Hemel Hempstead, Herts HP2 4TE, UK
40 Museum Street, London WC1A 1LU, UK
37/39 Queen Elizabeth Street, London SE1 2QB, UK

Allen & Unwin Inc.,
8 Winchester Place, Winchester, Mass. 01890, USA

Allen & Unwin (Australia) Ltd,
8 Napier Street, North Sydney, NSW 2060, Australia

Allen & Unwin (New Zealand) Ltd in association with the
Port Nicholson Press Ltd,
60 Cambridge Terrace, Wellington, New Zealand

First published in 1987

British Library Cataloguing in Publication Data

Grimshaw, Roger
  Interpreting policework: policy and
practice in forms of beat policing
1. Police – Great Britain
I. Title II. Jefferson, Tony
363.2'3'0941   HV8195.A2
ISBN 0–04–363010–3
ISBN 0–04–363011–1 Pbk

Library of Congress Cataloging-in-Publication Data

Grimshaw, Roger.
  Interpreting policework.
Bibliography: p.
Includes index.
1. Police – Great Britain. 2. Police patrol – Great Britain.
I. Jefferson, Tony. II. Title.
HV8195.A3J44 1987   363.2'32'0941   86–25935
ISBN 0–04–363 010–3 (alk. paper)
ISBN 0–04–363011–1 (pbk.: alk. paper)

Set in 10 on 11 point Imprint by Computape (Pickering) Ltd
and printed in Great Britain by
Billing and Sons Ltd, London and Worcester

CONTENTS

FOREWORD AND
ACKNOWLEDGEMENTS

Conducting research on the police is not easy. To get off the ground at all involves bringing together institutions, such as the police, universities and the Home Office whose interests are not coincident. To continue to a mutually satisfactory conclusion, therefore, involves the maintenance of a sometimes 'teeth gritting' harmony. And to write up involves bearing in mind one's debt to all the divergent institutional interests that made it possible, one's responsibilities to the next generation of researchers, and finally, and by no means least, one's responsibilities to one's conscience. Moreover, there is an (understandable) temptation, 'when it's all over', to remember, like summers of yesteryear, only the days when the sun shone brilliantly all day and long into the evening. In truth, past summers were always more variable than selective memory allows – as was the route taken by the research project upon which this book is based.

The project had its origins in a Home Office research fellowship, instituted at the Centre for Criminological and Socio-Legal Studies, Sheffield University, and taken up by Tony Jefferson in October 1977. Since the normal relationship between the Home Office and the research it funds is via direct contracting, this indirect form of arrangement, via a university fellowship, was an unusual initiative, only the second of its kind. As beneficiaries of that bold initiative, and the freedom it granted to plan and execute research completely untrammelled by Home Office policy-dominated interests, we are extremely grateful for the opportunity it gave us. Yet there is no doubt that that same freedom, given the Home Office's interest in policy *for* the police, and the universities in *explaining* (in our case and among other things) policies *of* the police, was the seed bed for later disagreements over our submitted report (Jefferson and Grimshaw, 1981).

By that time, Roger Grimshaw had long been a member of the research team (since October 1978); but also the status of the project had changed, when Tony Jefferson secured a lectureship in January 1980, to a piece of traditional contract research. So, whilst gratefully mindful of our opportunity, and not unaware of shifts taking place within the Home Office Research Unit itself, we were led to perceive a crucial axis of differentiation between the two institutions – the Home Office and the university – which could not be dissolved by good intentions. It is a difference which is, to anticipate a key theme of the book, *structural*. Not surprisingly then, our disagreements with the Home Office focused around the 'relevance *for* (rather than *of*) policy' of the submitted report; difficulties which led, in the event, to the completion of a supplementary Appendix drawing out the policy implications.

Similarly, the divergence of interests between the university and the police is structural. Any conjunction of an institution given the power to uphold order in a society undergoing profound and painful economic and social transformations, and one with the responsibility for examining and explaining the exercise of that power, can hardly be easily harmonious. It is not, therefore, paranoia that causes police to resist observation and examination on the grounds that whatever emerges will not be 'for them'; sociology of the police, as police know too well, *is* always critical – even when not conducted within a radical tradition. Since police apparently have so little to gain from opening their doors, we wish to express our real gratitude to the Chief Constable for the facilities and access granted us. It was unique in its extent, and, like the Home Office, bold in the current context which gives chief constables absolute powers over access decisions. Whilst we feel exceptionally privileged in the access we were granted, allowing us to reach into areas that other researchers hardly dared dream of, and enabling us to fully pursue the generality of our research, two points need also to be made; such access was not granted without considerable negotiations, and was not without some (albeit small) losses of particular access locations requested, a point we make not out of churlishness but to remind those who follow not to expect that doors will simply open, Ali Baba-like, on the production of some magic words. Secondly, to remind our readers of the important political point that, ultimately, such decisions, so crucial to the success or otherwise of a research project, lie with an unelected public official – a chief constable. It is this latter point which renders us ambivalent about our 'privilege'; quite simply, grateful though we are, it ought not to be a privilege in a society claiming the mantle democratic, but should be an expectation that researchers and others subject the exercise of power to objective and critical scrutiny. Hopefully our work, like that of other researchers, will help to demonstrate the value of that access.

Thanks are also due to those individuals within the force who fulfilled a contact and liaison role during the period of the research. And officers whom we accompanied on patrol and visits, etc., as well as those who consented to be interviewed, are owed our thanks for their co-operation. We hope that they will understand that our primary sociological interests are expressed in what might otherwise be seen as individious scrutiny of their daily work.

Studying the police in action always requires that a deep breath be taken before committing the findings to paper. The sharp splash of new experience, after entry to a normally closed world, is invigorating but transition to the stage of written report needs careful consideration, the more so the deeper the penetration of an uncharted territory. The writer's responsibility lies in handling this difficult process of making the invisible visible, all the while with the consent of those who usually maintain that invisibility in place. For such reasons our lengthy main report to the Home Office was preoccupied with theoretical clarification and general description; its completion, however, was delayed until a year after the project had formally ceased. In particular we had embarked on a further joint project that took up those theoretical lines of investigation but was applied specifically to the pressing issue of police accountability. Though material from the Home Office Report was published at around the same time (Jefferson and Grimshaw, 1984a), it was the accountability study that found book length form first (Jefferson and Grimshaw, 1984b). The involution of two research themes within the limiting scope of our work schedules meant that this more substantial, analytical version of our work on organization and control has taken some years to appear. While the intellectual fruits of longer consideration may be significant, we are aware that the presentation of particular empirical facts is sometimes felt to suffer from the passage of time, as identifiable changes serve to freeze some detailed patterns into the glacier of history. The major institutional innovation that has supervened in the interim is probably the Police and Criminal Evidence Act 1984, whose significance receives some attention in the latter part of the text. However, our concerns are not with the documenting of recent police history but with the elucidation of sociologically-defined structures that underwrite the development of modern policing. For this purpose the detail of observed policing more than retains its relevance into the mid-80s. Consequently after some consultation we have normally adopted the 'historical' or 'continuous' present tense in recounting our observations and in general discussion.

We should, however, draw attention to the fact that the Home Office advised the consistent use of the past tense because, like the researched force, they felt that inferences about subsequent events should not be drawn from data collected some years earlier. This point had been raised in connection with the final draft of our discussion of policy on community policing and racial attacks in particular, now slightly amended. Though we obviously cannot comment on empirical changes that may have taken place in the force's consideration of policy, nor any other changes for that matter, we must reiterate our concern to produce a structural analysis. The resolution of structural questions is not necessarily affected by the mere passage of time. The vital issue is whether any observed change would lead us to conclude that a structural alteration had occurred. On this point our material remains singularly relevant to any structural assessment of the present state of affairs, as Chapter 9 in particular seeks to demonstrate.

From the beginning the research process was overseen by a Steering Committee chaired by Professor Tony Bottoms, then Director of the Centre, now of the Institute of Criminology, Cambridge. We should like to thank him and other members of that Committee – Keith Bottomley, Maureen Cain, Ken Lidstone, Ian Taylor, John Westergaard, Paul Wiles, Sir John Wood and Ron Broome – for their sympathetic advice and support throughout the period of research. We also wish to acknowledge the long-standing counsel of others who have ventured into the hinterlands of police sociology, notably Stuart Hall, Mike Brogden, Joe Sim and Robert Reiner. These helped to sustain our belief in the validity and relevance of a sociology closely pursuing the detail of the police organization.

The crucial dimension of administrative and secretarial support was provided by Barbara Holland, Shirley Peacock, Lynn Rance, Vera Marsh, Annie Lutwama and Connie Goodwin. Family and friends endured the many phases of production in the making of this book; to them apologies, as well as thanks, would seem most appropriate.

We are grateful to the publishers of the *International Journal of the Sociology of Law* for allowing us, in Chapter 8, to draw substantially on our article 'The problem of law enforcement policy in England and Wales: the case of community policing and racial attacks', *IJSL*, vol. 12, no. 2, pp. 117–35.

Finally we must always turn to 'the public', especially people in police contact who tolerated our presence at times of anger or distress. We did not give them anything resembling succour. But we can offer, now, a form of knowledge that opens up for inspection some of the foundations of power in this society. Indirectly, the fulfilment of one duty to the public has therefore been attempted.

We are not the first academic researchers to reflect upon

discords – as well as harmonies – between universities and the police, as Jerome Skolnick can testify. What we hope above all is that the fruits of the research will on balance be felt to justify the efforts, stresses and sacrifices of all the various parties. But that judgement, of course, rests above all with the readers.

August 1986

PART I

Theories and Methodologies

CHAPTER ONE

Shaping a Structural Lens

Introduction

The police are currently the subject of controversy. Criticisms of the police have come to form a regular pattern, covering such issues as police–black relations, the use of firearms and other technology and the question of complaints against the police. At the same time defenders of the police are not slow to come forward, and it has recently become more frequent for chief police officers to take on this role – an intervention which critics have seen as a further cause for concern. The seriousness of the issues affecting policework has increased in the 1980s, most particularly because of the urban riots of 1981 and 1985 and the turbulent mining dispute of 1984–5, from which significant controversies have arisen about the use of police powers and the direction of police operations.[1]

The research on which this book is based took place in 1978–80, before the convulsions of the spring and summer of 1981. However, its scope and objectives were addressed to the kind of issue that has subsequently given rise to increasing anxiety. In dealing with a Metropolitan County Force, in an area of ethnic settlement and incipient economic decline, it could not overlook some of the key questions that presently occupy so much attention. At the same time the research was concerned to establish what routine policing in this context looked like rather than to investigate particular eruptions. It is this sense of the 'normal' that we hope will be conveyed, as an essential background for understanding the more explosive events that punctuate the history of modern policing.

The archetypal representative of the 'normal' in policing is perhaps the uniformed beat constable on patrol, available at all hours to succour the helpless or restrain the disorderly. This 'peace-keeping' image contrasts favourably in the eyes of many with the more coercive forms of policework which are on view episodically. Moreover the beat constable remains a predominant feature of British policing, numerically overshadowing the special departments, squads and administrative units which make up the rest of the force (cf. Jones, 1980). While the introduction of police support units has added a new dimension to the traditional role of the ordinary constable (cf. State Research, 1980), the demands of normal peace-keeping have maintained their importance, particularly in view of the rise of community policing philosophies which recommend just this kind of reassuring contact with the public. Indeed, the recent extent of publicized conflict in British society, in which the police have played a significant role, has increased the perceived requirement for a pacifying and tranquillizing influence, building bridges and healing community wounds in the aftermath of social strife.[2] The study of beat-work in its various forms represents a suitable empirical subject on the basis of which more general reflections on the theory of organized policework can be produced. In another work we have also looked at other parts of the police organization – the CID and the SPG (Special Patrol Group) – and our theoretical approach has thus been enriched by a wider comparison than we can encompass here (Jefferson and Grimshaw, 1981). However, on grounds of relevance and scope, beat-work forms our chosen illustration in the present book.

Our interest in routine policing was sparked by a dissatisfaction with existing texts variously 'explaining' police activity, in particular their collective failure to offer an adequate framework for understanding organized policework. It was also fuelled by the political implications of this failure. The research – which entailed a detailed examination of the policies and practices of one large metropolitan force – attempted to develop such a framework and to draw out the political implications. This book is the result.

The purpose of this opening chapter is preparatory to that task. Specifically, we intend:

(1) to demonstrate the inadequacies of existing explanations;
(2) to outline the elements culled from existing accounts that, transformed and developed, will provide the basis for a new framework, and to illustrate concretely how this might be achieved;
(3) to offer a new framework using these transformed elements;
(4) to produce a series of conflicting hypotheses, one series based

on the questionable explanations reviewed in (1) and one
based on our reconstructed framework;
(5) to overview the methodology and empirical scope of the entire
project;
(6) to outline the scheme of the book as a whole.

The political implications of all this will be dealt with in our
concluding chapter, Chapter 9.

Existing Explanations and Inadequate 'Problematics'

The influential work of Althusser, the Marxist philosopher, has
suggested that a study's theoretical starting-point sets definite
limits on the type of analysis that can be adopted, on the capacity
of the analysis to handle certain questions and on the 'theoretical'
answers it is possible to arrive at (Althusser, 1969). In short, this
theoretical starting-point defines a 'problematic': ' "a definite
theoretical structure", a field of concepts, which organizes a
particular science or individual text by making it possible to ask
some kinds of questions and by suppressing others' (Johnson,
1979, p. 201). The adequacy of a 'problematic' resides in its ability
to produce accounts or to answer certain questions in ways which
are consistent and non-contradictory. It is our contention that the
two main 'problematics' informing policework studies – 'sociological liberalism' and 'class functionalism' – fail on this criterion.
A primary purpose in our survey of the literature will be to
demonstrate this.

Even were this not so, we judge these problematics inadequate
on other grounds. In the case of 'sociological liberalism', studies
are plagued by the twin inadequacies of empiricism (the drawing
of inferences from the self-evident appearance of an arrangement
of given 'facts') and idealism (choosing a starting-point in the
realm of ideas rather than material reality); in the case of 'class
functionalism', the equivalent inadequacies are 'economism' (the
reduction of all political and cultural activities to mere epiphe-
nomena, 'superstructural' reflections of an economic 'base') and
voluntarism (the reduction of activity to the chosen 'will' of a social
class) – what Althusser and Balibar (1970, p. 114) have dubbed
'twin essentialisms'. Thus, a second focus of the following survey
will be these inadequacies and their repercussions: the inevitably
partial and selective notion of policework which emerges from the
empiricists; the assertive and essentially unexamined one which
comes from the idealists; and the 'reductive' functionalist picture,

one which elides or trivializes the specific content of actual police activities, bequeathed us by the class functionalists.

Additionally, we shall use the material to highlight those elements which, transformed and developed, will provide the basis for our own framework. In this respect we regard it as a mistake, made by many, to reduce studies to the 'essence' of the problematic underlying them and, on that basis, to discard them wholesale. Such is the 'rationalist' flaw in the Althusserian critique which has otherwise been so enlightening on this question. Rather, we follow the assumption adopted by Johnson that 'the concepts that constitute a given problematic are not "all of a piece" ', and that 'as elements, reorganised, they may constitute the basis for more adequate accounts' (Johnson, 1979, p. 202). In short, whilst the critique of existing problematics provides the starting-point, the basis of the new problematic can still be the existing conceptual elements, but *re*conceptualized and reorganized: 'elements taken from different existing problematics may, in a new order and constituting a new field, yield us greater explanatory power and political purchase' (ibid.).

It is our intention, then, to demonstrate in the following critique the various inadequacies of existing problematics and to offer the basis for a reconceptualization of policework – a 'new' problematic – by showing how some of the conceptual elements present in existing problematics might be profitably reworked.

Sociological Liberalism

We have found it most useful to group these studies of organized policework into three, according to their conception of the organization: the 'machine' model, the 'subcultural' model and the 'environmental' model.[3]

THE 'MACHINE' MODEL
The first of these implicitly or explicitly conceives the organization as a 'machine' in which individual actors within the organization simply execute the directives of superior authority. Knowledge of the formal organization or structure – its rules, procedures and policies – is thus sufficient to understand the normal functioning of an organization, since 'individual behaviour will directly follow organizational dictates' (Friedrich, 1978, p. 84). It derives, as Etzioni reminds us, from the 'classical theory of administration' or 'scientific-management' approach to organizations (Etzioni, 1964, p. 20) and has been widely criticized for its attention to the 'ideal' (how organizations ought to

function) at the expense of the 'real' (how organizations actually work).[4]

For our purposes, we can identify a 'legal' and an 'organizational variant' (Friedrich, 1978). The legal variant refers to those studies where law is seen as the higher authority dictating appropriate police action, best exemplified, as Bittner (1970, p. 14) suggests, in an article by Jerome Hall (1953, pp. 133–77). Whilst such an approach to the sociology of law enforcement has largely given way to the 'law-in-action' approach,[5] the organizational variant lives on in standard textbooks concerned with police management (cf. Bunyard, 1978). Though this approach is clearly idealistic in its failure to examine concretely the relation between individual behaviour and organizational dictates, we mention it to highlight the 'law-in-the-books' and the formal structure of an organization – aspects to which subsequent scholars, concerned with either the law-in-action or organization-in-action, have failed to give any serious attention.

THE 'SUBCULTURAL' MODEL

The 'subcultural' model of the police organization best exemplifies this last criticism. Concerned with the idealistic inadequacies of the 'machine'-model approaches, and committed to participant observation as the primary and sometimes exclusive methodological tool, studies produced from within this approach have focused on the occupational milieux of police officers. In relation to organizational theory, such studies in effect borrowed the notion of 'informal organization' – the principal concept of the human-relations approach to organizations developed in opposition to the notion of formal organization utilized by the scientific management school. This concern with informality emphasizes 'the emotional, unplanned, non-rational elements in organisational behaviour ... [and] the significance of friendship and social groupings of workers for the organisation' (Etzioni, 1964, p. 20).

From the perspective of subcultural theory, such studies can be seen as attempts to define and explain the nature of the norms, customs, values and practices of a particular occupational group: its occupational subculture. Later studies broadly within the same genre, though infused with the theoretical insights of symbolic interactionism and ethnomethodology, exhibit a greater concern for detailed ethnography and a heavier reliance on the shifting dynamics of situational encounters in explaining police behaviour (cf. Punch, 1979a, p. 103). Whilst we cannot do justice to particular studies here, it is interesting how similar themes recur across studies, with the overall picture being one of an embattled occupational group at odds with both the public and senior officers. This embattled self-image is a consequence of, in Manning's (1971) words, an 'impossible mandate': the contradictory organizational demands of high productivity, judged in terms of arrest, on the one hand, together with the requirement of strict adherence to legal rules, on the other. This conflict is resolved deviantly, by illegal corner-cutting. Routine deviance requires the 'cover-up'; hence cultural norms like secrecy and loyalty become important, the latter being reinforced by the need for group defence against a hostile, occasionally violent public. The peculiar structure of the work – often self-generated and all but invisible to supervisors – reinforces these characteristics. Across studies and through time, deviance, the cover-up, secrecy, colleague loyalty, mistrust of outsiders, cynicism and violence recur as characteristics – to which are opposed 'due process', senior officers and the public. Such a picture emerges from the early postwar work of Westley (1970), is continued in the later work of Skolnick (1975) and is still relatively unchanged in the more recent work of Holdaway (1983); across three decades and one ocean, little has apparently changed.[6]

But whilst we learn enormously from these studies about the daily grind of routine policework – about working practices, group values, colleague relationships, the situational dynamics of street encounters and routine stereotyping – we learn next to nothing about the law (except the supposed conflict between procedural rules and substantive law, which allegedly engenders much of the deviance; cf. Skolnick, 1975) or about force organization, policy and senior officers (except that the latter are committed to a kind of 'managerial professionalism' in line with the mandate that the organization is formally constructed to uphold; cf. Holdaway, 1977). In short, whilst the daily happenings, on the streets and in the locker room, are examined in all their apparently kaleidoscopic variations, the law, the formal organization, its policies and senior officers are all assumptive categories: essentially unexamined. In so far as these enter the analysis they enter as normative systems from which the police subculture deviates. Thus the relationship between the organization and the law, and between senior officers and the organization, remains, in Bittner's (1970) disparaging term, 'norm-derivative'; i.e. the behaviour of senior officers is 'derived' from the organization's presumed goals; and the organization's goals are 'derived' from the presumed norms embodied in law. Deviant police behaviour, minutely examined, finds its *alter ego* in an essentially unexamined normative system. The 'realistic' examination of rank-and-file beliefs and activities is, ironically, accompanied by a hopelessly idealistic conception of the beliefs and activities of police managers.

In general, what remains indispensable to all the explanations from within this approach is the notion that the organization itself, apparently committed to the highest ideals of integrity and legality, succeeds only in producing, as an apparently essential coping mechanism, the opposite, i.e. a subculture of deviance. Yet our next model, the 'environmental', demonstrates that this is not always the case.

THE 'ENVIRONMENTAL' MODEL

The 'environmental' model of police organization stands, in certain respects, somewhere between the two previous models. Uncommitted to the ethnographic approach as *the* research methodology, and hence to the prioritizing of the meaning systems of organizational actors, yet also critical of the reduction of the organization to its formal structure conceived in isolation from its social environment, the principal contribution of studies embracing this approach has been to attempt to conceive the organization itself – and not simply its agents – in a social way. In so doing, these studies conceive the behaviour of the organization – its structure, policies and working practices – as the product of a series of negotiations with what Reiss and Bordua call its 'environing system' (1967, p. 25).

Perhaps the best examples of this approach are the studies of Reiss and Bordua (1967) and Wilson (1968). The work of Reiss and Bordua represents what they call an 'orienting image' (p. 25) rather than completed research. It is none the less instructive. The discussion is centred upon 'a few basic environmental features' and their 'internal consequences' in terms of 'organisational transactions and internal processes, especially ... problems of production, strategy and tactics, and command and control' (p. 26). The environmental features they select for discussion are 'the nature of the legal system, the nature of violative activity and civic accountability' (p. 26). We do not intend to deal in any detail with the article, except to draw attention to the difference between the conception of law advanced here and the more abstract conception advanced by those who, like Skolnick (1975), regard the law as an abstract entity consisting of the substantive law and due process – a relatively common formulation. For Reiss and Bordua, with a more institutional perspective, the law affecting police organizations is a concrete legal system which 'is not a seamless web of tightly articulated rules and roles ... but a loose-jointed system held together at many points by microsystems of antagonistic cooperation and discretionary decisions' (p. 26). We do not have to agree with the particular breakdown of the legal system adopted – the 'legality', 'legal content', 'legal order' and 'government' components – to appreciate the advantages that such a concrete conception of law promises.

Although Reiss and Bordua also comment upon the relation between different styles of 'command and control' and the nature of 'civic accountability' to which police chiefs are subject, it is J. Q. Wilson (1968) whose work in this area is seminal and all but unique.[7] Wilson's work consists of an empirical study and not simply an 'orienting image'. What Wilson appears to have demonstrated is that there is an observable relationship between the working 'style' of officers, departmental policies and organizational codes, and the prevailing political culture. Whilst Wilson is concerned to suggest that much of what he says in the book is 'not proved' (p. 13), that the impact of policies on behaviour are 'gross' and 'imprecise' (p. 279) because of the existence of legal discretion, and that the political environment is more of a sensitizing than a governing constraint (p. 230), his approach remains, to our mind, important because it attempts to link police behaviour to organizational and legal constraints, and to the composition of the community and its prevailing style of political administration. Once again, we do not have to go along with the particular results achieved to appreciate the merits of the approach, especially the idea that different organizational strategies can affect at least some areas of police behaviour some of the time – an idea which flatly contradicts the findings of the subculturalists – and that the nature of the constraints imposed by the 'community' is an important matter for consideration along with legal and organizational constraints. Furthermore, Wilson's analysis reminds us that the community is not a single entity composed of a uniformly hostile public but consists of communities, sometimes homogeneous in terms of race and class, sometimes divided. Again, the particular characterization of communities described is less important than the recognition of a *differentiated* public with consequent differential effects on organizational strategies and police behaviour.[8]

Whilst the 'environmental' approach serves as a useful corrective to the 'machine' approach (with its exclusive attention to the formal structure) and to the 'subcultural' approach (with its over-reliance on observed behaviour and its meaning for organizational actors), its weaknesses represent precisely the strengths of the other approaches. Thus, despite the help of numerous research assistants, Wilson is unable to give the eight communities chosen for particular study the kind of detailed attention that constitutes the merit of the ethnographic approach. His statement that 'each of the cities included in this book was visited at least twice and usually three or four times for periods of no less than three weeks and in some cases for nearly two months by at least two researchers, who then compared notes' (1968, p. 14) might be considered by some researchers committed to a participant observation methodology as inadequate to achieve the kind of detailed understanding of police behaviour that they would deem necessary. Similarly, the understanding of the formal structure lacks the kind of detail that the 'machine'-model approach would appear to prescribe (although, in reality, it fails to deliver). Thus, the legal structure constraining the police role is reduced to the dichotomous distinction (reproduced elsewhere) between the responsibilities for order maintenance as opposed to those for law enforcement; and the organizational structure of departments is essentially a deduction from certain arrest rates that Wilson argues departmental policies can influence (for example, traffic, vice and gambling, juveniles), together with general comparative observations on the degree of specialization, the extent of training and community-relations programmes, the degree of bureaucratization, systems of evaluation and so on.

SUMMARY
None of these approaches, then – 'machine', 'subcultural', or 'environmental' – provides us with an adequate explanatory framework in itself. The 'machine' model fails to contextualize the machine or examine its working; the 'subcultural' model fails to examine the machine or the contexts in which it operates in anything like the detail it affords the working practices and meaning systems of the machine's agents; and the 'environmental' model gives insufficient attention to the machine itself and to the operating norms and practices of organizational agents. Moreover, these approaches have produced contradictory findings which have been left unresolved. The reason why the contradictory findings of police sociology ('the organization engenders deviancy'; 'the organization can control deviancy') can remain unnoticed or unsurmounted relates to the empiricism of the problematic of 'sociological liberalism' within which such studies are embedded. In Cain's words, such studies 'failed to define the police' (1979, p. 148). In other words, such sociologists define the police, if only implicitly, in an empirical or pragmatic fashion, while retaining idealistic normative assumptions, about law for example.

Class Functionalism

Marxism is a 'problematic' which is theoretically opposed to empiricism and idealism. From a sociological perspective it is a project committed to explaining the fundamental historical and material determinations underlying the *apparent* processes of human social intercourse or *immediate* empirical reality. But, as Althusser has tellingly demonstrated (though in his case with self-defeating rigour), there are many Marxisms, many of which retain elements from 'alien' problematics. Thus empiricism can exist within discourses which claim the mantle Marxist, as can idealism. But the most common problem in sociological studies of the police conducted within a purportedly Marxian framework is a 'reductionist functionalism' – a sort of mechanical materialism whereby the structured complexity of empirical reality is 'reduced' to the simple underlying economic class determinations; or, put the other way, empirical reality is said simply to 'reflect' the economic class struggle.[9]

Thus law, as part of the 'superstructures', is said merely to reflect existing property relations, characterized, in the capitalist mode of production, by the economic domination of the bourgeoise. The police as part of the state – a similarly epiphenomenal structure – have the function of law enforcement, which is, *ipso facto*, a mechanism for reproducing this economic class domination. In short, economic class domination is reflected in law, which is enforced by the police, who thereby reproduce existing relations of exploitation.

On the other hand, there is a recognition (which contradicts the above) of the empirical fact that not all laws reflect the economic advantage of the bourgeoisie, that some (such as laws concerning health and safety at work) embody working-class interests. How then are bourgeois class interests still ensured? The answer proposed is selective enforcement; laws reflecting the interests of the bourgeoisie are systematically enforced, while those reflecting the interests of the working class and designed to check the activities of the powerful and wealthy are leniently or under-enforced. But this requires a transformation in the conception of the police. They are no longer agents of the state whose action in enforcing bourgeois class laws is predetermined, but agents who choose 'voluntaristically' which laws to enforce and which to ignore – a choice premissed upon the class interest of the law in question. Voluntarism is thus substituted in the explanation when economism, its opposite, will not serve.

One difference between the sets of studies – the 'sociological liberal' and the 'class functionalist' – is that in the former the contradiction we uncovered passes unremarked (a function of its more pragmatic empiricism which can cheerfully accommodate the most contradictory findings); in the latter, the contradictory shift from 'economism' to 'voluntarism' is resolved (as the problematic demands), but tautologously, by explaining, in economistic terms, the particular pattern of selective enforcement 'chosen' – selection is a simple function of class interest. If this tautologous resolution is made possible by the fact that the contradiction between 'economism' and 'voluntarism' is only apparent (Althusser and Balibar, 1970, p. 114), both being part of an 'essentialist' problematic, it is made necessary by the inadequacy of the problematic, with its simplistic and reductive notion of a social formation, to accommodate the diversity and complexity of the empirical evidence encountered.

Towards a Reconceptualization

We can summarize what is needed in general terms by recapping on the main difficulties we have identified. While the class–functionalist approach has over-simplified the analysis of policework by relating its phenomena solely to a dominant socio-political order, the sociological liberals have investigated the nature of policework only selectively, and without attending to inconsistencies. What is needed, therefore, is an approach which is faithful to the profane details of daily policework, like that of the sociological liberals, but in a way which attempts to link these systematically, that is, in relation to the system as a whole, which represents the merit of the Marxist approach. We need to consider policing in terms of a *combination* of structures. Our general theoretical understanding of 'structure' is dealt with in Chapter 9. Here we are concerned to apply this approach in ways that illustrate its utility for our analytical tasks.

In line with our notion that the elements presently located within inadequate problematics, once reordered and reconceptualized, may provide the basis for a more adequate problematic with greater explanatory power, we need to review the resources available. Collectively, the models reviewed within the sociological liberal problematic offer clues – both formal and substantive – to the elements of such a new framework. Formally they alert us to notions of formal structure, working practices and environmental contexts; substantively, they alert us to the importance of law, work (a notion embracing organizational structure and colleague-group culture) and the community. On the other hand, the impact of the class-functional problematic is to suggest the importance of attending to the *relationship* between all the elements within a given social formation. In short, we need to draw on the substantive elements, suitably reconceptualized, identified by the sociological liberals – a requirement that ensures against reductionism – but materially, in relation to the foundations of the social formation as a whole.

One exemplary attempt to move beyond a reductive materialism is presented by Gramsci, the Marxist thinker and politician, and his followers. Neo-Gramscian conceptions of capitalist society have emphasized the positive role of dominant classes in shaping general features of society and winning consent from subordinate groups. This notion of 'hegemony' draws attention away from the simple and repressive towards the 'consensual' features of class domination and begins to explain why the political formations of the state, in government and so on, do not simply follow the entrenched lines of economic class interest (cf. Gramsci, 1971). Its relevance here lies in the possibility of constructing a conception of policing which recognizes that its conditions and effects are influenced by its position in an unequal society but does not assume this will have a simple repressive effect. In other words, the operation of policing within this conception partially cross-cuts divisions of interest. This conception does not lead us to a dilution of the argument that social inequality is an important determinant upon the pattern of policing; rather it encourages us to investigate in what particular ways this may be so.

Emphasis on the importance of attending to the particular in a systematic fashion brings us to Foucault, whose work has much to teach us in this respect. Whilst he shares with Marxists an interest in the question of power, his particular concerns have entailed a shift of attention from the traditional Marxist interest in the function of the single central source of bourgeois class power – the state – to its exercise, in manifold forms, within peripheral locations far from the centre (cf. Foucault, 1979). His analysis of the exercise of the form of power that he calls 'discipline', for example, identifies a series of characteristics – techniques of observation, regulation and training – which define it, but also an intellectual history of the logic or discourse which accompanies it. For our purposes, Gramsci and Foucault between them offer important breaks with reductionist conceptions of the totality: Gramsci in breaking with a reductionist conception of power and the social formation; Foucault in illustrating what that might mean in concretely analysing the exercise of power. With these anti-reductionist protocols in mind we can begin to approach our task. First, we need to suggest how existing elements – law, work and the community – need to be developed before they can become adequate to the task required of them. In particular these elements require examination as potential structures for the analysis of policework.[10]

Law – towards a Preliminary Definition

The conceptions of law as a determinant of police behaviour bequeathed us by sociological liberalism amount to three:

(1) a dual structure consisting of procedural law which is designed to regulate the conduct of state officials, on the one hand, and the substantive criminal law, which is designed for the main-tenance of social order, on the other (cf. Skolnick, 1975);

(2) a triple structure consisting of procedural law, and the sub-stantive criminal law comprised of 'law-enforcement' and 'order-maintenance' aspects, with the former applicable to situations which involve a 'violation of law in which only guilt need be assessed', the latter to those situations where, in addition to the legal infraction, there is 'a dispute in which the law must be interpreted, standards of right conduct deter-mined, and blame assigned' (Wilson, 1968, p. 84);

(3) a 'legal system' comprising four components – the 'legal-content' component ('the actual content of laws'), the 'govern-ment' component (the organization of the legal system 'poli-tically into larger or smaller, more or less centralised, units'), the 'legal-order' component ('the complex apparatus involved in the administration of justice, especially . . . the prosecutor and the courts') and the 'legality' component ('the procedural aspects of the exercise of legal power') (Reiss and Bordua, 1967, pp. 27–8).

A summary of these characterizations produces the idea of law divided into its procedural and substantive aspects; the idea of substantive law offering relatively clear (law enforcement) or more ambiguous (order maintenance) guides to action; and, third, the idea that the criminal justice system, especially the courts and the prosecutor, and the political organization of the legal system, should also be considered when thinking about the legal determi-nants of police behaviour. Whilst the addition by Reiss and Bordua of the latter aspects serves to make the whole slightly more concrete, their conception of the law governing police behaviour remains the conventional unrefined division into procedural and substantive aspects, which is not significantly advanced by Wilson's further distinction with respect to the substantive criminal law, that is, into 'clear'/'ambiguous'.

The legacy of the class functionalists is even more undiscriminating. Since law is regarded as reducible to its (bourgeois) class origins, the need to examine it in all its specific manifestations simply does not arise within the problematic. The net result is that we need to transform the notion of law in two ways: by *combining* the elements – procedural law, types of substantive law, legal system – bequeathed us by sociological liberalism; and by *developing* the new concept much more concretely. The essential move involved in combining the elements is to subsume both discursive and systemic elements within a single definition. In general terms this is in line with the formal definition of law as social practice put forward by Hirst: 'a social practice taking place within particular apparatuses and by means of a particular type of discourse' (1979, p. 112). Such a definition problematizes the traditional idealistic conception of law that focuses on the internal relations of legal concepts. But equally it problematizes the further distinction made between law-in-books and law-in-action, a distinction animating conceptions of law and its enforcement deriving from sociological liberalism. This initially attractive distinction has generated a dichotomy in the conception of legal practices which constitutes an obstacle to a more concrete definition of law, as McBarnet has lucidly shown (1978a and b). If, however, we define law as a structure comprising different apparatuses, legal discourse has to be considered as a total process of definition and interpretation, in which no single institutional site encapsulates the essence of law – 'the law'.[11] As Hirst succinctly put it: 'It is by being enacted, codified, subject to dispute and interpretation that laws and the nature of legality are defined and developed' (1979, p. 112).

In this sense, then, we employ the terms 'law' and 'legality' in the following sections. The law surrounding policework, which defines the duties and powers of constables and Chief Constables (in short their 'constitutional' position), is thus a product, at any moment in time, of statutory enactment, common-law right and successive, largely court-based interpretations of them. The result need be neither consistent ('Laws can be divergent and inconsistent in form and function and remain laws' – Hirst, 1979, p. 111) nor coherent ('assigning a definitive effectivity to legislation and legal practices means that law can outrun and redefine its discursive and categoric forms' – ibid., p. 112). No matter; it is with this legal structure as it currently relates specifically to policework, with all its significant diversity and complexity, that we are concerned here. Let us now spell out briefly the implications of this approach to law.

Take first the 'procedural' aspect of law. Rather than simply *assume* there is a set of legal constraints acting upon police officers, we need to ask the question: what are the legal powers of constables (and chief officers) in particular situations? Even a cursory examination reveals that the powers of officers differ between situations, in certain situations being highly discretionary, in others less so. To conceive procedural law as a unilateral set of constraints is to miss these points: the need for a concrete knowledge of the legal powers of officers in different situations, and for a knowledge of the degree of discretion embodied in these different legal powers. This opens up the prospect of law being more or less influential, rather than influential or not, depending on the powers available. If these are highly discretionary, the less constraining will be the law, and vice versa.

If knowledge of the actual legal powers of officers in particular situations needs to replace the existing idealistic conception of the 'procedural' aspect of law, the idea of the substantive criminal law as a unified body of law operating a unilateral (or bilateral in the case of Wilson, 1968) determination on the conduct of officers needs similarly to be replaced with a less idealistic notion. In thinking structurally about the criminal law as a constraining element we need, therefore, to ask the question: what are the legal demands of the various parts of the criminal law? Again, we need not rehearse here a full examination before suggesting that offences will *differ* in several ways. They will differ as to their *legal complexity*, which will be a function of the number of legally significant factors they encompass. They will differ as to the degree of *citizen involvement*, as witnesses or injured parties, necessary to meet minimal legal requirements. They will differ as to their *legal clarity* (a point that Wilson, 1968, does make, as we saw earlier). These differences mean that the effect of the law on police behaviour will be a function of the particular offences with which they routinely deal, with the more 'complex', 'citizen-involving' and 'clear' offences being more legally constraining, and the least legally constraining being those offences requiring only the discretionary subjective judgement of a single officer.

Finally, with respect to the impact of the criminal justice system as a whole, we need to ask what concrete use is made by citizens and legal authorities – such as the courts, the Home Office and Police Authorities – of their legal powers with respect to police activities, and how extensively, persistently and consistently these legal levers are employed. The implications of this are that, where powers are extensively, persistently and consistently used, they are likely to be more effective as a constraint on police behaviour than where the reverse obtains.

In thinking about legal constraints on policework, we need a thorough knowledge of the 'formal structure' of the relevant law – the legal powers of police, the legal demands made by the criminal law, the legal powers of citizens and legal authorities and the uses made of them – before we can begin to think about how 'law' affects police behaviour in particular situations. In other words, we need to be able to identify the legal constraints operating in particular situations if we are ever to be able to assess the role of the law as a structural determinant of police behaviour.

Work – towards a Preliminary Definition

With respect to the second major theme, the structure of work, it is generally recognized that this is opaque above a certain level in the police organization. In 1967 Reiss and Bordua complained at the lack of 'detailed description of the nature of command processes in a police department', and therefore of having 'to rely largely on published discourses that give information on the rhetoric of command and control' which, they admitted, 'are of variable and unknown validity as descriptions of behaviour' (1967, p. 48). Twelve years later, Friedrich echoed this complaint when he suggested that 'there is definitely a need for structured research into how policy set at the top of the police organisation is put into effect at the bottom' (1978, p. 95). Cain has suggested one reason for this lack of information: the fact that participant observation 'usually precludes understanding of the upper echelons of organisations' because the nature of the work of senior officers resists easy and economical observation (1979, p. 146). Punch has suggested another, oft recognized one: the fact that 'politics of access tend to deflect researchers downwards and away from the powerful' (1981, p. 35).

Police management is one area, then, about which all are agreed that nothing is concretely known. This conclusion is as applicable to the class functionalists – whose lack of interest in the specifics of organizational dynamics echoes their similar indifference to law – as to the sociological liberals. It is all the more surprising then that researchers, after investigating the occupational culture only of *lower* ranks, can talk of 'a major schism between the work cultures of the upper and lower ranks' (Punch, 1981, p. 26), of 'street cops vs management cops' (Reuss-Ianni and Ianni, 1983) and of 'managerial versus practical professionalism' (Holdaway, 1977). In truth, as we suggested earlier, whilst the occupational culture of line officers and immediate supervisors has been exhaustively examined, the organizational structure from which it purportedly deviates is an assumed category, taken from glances at the rule-book and the rhetoric, not from precise observations; or, worse still, taken, we suspect, from the rank and file's perceptions of the workings of management.

This point has important implications for an understanding of the determinacy of the occupational (or colleague-group) culture. The assumption of those that have examined the occupational culture is that it and the organizational structure represent *rival* sets of determination on police behaviour – with the former mostly winning out. Since the organizational structure has not been submitted to the same rigorous observational examination that the occupational culture has, the empirical possibility remains that the two might not be universally in conflict. For this reason we wish to distinguish two structural determinants of police behaviour which might be termed *organizational* and *occupational*. These form elements of a work structure. In other words, we wish to suggest that this structure is best studied as a single one with two dimensions: an 'organizational' one – referring to the vertical dimension of rules, policies, approved procedures, command and control – and an 'occupational' one, referring to the horizontal dimension of the norms and practices of colleague groups.

Given the idealistic assumptions made about police manage-ment, the first transformation required is to conceptualize this vertical dimension as a series of specific practices – supervision, policy, deployment and so on – which require a material analysis as they relate to the specific tasks assigned to officers. Whilst some of these practices have simply to be brought to visibility (but not only as seen 'from below'), others, like policy, a key management practice, need first to be reconceptualized in a thoroughly material fashion. The conventional view stemming from the 'machine'-model approach is that policy is an authoritative statement of the organization's specific goals, carrying a clear meaning and rele-vance for all subordinates which it is intended they should automatically put into practice: policy as 'rational authority', we might say. The 'subculturalists', on the other hand, imply that policy is a mere declaration of some orientation favoured by policy-makers, an expression of the organization's general inten-tions, issued in various degrees of good faith, which is in practice impotent: policy as 'irrelevance', we might say. Rather than simply operate with either of these notions, we need to look closely at the activities (for example, conferences) in which the term 'policy' is accorded meaning and to explore how these can be categorized. This examination may lead us to propose an account of policy which arbitrates with more accuracy between the polarity suggested by existing views. We need therefore to discuss the *activity of 'policy-making'*, to look at the possibility that policy is produced out of a routine process of consideration in which policy-relevant matters are regularly placed under scrutiny (with no necessary innovation or 'making of policy' on each occasion). We also need to examine the concrete forms in which such considerations are disseminated for the attention of subordinates. Policy consideration and dissemination in this sense will be a much more complex and comprehensive structure than would be supposed by those who operate with a simplistic conception. This will also enable a realistic assessment to be made of the relationship between policy and working norms without prejudging the issue as one of difference or conflict. It will examine the alleged 'gap', not between policy and practice, but rather between particular types of policy and particular types of practice.

Democracy – towards a Preliminary Definition

The 'community', the third substantive element identified, has largely been conceived either unilaterally – the 'hostile public' – or as differentiated along conventional lines relating to population composition (homogeneous vs mixed; middle class vs working class; black vs white and so on), 'crime-proneness' (law-abiding vs criminal), or attitude to the police (hostile or supportive). These differentiations are not unimportant, but they remain insufficiently developed as a means of understanding how 'the public' or 'the community' affects police behaviour. Moreover, the notion of 'the public' is itself too vague for our purposes. In a 'democratic' society like that of Britain, formally speaking, the people or 'public' are supreme. Now whilst the nature of British democracy has still to be elaborated, showing the way such a formal system works, we none the less wish to reconceptualize the role of the public in relation to policework practice as a democratic structure. In other words, we are suggesting that policework practices are determined not only by a legal structure and a work structure, but by a democratic one too.

The concept of democracy has a long historical pedigree, as political theorists from Plato to Lenin have sought to establish and re-establish its meaning. It has in consequence a variety of meanings, being claimed by a variety of different societies to be a characteristic of their political systems – be they 'capitalist', 'communist', or 'underdeveloped', as MacPherson (1966) has eloquently reminded us. In order to clarify our usage we have found it helpful to draw on Hindess's work on parliamentary democracy (Hindess, 1980). In this work Hindess rejects those conceptions of democracy which rely on the 'democracy/ sovereignty couplet' (1980, p. 105) – those conceptions which take as their problematic the question of making the sovereignty of the state 'adequate' to the natural sovereignty of individuals – since they detract attention from the 'specific determinations and limitations' of 'any putatively democratic mechanism' (p. 105). What Hindess points to is the need to look at concrete practices and discourses ('mechanisms') in relation to particular institutional sites. Policework may not possess democratic mechanisms in the Hindessian sense, but his stress on mechanisms, their scope and organization and, most importantly, the conditions under which they operate, when transcribed to police decision-making, allows us to ask, in relation to decisions made, be they policy decisions or the decisions of individual officers to invoke the legal process or not: under what conditions are various 'publics' ('constituencies') able to have an effect on policework practice? Put another way, which decisions in relation to which constituencies and which conditions are subject to extra-legal, 'non-police' determinations? Thus our conception of the democratic structure in relation to policework practice amounts to being able to specify the relationship between 'constituencies' (or 'publics'), decisions (or 'practices') and conditions. But for this we need to spell out the nature of police 'constituencies'.

Proceeding negatively, we can see that the existing gross divisions in the literature do not differentiate between the *roles* in which the community – middle or working class, black or white and so on – can come into contact with the police, and, through such contact, potentially influence police behaviour. Thus, it does not distinguish contacts between police and citizens, as individuals – as potential witness, injured party, complainant, caller, or refreshment 'spot' – as representatives of the community (either elected or self-appointed leaders of community or pressure groups), or as members of organizations with whom the police have institutional contact (the social services, housing departments, schools, or the media, say). In line with our orientation, we would expect some difference in the ability of citizens, according to the nature of their 'contacting' role, to influence police behaviour, with, for example, contacting roles spelling 'trouble' or 'inconvenience' less likely to influence behaviour, since they are resisted, than those offering more desirable prospects. Further, in relation to each of these 'citizen roles', there are a number of further ways in which potentially significant differentiations can be made. Citizens in each 'contacting role' can be seen as respectable or otherwise (a point which subsumes many of the community distinctions made previously in the literature), known locals or unknown strangers, community representatives or individual citizens. The nature of the contact can be reciprocal, with each party having items of value to exchange, or one-way, and can be either sporadic or recurrent. Furthermore, the nature of the issue bringing citizens and police into contact can be one about which there is a high degree of consensus, or it can be highly contentious. Once again, we would expect least influence to be exerted by non-respectable individual strangers who have nothing to exchange and with whom contact is sporadic and contentious. Study of these concrete conditions will allow us to pose clearly and specifically the extent to which other fundamental conditions, notably the key social characteristics underpinning the social order, affect the decision-making of the police. In short, contact between police and citizens can take a variety of forms, and each form of contact can vary in numerous ways. This recognition underlies our notion of the 'community' and its influence on police organization and practice: our notion, in other words, of a democratic structure as a potential constraint on police policy-making and practice.

A New Framework

The final question in considering these reconceptualized elements – the structures of law, work and democracy – concerns how they may be understood in relation to one another. We have already rejected the 'a priorism' of a class reductionism which spells out, in advance of an empirical investigation, the relations between elements in a system. Such rigour, we argued earlier, is self-defeating since it produces a spurious theoretical unity at the expense of doing justice to the structural diversity and complexity of policework practices. But we also rejected the failure of the sociological liberals to produce a systematic unity out of the otherwise bewilderingly diverse findings they have collectively produced. Our approach is premised on the need to avoid the twin pitfalls of empiricism and a reductive materialism, and on the belief that it is possible to grasp the unity of organized policework – its relationship to a determinate social formation – in all its significant diversity at one and the same time. We have cited Gramsci's work as exemplary in delivering examples of concepts which break with reductionism without resorting to empiricism, and Foucault's as illustrative of how attentiveness to the concrete detail of specific practices need not be executed unsystematically. It may be salutary to note that others have also linked both authors in their attacks on reductionism (cf. Mouffe, 1979, p. 201). For present purposes, we need to be able to suggest a relationship between the structures which allows a unified sense to be made of all the particular empirical findings, but one which does not foreclose on the variety of empirical possibilities. The proposed relations must also be empirically testable. What we propose in this regard is to follow Althusser and Balibar (1970) in making a distinction between 'determinant' and 'dominant'. The structure which is determinant need not be the immediate empirical one. With this in mind, we suggest that the key to understanding the relationship between the practices is to be found in law; this, we suggest, is the determinant structure, in that it will determine which of the structures is the dominant one. The subsequent chapters will explore aspects of this thesis.

The prima-facie reasons for suggesting law as the determinant structure are numerous. In the first instance, at the level of common sense, public conceptions of policework are largely founded on a notion of police officers as agents of the state upholding the law. 'Philosopher, guide and friend' they may be on occasions (cf. Cumming, Cumming and Edel, 1965), but it is as law enforcers and prosecutors that they come to be defined as specifically police officers. It is this aspect of policework which is seen to define the *specific* nature of the relations between police and public. The police themselves also embrace this traditional common-sense conception of themselves; preventing or detecting *crime* is the fulcrum of their self-conception. The prestigious work has always been that which involves most involvement with crime, namely the Criminal Investigation Department (CID). Police priorities reinforce this conception, though we should not overlook other significant legal domains such as public order.

This common-sense view of the importance of the law in understanding policework is echoed in the class functionalist's definition of the police role. As we saw, the use of police discretion or selective enforcement is 'explained' by reference to a definition of police as state agents reproducing exploitative class relations via a discriminatory use of the law. We have already indicated our objections to the reductionism of this particular definition; but we have never objected to the idea of a *definition* of policework *per se* that allows linkages to be made to other social practices and the social formation as a whole, rather than some more pragmatic definition, based, for example, on what police spend most time doing. That common sense and a version of Marxism agree on the centrality of upholding the law does not, of course, mean that both work with the same notion of law – far from it: Marxism is far from being the 'common sense' of the age – but it should raise the claims of law as a central practice in understanding policework.

However, we need not rest there with a perhaps fortuitous coincidence. In trying to specify more concretely the relationship between police and state, we are drawn not only to the substantive criminal law as crucial mediator, as the above accounts indicate, but also to those legal duties and powers which spell out the obligations and mechanisms of control to be exercised on the police – those laws which collectively constitute the system of police accountability. Though we can only gesture towards an analysis here, what this reveals is that each structure we have identified is reflected in elements of the accountability system. The Police Act 1964 refers to a tripartite structure of supervision in which the Home Secretary and the police committee (in the provinces) bear cognate responsibilities for the adequacy and efficiency of a force, but the Chief Constable is responsible for the direction and control of the constables under his command. At the same time, case law decrees that the Chief Constable is responsible to the law and the courts for upholding the law in his area, though questions of deployment are his to decide (Jefferson and Grimshaw, 1984b). This system contains elements that reflect the fundamental practices of policework. First, in respect of the law, note the legal obligations of the Chief Constable; secondly, the structure of work manifests itself in relation to the demand for adequate and efficient policework supervised by the Home Secretary and the police committee; these offices also bear on the third structure identified here, since they are representatives of democracy. In this system, then – a system fundamentally of *legal* accountability – the three structures converge and combine, but the relationship between them is structured by law. Moreover the *central* responsibility of the police themselves in this system is to uphold the law, as interpreted by the Chief Constable in particular instances.

In the absence of pressing counter-claims, we have to submit that the relationship between the structures is structured by law, and that upholding the law is the principal obligation of the police themselves – without that in any way implying that law will be the *dominant* structure of organized policework in particular instances. The observable importance of practices and ideas which do not carry an obvious link with law, such as police 'scientific management' or 'common sense', will thus be conceived as a secondary function made possible by a primary legal structure which also constrains their appearance within definite bounds of relevance. This approach, which might at first sight appear paradoxical, offers a coherent means of conceiving policework as a systematic whole while doing justice to the particularity of subsidiary structures and ideas. An illustration of this argument is presented in the subsequent chapters.

Alternative Hypotheses

In this section we present a series of hypotheses based on the competing models of policework which it will be the function of subsequent chapters in Parts II and III to explore.

The 'machine' model is based on the idea that organizational dictates coincide with the law on the one hand and with rank-and-file behaviour on the other. Consequently, a manifest failure for all – law, organization, rank and file – to be synchronized means either a failure on the part of management to translate legal requirements into policy, or a failure to get the policy message across. In terms of a pair of matched alternative hypotheses we might suggest the following. If the 'machine'-model approach is correct, any observed discrepancies between organizational requirements and rank-and-file behaviour are best explained as part of a 'communications blockage'. If our framework is correct, observed discrepancies between organizational requirements and rank-and-file behaviour will best be explained by examining how the three structures relate to the particular behaviour in question, and explaining the role of the legal structure in organizing the relations between the structures.

The 'subculture' model, in contrast, offers the possibility of a series of connected hypotheses. Centralizing the importance of the rank-and-file subculture as the key determinant of police behaviour, and stressing its relative impermeability to management values and policies, has produced a series of notions: that any serious supervision is doomed to failure; that there are two subcultures, that of the rank and file and that of management (variously characterized); and that these are invariably opposed. As a series of hypotheses, these would read as follows. If the subculturalists are correct, we would expect to find:

(1) two broad subcultures, one comprising that of the rank and file, or operational officers, and the other comprising management;
(2) that these subcultures are opposed, one favouring a tight-managerial 'professionalism', the other a more practical, commonsensical 'professionalism';
(3) attempts at supervision routinely failing.

The alternatives, based on our framework, would read as follows. If our framework is correct, we would expect to find:

(1) the structure of law in relation to any given task determining the degree to which other structures, and their related discourses or values, can come to the fore. Those tasks involving a legal structure which is in any way limited or permissive will enable work-related values to prevail; those tasks involving a substantial and precisely articulated legal structure will not be so open to the influence of work-related values. Since tasks involving different legal structures cut across the management/rank-and-file divide, the corresponding task-related value systems will also traverse the divide;
(2) that since the tasks involving a limited or permissive legal structure are those dealing with operational and related matters, it is these tasks which will more often be subject to the operation of occupational, common-sense values than those dealing with administrative matters. And the more discretionary and ambiguous the legal matter, the greater the opportunity for such common sense to enter. Thus the possibility of coexistence is as important as the possibility of conflict, the outcome depending on the interrelation of tasks;
(3) the effectiveness of supervision to be related to task. In some tasks, where the legal or work structure is limited or permissive, supervision will need to recognize rank-and-file values in order to be effective; but in others, where the task is strongly determined by law, administrative systems, or managerial directives, supervision need not fail.

The 'environmental' model produces the hypothesis, broadly, that the 'environment' shapes police behaviour, but works with an underdeveloped conception of the environment. Our approach takes up and develops that point. In so far as the environment can be reconceptualized to mean the structures of law, work and democracy, the particular relationship between them being structured by law, it is of course identical with our approach. Clearly, then, the question of alternative hypotheses is inappropriate here; our job is to demonstrate the superior ('more precise', less 'gross') explanatory and hence predictive power of our framework over Wilson's, in order to develop the approach.

The same can be said of the class functionalist's approach. Our relationship with this position is as our relationship with the environmentalists – development, refining, making more precise. The notion of law and its enforcement held by the class functionalists, based on the notion that class determines both, is too simple, as is the hypothesis that stems from it: broadly, that 'class determines police behaviour'. Once again, the question of specific alternative hypotheses is inappropriate here; our job is to rethink the ways in which class (and other social factors) is *complexly* related to law and its enforcement. Combined together, the 'environmental' and 'class' aspects of policework allow us to postulate a democratic structure, the influence of which will be conditional on the other structures.

With this new framework and these hypotheses in mind, we can now turn to the empirical material: first the methodology and scope of the project as a whole, and then an outline of the chapters of the book.

Methodology and Scope

Method

The methods adopted have to relate to the theoretical object of inquiry. We have attempted to explain what we think are the necessary elements to be clarified by a theoretical framework for understanding organized policework: our object of inquiry. What we now need to explain is why we chose to examine the policies and practices of one large metropolitan force, in the way that we did, in order to accomplish this. The methods adopted had to be such that they were capable of illuminating in one movement the form of the structures *and their interrelationship*. To do this demands an approach that is alert to significantly contrasted features of organization yet has regard to common foundations and conditions. The dimensions of the task are equally empirical and analytical, making distinctions, marking limits, setting out conditions and reducing processes to their elements. To do that requires an integrated case-study approach because it is this approach, *par excellence*, which enables the adequate tracing of differences and connections.

It is important to stress this, and the difference between the case-study approach and another major methodological approach:

representative sampling. The sampling approach is designed to produce, not an account stressing forms of distinction and connection, but empirical generalizations. To be successful, such a method must already have an analytical framework of sufficient clarity to make the results adequately comprehensible – as Rees, Stevens and Willis (1979), who employ this sampling method, are forced to concede. Central factors in police organization are ignored, neglected, unknown, or misconceived in the existing literature employing this method.

Linking the data together in a plausible manner proves difficult for research on police 'effectiveness' in which 'input' and 'outcome' are measured without a specification of the *process* by which one is said to give rise to the other (Wycoff, 1982). Not surprisingly such methods would seem to bear an affinity with the 'machine' model, in which such a process is assumed rather than demonstrated.

If the case-study method, unlike the sampling approach, enables connections to be made, it is important to differentiate our own use of the case study from its conventional usage. Such a distinction relates to the question of *which* connections are central. Conventionally, the case-study approach has been associated with those studies we have loosely termed 'subcultural'. In these case studies, which prioritized the examination of the working situation of police officers, the object was to trace the connections between working practices, situations and the subjective meanings, for the actors involved, in order to produce a coherent, over-arching account able to 'explain' all the kaleidoscopic variations observed, experienced and intuited: a theory of the occupational culture, the informal structure, or 'organizational reality' (Manning, 1979).

There are two problematic aspects of this general approach relating to the question of connections. The first concerns the subjectivist and pragmatist theoretical presuppositions of interactionism which informs a good many of these studies. According to interactionism, the primary explanations of society are to be found in the goal-seeking of empirical individuals in social groups, which sustain structures of subjective meaning that make sense of their common world (Blumer, 1969). There is a wholesale rejection of the assumption that society is an orderly conglomeration of discrete social facts. Instead, there is a movement in interactionism towards the rooting out of meanings *in situ*, where the 'action' is. Consequently, the connections they were committed to establishing, through detailed, direct observation and interviewing conducted in case studies of actors working in particular organizational sites, necessarily prioritized the structure of meaning as the central point connecting up and explaining working practices, operating norms, situational rules, relations with others and so on. Manning, an exponent of this approach, makes essentially the same point when he says that the organizational reality 'operates as a transducer, filtering the meanings of behaviour elicited from audiences and clientele, as well as from other members' (1979, p. 46). By prioritizing structures of meaning, organizational sites or social practices which were excluded or marginalized in the structure of meaning (that is, were not given much thought by the actors themselves) became excluded or marginalized in theoretical accounts and methodological practice. Theoretically this had the effect we have already mentioned of neglecting the role of law and the organization as important determinants of police behaviour; methodologically, it excused the exclusive attention to groups of junior officers at the expense of other areas of organizational life.

The second problematic aspect of this approach follows from the prioritization given to the structure of meaning and directly concerns the question of actively making connections with other social structures marginalized by the structure of meaning. We have already argued that for the pure interactionists this presented few problems since theoretical accounts were obliged to follow the contours suggested by members' accounts. But, for those studies of a more hybrid nature, which adopt some of the protocols of interactionism but still posit the relevance of structures 'outside' the perspective of occupational groups, some attempt had to be made to connect the occupational culture to the organizational elements and to the law. Skolnick's study (1975) falls squarely within this category. The problem, however, is that the exclusive *methodological* attention to working groups precludes other than an abstract prescriptive account of the law and the organization which inform working practices. As we saw earlier, the connections traced by Skolnick between working 'reality', the organization and the law rely on an essentially presumptive picture of the latter elements.

These case-study approaches, because of certain theoretical presuppositions, make connections solely on the basis of members' perceptions, which effectively exclude other structures, except in so far as these were indicated in the particular discourses of empirical individuals. Or they make connections between a closely observed group reality and an unobserved and essentially assumed set of 'external' structures. In either case, the methodological predilections significantly skewed the resulting theoretical accounts.

Other methodological approaches entail the comparison of a *range* of cases, supported by statistical inquiry. Broadly, these are associated with 'environmental' theories of policing, and under-standably so, since they reflect the possibilities of discovering complex interactions between organizations and environments in a systematic manner. However, as we shall see, such attempts rely heavily on empirical induction, on pursuing a number of impressionistic hunches with considerable investigative vigour.

An interesting attempt to utilize a broad analytic framework incorporating sampling methods over a wide empirical field is represented by J. Q. Wilson's study (1968). The eight cities covered in detail were chosen by Wilson because 'they seemed to exhibit important differences in police behaviour and political culture' (p. 12), that is, they 'represented' some of the important differences that Wilson was interested in explaining. Qualitative and quantitative data relevant to police behaviour and political culture were collected from these cities. Empirical generalizations or categorizations were made on the basis of this patterning of empirical data, discovering empirical similarities and differences between communities, city administrations, police departments and police behaviour. These differences and similarities provided the basis for the initial categorizations (centralized or 'reformed' police departments versus decentralized, relatively unbureaucratized 'traditional' ones; professionalized civic administrations versus party-political administrations and so on). The patterning of categorizations – which categories of community were associated with which categories of city administration, police department and police behaviour – then provided the basis for the final master categorization – the three styles of police behaviour: watchman, legalistic, service. As Wilson says, summarizing this process of analytical hunch and empirical generalization: 'Such categorisation as is offered in this book was arrived at more or less instinctively, not deductively, and reflects the empirically observed patterning among places initially picked much at random' (Wilson, 1968, p. 12). We would not wish to dispute that empirical generalizations within a perceptive framework can achieve a high degree of insight and plausibility. The problem, however, remains one of analysis: has a crucial dimension been omitted or neglected in the attempt to produce a general model?

Wilson does attempt to make adequate connections, that is, to explain the relation between these categories: to explain *how* particular police 'styles' relate to particular departments, the law and so on, and why. But this attempt is dominated by an inductive method primarily drawing conclusions from observations. He fails to examine sufficiently his concepts of law and of the police department which, as we suggested earlier, are essentially 'normative prescriptions' or 'ideal formulations'. Thus the connections traced are between a series of empirical generalizations, derived from empirically observed patterning of certain data and essentially abstract prescriptive notions of the law, the department and so on. The result is that the theory produced is a mish-mash of tenuous connections between empirically derived categories and presumptive, idealistic categories. At its ambitious best, such work can be an important source of insights and general description; what it cannot do is produce the elements of an adequate explanatory theory.

The question of method presents itself rather differently when we turn to the last of our principal models: the class functionalist. In so far as this perspective has empirical (as distinct from theoretical) implications, they lie in the documentation of abuse and discrimination at the hands of the police. Methodologically this approach entails an accumulation of instances based on case studies and records. Not surprisingly such a method includes a strong historical dimension, since much lies in the public domain that can be interpreted in this way. Alternatively, analysis of police statistics might provide a method also relevant to the task. However, it is in the realm of case-by-case documentation that this approach finds perhaps its most characteristic expression (cf. Bunyan, 1976). A problem must then be raised about the analytical adequacy of case recording, since the structural context of events will tend to be reduced to their 'class' significance, rather than including the many determinations necessary to comprehend fully those particular events. In the absence of a broader methodology, placing particular events in the context of other developments and comparing them with other events more generally, the class-functional method remains narrow and predictable. Case study must in our submission contain sufficient breadth to produce significant contrasts and connections, a conception which we must now outline in more detail.

If the case-study approach has clear advantages for our purposes it is not without its own problems. What is required is a case-study method, but developed in certain important ways.

One resource for the task of constructing an adequate method for developing theory through investigation lies in a critical evaluation of the work of Glaser and Strauss (1967). Their interest lay in encouraging the generation of theory beyond the suggestions of the 'grandmasters' of sociology. Such an enterprise bears some resemblance to the approach of Wilson (1968). Thus they advocated an inductive method of producing theory – *grounded* theory, in which concepts were clarified and substantiated by empirical inquiry and analysis. Our task by contrast is to develop and enrich our fundamental theoretical categories by means of a research investigation. In this regard Glaser and Strauss offer useful insights. They reject the notion of research as *simply* an empirical verification of logically derived theories, and instead regard the development of theory as a proper objective for a research investigation. They recommend the use of comparison groups in order to carry forward the analytic task, exploring basic categories by examining distinctive social milieux. Looking at these differences is intended to throw up significant connections and discontinuities among the sociological terms in play. They also reject, as we have done, the logic of statistical sampling, preferring instead to refer to *theoretical* sampling – the selection of empirical cases sufficient to substantiate without significant contradiction a theoretical point. The relevance of their work is also heightened by the further refusal to be bound by narrow formulas of proof and to argue for a multi-faceted investigation which provides material for adequate cross-checking. However, the inductive basis of the approach, reminiscent of 'environmentalism', requires modification, firmly acknowledging the contribution of theoretical criticisms to the formulation of categories for investigation.

This modified form of case study we shall term a *theoretical case study*. Its distinctive features are as follows. (1) The case chosen most possess a sufficient range of empirical differences and interconnections to constitute a starting-point for the task of elucidating theoretical concepts generated through a critique of existing theory. (2) Since the study is concerned with the systematic articulation or connection of social structures, it will not be confined to comprehending structures of meaning in the interactionist sense. Rather, it will also use these meanings as indications of multiple points of connection. Thus it will not be confined by the methodological prescriptions of interactionism – the triangulation of observation and conversational meanings in a jointly held-in-common universe. That form of study needs to become part of an enlarged design which will include attention to points of connection not immediately recognized by participants.

In practice these methodological protocols required that we select a force operating within an environment displaying the kind of characteristics likely to promote the fullest significant range of policework responses. Specifically, this meant a large urban force, policing racially and socially mixed areas, seriously deprived areas and prosperous suburban fringes. It also meant a force exhibiting all the structural features associated with modern policing: a large establishment, recently amalgamated, possessing a range of specialist departments and a large, centralized command structure.

Beyond that it required that we conduct detailed observational work at strategic sites in the organization designed to elucidate the full range of practices: from policy consideration, through operational command and supervision, to operational duties of various kinds. It meant detailed attention to the written statements relating to working practices: standing orders, policy files and operational orders. It also meant acquiring a detailed knowledge of the background legal structure informing the whole: the powers and duties of constables and Chief Constables, the relevant Police Acts, common law, statutes and their interpretation in the courts and so on. Finally, it meant special attention to police–public contacts of all kinds: to contacts with complainants, victims, arrestees, letter writers, petitioners and organizational agents, since these provided one important empirical indicator of the presence of the working of democratic elements.

Once collected, the analytic strategy consisted of perusing the data relevant to particular practices, proposing a concrete idea structured around the question of the relationship of the original theoretical concepts, then 'testing' the idea by searching for aberrant cases, reformulating the notion, if necessary, until a thesis about the relationship between the determinants of a particular practice had been achieved. *Analytic Induction/grounded theory*

We ought also, before leaving this section, to add something about the particular sites chosen for observation, the particular policies and practices selected. We have suggested already that these should be varied enough to encompass a range of responses. But 'range' is not the only criterion, since, on that criterion alone, diversion signs and sudden deaths might be deemed as significant as crime and community relations. In fact our interest was guided as much by criteria of significance as by variation: significance in terms of likely theoretical import, but also in terms of political pertinence. By political pertinence we intend those aspects currently posing the most urgent demands on modern policework. Those aspects in which change and 'strain' are exhibited are particularly significant as these offer the most searching test of current theoretical assumptions about policework – since an adequate theory must comprehend political change and development. Such considerations explain the particular divisional location for our research in a predominantly working-class town with significant deprived areas and a degree of racial tensions, *and* our choice of operational beat-work – patrol and resident beat officers (RBOs).

Our choice of particular organizational sectors was thus determined by the wish to establish *pertinent* comparisons. We chose two contrasting forms of beat-work – the unit policing system and the resident beat system – which have become significantly differentiated in recent years, both in the theory of police management and in public debate about the future of the police. The concept of 'community policing' in particular has placed emphasis on the role of RBOs and has distinguished its approach from the allegedly more remote and technologically oriented style of policing associated with the 'panda' car. Exploring the differences between these groups thus involved reflection on the main categories of current thinking on police organization and practice.

Our theoretical case study thus involved a multi-faceted inquiry aimed at developing theory by exploring pertinent connections and differences within an integral case – a large urban police force. Various kinds of data were brought to bear in order to expand our understanding of the conditions affecting beat-work in its distinctive forms. In these ways it was hoped that the theoretical objective of the research could be sustained.

The Empirical Scope of the Project

The empirical scope of the research can be outlined by listing briefly the main activities which contributed data for subsequent analysis. In the first place, a pilot study was conducted within the selected force which helped to identify a suitable location for the main observational study. The pilot study, which altogether comprised 268 'field contact' hours, was conducted during a ten-week period in 1978. Of this, two weeks were spent at Force HQ, five weeks at two different subdivisions[12] and one week each with Traffic, a divisional Public Liaison Department and the SPG. These observations included all significant functions of interest within each location, and covered all rank levels in the organization.

The pilot study was followed by the major examination of beat-work on a selected subdivision, comparing the unit beat and resident beat systems simultaneously over three to four months (October to January). Observed periods of normal working comprised 28 in the case of the unit and 29 in the case of the resident beat officers. (Further details of the method are given in the following sections.) The observations were supplemented by semi-structured interviews with all significant ranks on the subdivision. (See the Appendix for the interview schedules.) From the particular unit observed, three sergeants gave tape-recorded interviews totalling approximately 5.25 hours in length, as well as five police constables (PCs) (8.25 hours); in addition, two PCs gave interviews that were noted in writing. Taped interviews were obtained from RBO personnel, comprising the sergeant (2.25 hours), eight PCs (15.75 hours) and the detective (3 hours). Four subdividisonal Inspectors were interviewed (providing 9 hours). At the rank of Superintendent we branched out to include the neighbouring subdivisions that together made up the division, interviewing three Superintendents (8.25 hours) as well as the divisional Chief Superintendent (3.75 hours).

For the study of policy, a number of regular meetings and conferences were observed, ranging from the locality of our observations up to force-wide and high-level meetings. These were attended over eight months, producing a total of twenty-three observed events. We sampled the more frequent meetings and visited as many as possible of the less frequent. Also relevant to policy were the policy files in which records of correspondence and meetings were deposited; a three-to-four-month study of these produced a total sample of sixty-three files for analysis. Interviews with the force leadership also took place, including the Chief Constable (6 hours), the Deputy (3 hours), the Assistant Chief Constable (ACC) in charge of operations (4 to 5 hours) and the ACC in charge of organizational matters (2.25 hours).

The Scheme of the Book

The manner of presentation we have adopted in the substantive chapters which follow is related to our previous critical exposition. We begin by listing the relevant matters highlighted by the 'machine' model: official rules, functions, training, supervisory responsibilities and so on. We go on to present material in an ethnographic or descriptive manner, thus introducing themes relevant to the other main approaches. In the analytical sections, the 'system at work' is given a theoretical interpretation related to the structures identified by the theoretical criticism. We end each examination by submitting rival interpretations to the test of our original hypotheses. This means our analysis of each part of the organization will highlight the principal structures that were earlier brought to light – the structures of law, work and democracy – which will thus form a repeated series of themes in the presentation of the main body of the research.

Given this general framework, we follow this opening 'ground-clearing' Chapter 1 with Part II, 'The Unit Beat System', which comprises a look at the system's formal elements and some ethnographic exemplification in Chapter 2, and then our sub-sequent interpretation and hypothesis testing in Chapter 3. We continue with Part III, 'The Resident Beat System', similarly splitting our examination into two – Chapters 4 and 5. The 'Conclusion to Parts II and III' draws both forms of beat-work together in summarizing our key findings as they relate to the starting hypotheses.

In Part IV we shift our attention to 'The Policy System', commencing with a general reminder of the hypotheses and how these apply to the specific question of policy. Subsequently, we spell out the formal elements, in Chapter 6, an enterprise which devotes substantial attention to the production of an acceptably specific definition of policy. Chapter 7 continues this examination by looking at one key institution for the consideration of policy – meetings – and then at the consideration of particular policy issues. This examination constitutes both an exemplification and an interpretation of one part of the policy system at work, and is repeated in Chapter 8 in relation to a second key institution within the policy system – its record files. Once again, we attempt to summarize our findings here, through a concluding look at their relationship to our opening hypotheses. We end by briefly con-sidering the relationship between a key theme of the final chapter, the concept of structure, and policy.

Part V, 'Conclusions', Chapter 9, first addresses theoretically the notion which has provided our orienting focus throughout, namely structure, and then draws out the political implications of existing approaches to the sociology of policework. There follows a structurally informed critique of political positions within the debate on the police, and the chapter ends by spelling out the political implications of our structural interpretation of pol-icework.

Notes

1 The literature covering the various concerns about policing is now voluminous, but the following selection of more recent writings provides some useful starting-points. On a variety of 'problems with modern policing', see Baxter and Koffman (1985); on the politici-zation of the police, Reiner (1983); on police–black relations gen-erally, Reiner (1985a); on the 1985 riots, Hall (1985), and Sivanandan (1985); and on the policing of the 1984–5 miners' strike, Fine and Millar (1985), and Jefferson (1986).

2 The conference proceedings that collectively comprise Cranfield Papers (1978) illustrate a range of community (or preventive) policing

philosophies. The article by Newman (1978) demonstrates well the enhanced importance of such philosophies in times of conflict – as, of course, does Scarman (1982).

3 We shall be treating a variety of distinct studies in terms of their similarities for our purposes, that is, in so far as they fall broadly within the problematic of 'sociological liberalism' (Rosenberg, 1971). Such studies also exhibit certain theoretical and methodological differences which we cannot address here.

4 Bittner (1970, p. 6) calls this idealistic approach 'norm-derivative' – the derivation of actual behaviour from the norms intended to guide conduct rather than attending 'to a level of social reality that is unrelated to ideal formulations'.

5 First exemplified seriously by the United States studies in the 1960s concerned with the practical exercise of police discretion in which deviation from 'law-in-the-books' appeared to be the rule (cf. Cain, 1979, p. 144).

6 Though cautiously confining himself to the British context, James (1979, pp. 66–9) similarly concludes as to the picture of 'normal' urban policing depicted by successive police researchers. If Punch (1979a) is anything to go by, the picture holds true in Amsterdam too.

7 Though the similarly 'environmental' work of Sherman (1978; 1983) should not be forgotten.

8 It should not be overlooked that the 'subcultural' literature dealing with police–public interactions also has a sense of a public, differentiated by race and age, for example, producing, under certain conditions, differential police responses. See, for example, Piliavin and Briar (1964), and Bouma (1969).

9 Marxist work in this area is noticeable largely by its absence compared with the range of work available in the sociological liberal tradition. Moreover, the tag 'conflict theorists' might be a more accurate characterization in certain respects (for which, see, for example, Chambliss and Seidman, 1971). At least in the USA, with its lack of a developed Marxist tradition, 'conflict theory' and 'reductionist' Marxism are bedfellows. The following is based heavily on the work of the Center for Research on Criminal Justice (1977), which is taken to be the paradigm example.

10 In an important study of patrolwork Ericson (1982) has developed a 'social action' approach in a way that seeks to incorporate 'structure', emphasizing the influence of the law, the organization and the community. Our approach develops 'structure' in a systematic fashion that reflects our initial premises.

11 In so far as Hirst refers to law as a social practice rather than a structure, as we do, he draws attention to the aspect of historical development through which the properties of a structure are manifested. We return to this issue in Chapter 9.

12 One of the subdivisions subsequently became the research location of the main study.

PART II

The Unit Beat System

CHAPTER TWO

Patrol Report

The Formal System

We begin this account of unit work with an outline of the formal elements which go together and make up the skeleton of operational unit policing. Such a description will, we hope, make comprehensible the more detailed narrative which follows. These elements also remind us of the determinate nature of such operations – that the system contains definite possibilities and characteristic features, which we shall demonstrate more clearly later. These then are the basic resources and lines of connections within which officers construct their version of policing.

PERSONNEL
Personnel are appointed to and transferred from units by a number of means. The first means of entry is by appointment as a police constable within the force; all officers on leaving training school join a uniformed unit on a subdivision. Another mode of entry to a unit is by transfer from other units, sections, or departments, for a variety of specific reasons – some voluntary, and others, such as disciplinary action, imposed. Normally there is an assumption that members will stay on a particular unit, unless there are exceptional reasons to the contrary. Officers move out on transfer to a specialist section, while specialists may return to a unit, on promotion to a sergeant, for example. A unit is therefore a broad channel fed by a mainstream of recruits and by several smaller conduits from different sources.

This appointment pattern has effects on the training background of the unit members. All officers who join the unit have received several weeks' basic training at the District Training Centre. During a two-year probationary period spent on a unit they are required to take courses of instruction which may draw them temporarily away from unit work. The unit also contains more experienced officers with greater in-service training – for example, in driving. Senior officers in particular will have passed police examinations for the ranks they currently hold, these qualifications being focused on legal powers and duties. There exists therefore a specific range of personnel on the unit with various degrees of training.[1]

TIME

Officers are allocated to a unit which forms part of a rotating shift coverage, based on an eight-hour turn of duty during three fixed periods of the day: 6 a.m. to 2 p.m., 2 p.m. to 10 p.m., 10 p.m. to 6 a.m. (cf. Smith and Gray, 1983, p. 21). One shift rests during a day when the other three work. The four shifts work in turn a continuous week of night duty while the other periods of the day are worked according to a non-continuous rhythm; rest days and rest weekends are interspersed in this cycle.

Officers begin the shift with a parade and briefing by sergeant or Inspector, comprising information relating for example to missing persons or to those wanted by the police. Patrolling officers then leave the station to take up their various duties, while station officers run the command-and-control system, incorporating radio and telephone communication, and the desk which the public can visit directly. The shift is usually split into two by the Inspector to accommodate two adjoining three-quarter-hour meal breaks, when the actual shift patrol coverage is reduced by half, subject to the recall by unit control of the group taking refreshments. As we shall see, the organization of time produces significant effects on unit work.

SPACE AND RESOURCES

The unit is, for the period of its turn of duty, responsible for the policing of a territorial subdivision. Any matter requiring police attention during that period can be brought into the scope of unit work. The unit can call on the assistance of the specialist officers present on subdivision, including subdivisional RBOs and CID, and the non-divisional units: CID squad, Traffic, SPG.

Unit officers occupy the central station and any section stations on subdivision. The communication facilities, lock-up, supervisors' offices and parade room are typically (though not always) located on the same premises. The parade room is available to all unit members; the sergeants have access to one office, and the inspector is the sole occupant of another. The command-and-control system is located in a station office. Telephones are supplied in all offices, channelled through a central switchboard.

The unit is provided with marked vehicles, divided into two classes: standard 'panda' vehicles for patrol and service calls; and better-performance vehicles dedicated to 'first response' to serious incidents. Two first-response cars are assigned per unit, with up to four pandas in addition, making in principle a basic complement of six vehicles. There are supervision vehicles for the patrol sergeant and Inspector.

Some officers are assigned to duties that generally confine them to the station. Constables deal with station inquiries, communications and the lock-up, working with unit supervisors as necessary. The system of beat-working formally allocates the mobile elements of the unit, including car drivers and walking officers, to particular areas. Walkers are assigned to the small concentrated beats in urban centres, where there is a concentration of valuable property and a great deal of pedestrian traffic. Panda drivers are assigned to collections of adjoining single resident beats – a territorial area covered by a single RBO – on an equal basis. Superimposed on these are first-response vehicles which cover equal collections of panda beats. The two levels of driver coverage separately encompass the whole area of the subdivision.[2]

COMMUNICATIONS

The central communications control is used to organize responses to matters relevant to police which come to attention. The system feeds on information which is relayed to the controller.[3] On receipt the controller interprets the messages and gives instructions to unit officers. Information enters the system from various sources, including public and police, unit and non-unit officers. Some calls from the public are answered initially by station officers assisting the controller; however, some are conveyed by a wider area control to first-response cars. The status of incoming messages is interpreted by controllers as to their relevance to police. Thus some public calls can be excluded. The controller's imprimatur determines the attendance of a mobile resource which assesses the situation and takes action, calling on assistance if necessary. Any paper reports then have to be completed, from a simple occurrence-book entry to formal reports of crime, etc.

SUPERVISION

Supervision for the unit is provided first by several sergeants who take individual responsibility for the station premises and lock-up, communications control and patrol supervision. The Inspector exercises control over all the aspects of unit work. The Superintendent is generally responsible for ensuring that force and divisional policies are made known to unit Inspectors, for the effectiveness of the units and for the allocation and re-allocation of personnel to units.

All paperwork generated by unit officers comes within the scope of supervision, the passage of material to and from the unit being relayed through the Inspector. Paperwork is organized according to central administrative categories. Pro-formas are supplied for routine reports: crime reports, accident report books, identity records, etc. Pocket-books are provided for note taking, and should be regularly examined by unit supervisors. These administrative procedures are supported by standing orders which oblige constables to observe them and supervisors to ensure compliance. The rules relating to administrative procedure are fundamentally invariant and non-discretionary.

The controller sergeant is the centre of the communications control system and has to maintain central records relating to public calls and incident response. Demands for service are met by the assignment of resources by the controller, who therefore generally supervises the deployment of unit resources to meet known demands. Patrol supervision is exercised too by senior officers – the patrol sergeant and, at discretion, the Inspector. Station supervision is specifically the job of the station sergeant. The processing of those taken into custody is supervised by a station sergeant, who completes records of procedure and charges prisoners. The Inspector has an ultimate authority over all these aspects of supervisory work.

A RESUMÉ OF DUTIES

Constables on station duty deal with public inquiries, pass messages to the controller and assist the station sergeant. Constables walking beats are deployed on the streets to attend service calls relayed by the controller, and to prevent crime and disorder by maintaining a public presence through patrol. They should meet requests for service addressed to them by members of the public. Constables driving panda vehicles have a similar role. The greater mobility of the panda driver allows him or her to deal with a greater volume of calls, spaced more distantly apart. Similar functions are assigned to first-response vehicles, though, as their name indicates, these are designed to ensure an efficient response to grave and urgent matters – emergencies and crime in progress. All patrol constables are responsible for the completion of the paperwork relevant to matters with which they deal.

The controller sergeant is responsible for the communications control system, for deploying and supervising unit resources and for maintaining a log. The patrol sergeant visits the constables on patrol and supervises their work, offering advice and directions as required, and overseeing the paperwork submitted by constables. He or she also has a responsibility for any cases that, because of the difficulties or complexities involved, he or she is assigned to or chooses to deal with personally. The station sergeant supervises the process of dealing with prisoners, and in particular charges them. Beyond that he or she is generally responsible for all matters relevant to the running of the station, including the care of plant and equipment.

The Inspector is responsible for the efficiency, welfare and discipline of the unit as a whole. Each shift requires the Inspector to deploy available officers to unit roles. Inspectors must attend sudden deaths and deal with fatal accidents. They also have to administer formal cautions, make inquiries about potential recruits and conduct inquiries and checks as requested by the Superintendent, in licensing matters, for example. Supervisors, it is clear, have a workload of their own, over and above their supervisory duties.

A UNIT OF CONSTABLES

We have so far delineated some differences among officer duty assignments but we should not neglect one thing they all share. All members of the unit enjoy the powers and bear the obligations of constables (Leigh, 1975). In law there is no distinction between the initial recruit and the experienced officer. Nor is there any distinction between the supervisor and the lower ranks, though the lower ranks are obliged to obey all lawful instructions of supervising officers. The common possession of constabulary status effectively flattens the rank structure of the unit in law. It produces a common identity and at the same time represents an individual possession which qualifies the holder for membership of the police occupation. This bedrock of constabulary status should not be overlooked, because in organizational terms the unit is strongly differentiated internally, with experienced senior officers and less experienced junior officers. While the unit is also organizationally distinguished from specialist sections which can in their own field override the responsibilities of the unit for general policing, the common possession of constabulary status cuts across all these distinctions. However, the legal operations of the unit officers cannot be specified in advance of further inquiry. For patrol officers, the formal specification of their duties clearly indicates that the potential range of their legal duties and powers is both wide and varied. We should also expect a corresponding variability in the capacity of 'the law' to constrain action – and likewise the same variability with respect to the control potentially exercisable by courts and citizens.

RELATIONS WITH THE PUBLIC

Similarly the formal remit of the unit prevents a ready specification of exactly what form contacts with the public will take. Contact with the public is a result of deployment on public service or police calls and also a result of independent patrolling; for the latter also, the initial impetus can derive either from public request for service or from police inquiries. The instruments of communication and mobility thus form systems open to many demands from any quarter, with the public (potentially) performing a central role in the working of the unit organization. The system of telephone and other requests for service allows the public to define its need for police services, while the system of patrol inquiry and response to police calls puts the onus on the police to define their own needs. The general responsibilities of the unit for policing a territorial population would appear to admit potentially wide outcomes when taken in conjunction with the processes, outlined above, which set unit work in motion. In other words, the role of the public as a determinant of police action is not easily predictable.

We observe at the outset therefore a definite and highly developed organizational structure, in contrast with a generalized legal structure and an equally generalized relation with the public or democratic structure. Let us now glimpse it in action.

The System at Work

In what follows, we shall present a series of accounts showing several officers at work, selected so as to represent a range of officers and a mix of shift periods.

Panda car duty	(10 p.m. to 6 a.m.)	EM
Panda car duty	(6 a.m. to 2 p.m.)	BJ
Panda car duty	(2 p.m. to 10 p.m.)	FN
Panda car duty	(6 a.m. to 2 p.m.)	CK
Foot patrol duty	(6 a.m. to 2 p.m.)	GO
First-response car duty	(10 p.m. to 6 a.m.)	DL
Patrol sergeant	(6 a.m. to 2 p.m.)	HP

These observational accounts were selected from twenty-eight such periods of normal working, occurring from October to

January. They included six sessions with supervisory ranks (acting sergeant, sergeant and Inspector); the remaining periods with PCs comprised fourteen panda car duties, four first-response car duties and four foot patrols. The twenty-eight periods covered eleven duties from 6 a.m. to 2 p.m. nine from 2 p.m. to 10 p.m. and eight from 10 p.m. to 6 a.m., though the whole of the shift was not necessarily observed, particularly in the 'quiet' time from 4 a.m. to 8 a.m.; the twenty-two periods with PCs were distributed over the duty times listed above in the ratio 7:9:6 respectively. The most frequent focus of observation was thus the panda car driver, with the other major roles sampled on a comparative basis. Observations generally covered the majority of the operational duty periods of the unit.

PANDA CAR DUTY — 10 P.M. TO 6 A.M.

A 'Reclaiming the Night' feminist demonstration is taking place in the city centre. The senior officer on duty is to go there and is heard to remark that the organizer of the demonstration is a nice girl, a nice bit of stuff. A similar set of assumptions about women is evident at the unit parade where the sergeant remarks that the women on the demonstration can't be cracking birds, because all of that sort will be at home doing their duties. But this event does not impinge on the panda driver, EM, whose activities are to be shadowed on this night duty.

After parade beginning at 9.45 EM travels to a block of flats to obtain a statement from a moped owner in a case of theft that he has been working on. At least five minutes are spent trying to locate the particular flat. The owner is a female 'general assistant' at a local higher education institution. We sit down in a pleasant flat, and EM writes the details down. Remarking that the moped is now a wreck, the owner says the penalties for the offence are too light, and EM agrees. He drives back towards the area around the station when he receives a call from subdivisional control. The moped owner has told Control that EM has left his torch behind. EM and I are both mystified but he says he will check it out and he takes a route which eventually arrives back at the flat; it turns out not to be his torch. During these comings and goings he checks out a call regarding a stolen vehicle reported at 9.51; the person has said he will be at a given location for five minutes only to wait for a police car. After some difficulty the place is discovered, but predictably by this time no one is there, and EM drives away.

It is 11.15 when EM leaves the flat and, following up a call, he drives to an address where at 11.35 an elderly woman explains she has returned home late and found the meter doors open, small signs of disturbance and her pension book missing. Small amounts of money remain, and her valuables are intact. EM agrees that intruders must have been disturbed and examines the garden. He asks her to check any lost property. She offers coffee, and EM accepts; we sit down as the woman checks her property. He says he will note the loss of her pension book, though they agree it is of no value. All valuables prove to be intact. EM feels confirmed in his theory of 'intruders disturbed', thinking that the meters were their objective. The owner and EM have thus 'talked through' the events and the evidence together, she appearing co-operative and intelligent. After taking the details he drives back to the station for petrol. It is now 0.05, five minutes past midnight.

It appears that an indecent assault has been reported. A woman is waiting in the station entrance, and a WPC and a second woman are found in the parade room, presumably in connection with this incident. Talk among the station staff suggests the 'Reclaiming the Night' march has passed off without incident. The sergeant tells me that he has put it to the indecent-assault complainant that she is trying it on to get publicity. But she has no connection with the march. Sympathetically he calls her a 'poor girl'.

EM reports to the controller sergeant, who is making an incident log for the purposes of a Management Department review. He reports that he went to the rendezvous concerning the stolen car straight away and waited for five minutes. (But he definitely did not attend the scene straight away. I speculated whether he had preferred to obtain his moped witness statement first rather than delay this contact and still probably miss the rendezvous. Later, at 2.10 a.m., the controller makes a Police National Computer (PNC) inquiry and hands the owner's name and address to EM.) The 'break' (break-in) EM has just attended will not require a visit from Scenes of Crime, he tells station staff.

About this time EM visits a small subdivisional station to do some work on the moped thefts file; there is some talk about the station PC's recent dog bite. On their leaving together, the small station is locked up.

At 1.15 a.m. there is a call to a domestic dispute. We arrive at a house to find a woman, slightly marked on the face, comforting a child. There are two men, one of whom talks, telling EM he is a dealer, explaining *en passant* that he has convictions including assault. EM, whom the woman calls 'Officer', clarifies whether they are married or not, telling the man not to raise his voice. The husband explains she won't let him correct her boy. EM is told that the wife's children have not been adopted by the husband. He listens, very much the arbiter, and advises them to separate. He tells the wife she can summons the man but that the matter is not serious enough for police intervention; he tells her he can't ask the man to leave, because his things are still here and it's late.

'But there'll be no more trouble tonight, will there? Or I'll be back.'

The man agrees, saying, 'If you'd been in my situation, you would have done the same.'

EM replies that he never hits women. The man says that his mate – the silent witness to this altercation – is the same. We leave and chat briefly with officers in two more panda cars that are waiting outside.

A general tour follows. EM remarks that people like that are pigs and animals. He subsequently makes an entry in the station 'violence-in-marriage' book, recounting the circumstances and the action taken – 'advice given' in this case. There is a call about a man 'thieving in a car' in a particular street. As EM drives, he notices two men pushing a pram; he turns back, stops them, asks their names, the address whence they've come and their destination. The older man, possibly drunk, gives the information. EM asks to see the pram's contents – one folded plastic mat. It is about 2 a.m. EM is satisfied for the moment but says he will check out the address later. He visits the place of the reported 'thieving', but no car of that description can be seen. Its number is not on the PNC, he tells me. He thinks it's some sort of grudge call. He tells me a story about an Irishman who was seen walking along the road carrying lead. On being questioned by EM, the man said where it had been obtained and was promptly arrested. He had said something like 'Oh dear' when told it was an offence. EM returns to the station.

By 3 a.m. EM is back on patrol, touring the subdivision with no result. At 4 a.m. there is a call to an incident. EM arrives to find an officer in the dog van searching for the address. They proceed down the street to find two men and a car. The men explain that a youth living close by has been spotted in this car by a neighbour. When hailed by one of the men, the youth ran round the block and back to his house. EM goes to the youth's home. It emerges that the youth is already charged with burglary in conjunction with an adult. Two other subdivisional panda cars have arrived, with four officers. One driver goes round the back of the house; the dog van takes no further part. A woman responds to the knock on the door, and protests when EM and a colleague explain. However, she invites them in saying, 'I'll sort this out.' She asks who's accused her son, but they reply that they can't say. She invites the officers to wake the youth, because he might climb out through the back

window. EM and his colleague go up and find the youth in bed;
they ask him where he's been. He says something I cannot discern.
They say, 'Get your clothes on. You're coming with us.'

Accompanied by the police, the youth comes down to the sitting
room with his clothes. His mother protests, saying, 'I like to see
fair play.'

EM tells her it's a bloke down the road, mentioning the man's
name. She says the man has nothing else to do but be nasty.
'You're not taking him,' she says.

EM obtains from the owner details of the car and the circumstances it was left in; the owner is told he will be interviewed later.
EM then takes the mother down to the station while her son is
driven in another car. Subsequently EM tells me that the youth
was never asleep.

At the station the patrol sergeants and the station sergeant take
the youth into the charge room and close the door. After a few
minutes these three are seen in whispered conference, and then the
station sergeant telephones the night duty detectives.

The mother, sitting in the foyer, remarks, 'Aren't you supposed
to interview him in the presence of a parent?'

EM answers, 'He's not being interviewed. He's in the charge
room.'

She makes no reply. EM and the youth are seen chatting. The
boy smiles. It emerges that they are discussing the local football
team. The two night detectives arrive after a long interval and
enter the charge room. One of the constables on duty, a probationer, has taken a statement from the witness in the presence of
a panda car driver and gives it to the station sergeant. After
examining it, he takes it to the detectives. After some talk, the
mother is invited to join the youth and the detectives, who depart,
presumably for the interview rooms.

The rest of my visit is spent in the station, chatting mainly with
the station sergeant. He asks me if I'm familiar with the Judges'
Rules. I say, 'Not exactly. I know you're not supposed to interview
a juvenile without the presence of the parent.'

Interrogation of a juvenile with a parent present is difficult, the
sergeant replies. He and the station PC agree that you get a parent
who is obstructive and tells the lad what to say. 'So this is what we
do', he says, referring to what I have seen. 'It depends what you
mean by interrogation.' The detectives have just now read the
statement to the youth, and he has 'coughed it' (confessed). The
sergeant says that the detectives were called in because previously
he had not 'coughed it'.

I mention the evidence of the Superintendents' Association to

the Royal Commission on Criminal Procedure asking for more
police powers.

The sergeant says, 'The association wants to get the law to fit
what we do. I want more powers, but then I'm a policeman.' He
quotes some difficult cases where powers were in question.

An audience of two or three PCs is now gathered, including EM.
At 5.40 a.m., twenty minutes before the official end of the shift, I
depart.

PANDA CAR DUTY – 6 A.M. TO 2 P.M.

At 8.10 a.m. I join BJ, who begins patrolling his set of beats. He
stops the car to note down in his pocket-book details of a
missing-person inquiry referred to him by Control. He visits the
house, to be told by a mother that her son ran away when the car
arrived. In fact, the boy had previously returned home, and the
mother tells BJ that he was ready to go with the social worker who
called. BJ notes this information but does not report back to
Control. As we leave he says that he has noticed a different attitude
when I accompany him; people's minds tick over and try to work
out who I am, he says.

Patrol is then resumed, but BJ returns to the main station to
replace his radio after a call has failed to make sense. This is the
first of three such replacements that morning. At 9 a.m. he takes
breakfast bacon to the sectional station, where I meet the new
station sergeant, an older man, returning to duty. He philoso-
phizes, 'Ambulance service – that's what the police are now.
There's no preventive policing like in the old days.' I mention
RBOs, but he demurs: 'That's all there is.'

BJ is given forms requesting petty cash. The forms are to be
dispatched to the Chief Inspector and the cash is to be delivered
this morning. The forms concern identity parades (participants
each receiving £1) and CID expenses (covering periods with
informants, amounting to £2 a time). The total sum is £22.10. BJ
returns to the main station, where the Chief Inspector asks me to
contact my research colleague at HQ. BJ comments ironically on
the senior officer's agitation at mention of the upper echelons of the
force.

A break begins at 9.30. Two card games develop among unit
members – Crib and 'Chase the Lady'. It is about 10.30 when BJ
resumes patrol, first delivering the petty cash to the sectional
station. It's tenpence short of the total, and BJ pays the difference
from his pocket. The station sergeant prefers the cash in pound
notes. BJ obliges by volunteering to go to the nearest bank to
change the money.

At about 10.50 a.m. BJ leaves the section station to visit the home of a complainant in an inquiry concerning unlawful sexual intercourse (USI). He has just spoken to a woman detective constable, who has advised him that the required birth certificate can be tacked on the file later after submission. He tells me the story of events which began when the mother of a pregnant 15-year old girl complained to the police. BJ asked her boyfriend to come down to the station (the offence not being arrestable, he explained), and the youth broke down in tears and gave a statement of admission. The girl has recently given birth. It emerges that the boy is black and the girl half-caste, an aspect of the case BJ mentions at the end of his recital. His attitude is philosophical, based on his impression that USI happens quite often. He thinks the mother of the girl will give the baby a good home even though it is an unfortunate start in life. He has a full file of statements and now wants the girl's birth certificate. Probably the boy will be cautioned formally, he thinks, because there is no history of sexual offences, though the youth has form for burglary.

At 11.10 a.m. BJ visits the home where he finds the girl and her mother, who is white and does the talking. She complains that the youth won't get much in the way of punishment; he's broken her windows, but no one saw him do it. My impression is that she wants to rid him from her life. BJ sympathetically explains the possible outcomes but stresses that it is not his decision whether to prosecute. At least a caution will make the boy think. The mother says she's been tied up with the baby and will get a copy of the birth certificate when the baby is registered. We leave and arrive at the section station at 11.30 a.m. BJ visits the CID office only to find the WDC gone. He explains to the secretary that he will leave the file and await the certificate in due course. He completes his pocket-book, a matter in which I note him to be very conscientious. At 11.45 a.m. we return to the main station for petrol and leave at 12 noon on patrol.

At 12.15 BJ calls on a shopkeeper on his unit beat area. The shopkeeper is known by his first name and offers coffee. BJ tells me that the shopkeeper is an old 'tea spot' (place to stop for a cuppa), the only one except for private homes on the RBO area BJ used to work. The other commercial establishments would shop you, BJ says to me; meanwhile customers are being served, and one says jokingly as we sip coffee, 'You're not supposed to do that.'

The shopkeeper describes how he was nearly mugged when leaving the local football ground recently. A group of youths – white – surrounded him and his two children as they walked. Feeling jostled, he threatened them with a kick. They mumbled something like, 'We've got a hard one here', and left. BJ sympathizes. A discussion about strikes takes place between BJ, the shopkeeper and a customer – terrible, they all agree. When we depart, BJ tells me that he thinks trade unions have to be restrained. The shopkeeper is a good source of information, he says later, and it emerges that BJ's neighbours happen to be the shopkeeper's relatives.

BJ then patrols, stopping for a few minutes to have a smoke and to write up his pocket-book, then recalling he's already done so. At 1.05 p.m. there's a call from Control asking BJ to return immediately to the main station to see the Chief Inspector. Duly returning, he is given the tenpence by the Chief Inspector owed him from petty cash. The Chief Inspector makes a heavy joke about BJ showing me round the police: 'You'll see that with all the rumours about the police, only half are true.' BJ smiles. I break off and leave at 1.20 p.m.

Bearing in mind the relative absence of concrete work in this period, BJ has the opportunity to talk with me about a wide range of matters, of which several are pertinent to unit work. One of the probationers on the unit has resigned following disciplinary investigation. He tells me the man threatened over the phone to commit suicide. He used to leave his current inquiry folder empty, which looked good. But then files would come in later, and the patrol sergeant would be asked about the delay. It turned out that he would take those files home. I mention a story I've been told about a 'blag' (joke) played on the man, in which he was told to put on a gas mask and ride to the station on a bicycle, as part of a supposed civil defence exercise. But BJ is unaware of this story. The probationer was not liked because of his bragging, he says.

He tells about the contrast between RBOing and unit work. As an RBO you get to know the exits and entries of an area, which is useful knowledge for a driver. He missed the comradeship of a unit, however, and gives this as one reason for giving up the RBO work. Another was passing his driving test. He didn't want to be labelled as someone who had not done ordinary panda driving. So he returned to the unit and enjoys it. With more men coming in the force, the areas could be made smaller and the number of RBOs doubled.

BJ mentions the problem of panda drivers 'balling up' RBO work. 'You might get in with a family through solving a minor complaint or nuisance and then find some hard panda driver messing it up, and the family don't treat you the same any more.'

I ask how the officer arrests someone in a family he's got to know.

He says, 'It's OK', and describes how he cleared up a family's complaint about indecency, for which they were grateful. He later had to arrest a boy in the family for assault, following an incident in school. BJ invited the parents to accompany them to the station. 'Yes, certainly,' they replied. BJ put it to the boy that several witnesses had seen him strike the victim. When the boy denied this, his father said, 'Tell the officer the truth or I'll give you a thick ear.' So he admitted it. BJ explains that his approach on arresting is to ask people to come with him. If they refuse, he says, 'Right, I'm arresting you', and takes the person's arm. Some policemen would put them across the car bonnet (an over-dramatic approach, it seems). On the other hand, he says, you have some criminals who you can't soft-soap. If you do, they laugh at you.

He mentions how he deals with complaints about games-playing in the street by children. After unsuccessful warnings he took the names of twenty or so, and they were cautioned. That stopped it for a while, but it has been resumed. Even cautioning helps, because parents don't like to have to go to the station with the kid.

It is interesting to learn after this discussion of RBOing and unit work that BJ enjoys the night van patrol. 'You get drunks, and that's where the punch-ups occur. It really gets the adrenalin going.'

PANDA CAR DUTY — 2 P.M. TO 10 P.M.
FN begins the afternoon shift by transporting a WPC 'walker' to the neighbouring subdivision so that she can obtain antecedents for court from a woman she arrested for prostitution about a week ago. But the woman is not at her address, and FN drives the WPC back to the station. A call comes. The Inspector needs the WPC to check a mock-auction, I learn later.[4] The WPC talks about an incident involving the Inspector. One day the Inspector said to her, 'You haven't had a complaint, have you?' Soon after, she did have a complaint, after she and the Inspector had arrested a man for importuning for immoral purposes. The 'queer' became 'hysterical' in the police station, and formally complained that the Inspector and the WPC had used violence against him and that she had abused him. However, the case against him was sustained in court.

FN drops the WPC at the station and drives to the subdivisional section station to fill in a road-accident book – a pro-forma report for one incident. He has two witnesses to visit, each having slightly different descriptions of events. But, he explains, he has nothing on his plate; his unit beat area is normally quiet. Drivers are circulated round these different areas, he explains. He talks about a fight in a pub which the unit attended a few nights ago, which could have turned nasty.

At 3.15 p.m. FN departs on a general patrol around his area. He explains that the accident books have a statistical purpose and are filled in at the time of the event. When I ask him about this continuous patrolling, he says he might have packed up if I hadn't been with him. Commuter traffic often presents a difficulty when one patrols between 4.30 and 6 p.m.

At 5.20 p.m. FN gets a call to assist an ambulance through traffic. Control is setting up escorts for this vehicle to get to the hospital. But by the time we arrive the vehicle appears to have gone. FN then gets a call to attend an injured dog on a main road. The dog is lying on the pavement in a bus shelter when FN arrives. He wants to call out a vet, but Control says the vet can't come yet. FN appears nonplussed, and we wait for the vet.

Suddenly Control calls FN to a snatch of money outside a town-centre bank. Using the car codes, Control says that another of the panda drivers is to take the description, and FN is to 'do the crime'. When we get there, FN sees his colleague's car parked outside the bank and cruises past and round the town centre. He feels the thief could have taken one particular route, as has often happened previously, or could have boarded a bus. FN seems to have taken a fatalist attitude and does not check these theories. At 6.15 p.m. he returns to the injured dog. On the way the controller, learning that the dog is incapacitated, tells FN to remember what's in his back pocket (i.e. his 'staff' or truncheon). FN tells me he won't smash the dog, however. It takes a few minutes to find the dog, which has moved. FN is reluctant to touch it because of a possible bite.

The vet still can't come, it appears. At 6.30 Control asks FN to visit the bank where a witness is waiting to make a statement. FN asks me if I heard the previous instruction. I say that I heard that the other car was to take the description (though I had thought the words used, 'doing the crime' or 'criming it', suggested that FN should write the crime report). At 6.45 we arrive at the bank again to find the manager and the witness – a young woman. FN takes a statement from the young woman in the bank. She was depositing money in the night safe when a white youth grabbed her. She shouted, 'Stop! Thief!' He grabbed her shopping bag, giving her time to drop the money in the safe. She had little chance to catch details of his appearance as he ran away. FN goes through the events with her, concerned to be sure of exactly what she has seen, then writes the details down and asks her to sign. At 7.15 we leave the bank and go to the station for a break. In the parade room between 8.30 and 9.00 p.m. FN types up the crime report for the robbery attempt, after which I leave.

PANDA CAR DUTY – 6 A.M. TO 2 P.M.

CK collects me around 8 a.m. and drives to the main station where he picks up the bacon for the section station canteen. I learn that only three pandas, one walker and one area car are operating today (because of examinations, leave and attachments), compared with a theoretical strength of four pandas, eight walkers and two area cars. CK has three years' service and wants to join the Traffic Department. After visiting the canteen, CK drops in at the CID office and discusses the progress of a case concerning theft from vending machines. He discovers that the defendants have elected for trial, a process that can take twelve months to occur, he tells me. On returning to the main station he retraces his path once again to the section station to obtain keys in order to open a car locked by accident. At 9 a.m. he visits the scene of a reported 'break' – a clinic – but no one seems to be present. CK reports this to Control, only to be interrupted by a cleaner opening the clinic door. A window in the kitchen is broken, and the cleaner tells CK that a kettle has gone. Unlike EM, CK fills in the crime report directly rather than making notes and completing the form later. During the conversation the cleaner reveals that the window was broken a week ago, a point CK has not asked about. She says the broken window was not covered so as not to draw attention to it. It appears that attenders at a nearby disco may have had something to do with the break-in. CK says he will report this to the RBO.

CK's next task is to visit a garage which has reported a car stolen. The manager is not present when CK arrives, so he speaks to the mechanics. The car was taken in for repairs and discovered to have a hopelessly poor gearbox, so the owner was asked to take it away. It is still in the car-park, suggests the mechanics. This inconclusive incident is later reported in the station occurrence book.

CK turns to an ongoing inquiry into an 'elopement'. It appears that a middle-aged man has run away with a 'mentally retarded' girl. CK visits the home of a boy who apparently worked with the man. The boy, it turns out, has also run away. The mother, together with another boy (a relative or a boyfriend of her daughter) shows CK a letter from the runaway boy. The letter is from a location within another divisional area of the force; it says he is OK. There is a consensus that the couple and the boy are living together in a caravan. CK then visits the parents of the 'retarded' girl. The home is in particularly poor condition. He finds that a similar letter has been received from her, originating from the same area and assuring the parents of her safety. The father explains all this to CK, saying that rumours imply she is pregnant, but he saw no evidence of this prior to her disappearance. He says he is sceptical about the statement in his daughter's letter that the man concerned now has a job. The man was always self-employed, and anyway would get tax refunds (as an income). CK makes his third visit, this time to the home of the man concerned. A boy there tells CK that the man's wife is out of the house. The boy says he knows nothing further. On his return to the station CK rings the relevant division to find if the caravan could have arrived at any particular site. But there isn't a site. The local social security office is then telephoned to find out if anybody involved in the case has signed on for benefits, with no apparent result. CK asks the Inspector about his next annual leave as he needs to fix a particular time for it. Calling CK by his first name, the Inspector takes him to the subdivisional clerk's office to look at the leave list but cannot find the details.

A sergeant sends CK, accompanied by a walker PC, to find a missing little boy, while the sergeant himself uses another car. CK is simply told to search the town centre. He photocopies the boy's photograph, after first asking the sergeant's permission. He is also shown the details about the boy and finally given the original photo to use. CK explains to the walker that the little boy is 4; it appears that on a previous occasion the boy left his home and was found in the town centre. He is 'mentally retarded' and doesn't like his school.

CK arrives at a big cleared space to look for the child and meets a second walker, who is shown the photo (but not told the child's name). CK drives round a local park and near some waste ground. Then he goes to the skateboard park and asks the owner, but he has not seen such a boy. We walk round the skateboard park and are stared at by children. I notice that CK makes no general appeal to the skateboarders, though he reacts in a friendly fashion when one boy speaks to him and when he avoids bumping into another boy. The owner finds two boys – one black, one white – who look at the photo but don't recognize the face. I suggest looking at the joke shop in the town centre, and CK asks the walker to check this possibility. The walker doesn't take the photo into the shop, and there is no apparent result. They visit the rail station and have a word with the guard at the entrance before checking the platforms. Then the pair check out a children's toy store, walking around oblivious to stares. There is no response when a store assistant approaches CK as if to speak. When another assistant finally says something like, 'Find what you're looking for?', CK smiles and says 'No.' He then visits another toyshop, explaining his interest, with no result.

Finally, CK visits a cinema, goes inside and says, 'We're looking for a lad.'

Two men say, 'No, we've not seen one in here. We're not open. Kid gone missing, then?'

'Yes,' CK replies.

At this point, with the search still inconclusive, I am due to leave.

FOOT PATROL DUTY – 6 A.M. TO 2 P.M.

Snow leads to my late arrival – at 10.35 a.m. There's been some playing in the snow. No cars are being allowed on the road. BJ is staying in to do reports, and I decide to accompany GO. Before he can patrol he has to make tea for one of the senior officers in charge of the subdivision and for his party. The acting sergeant takes the tea upstairs. GO is then sent to buy newspapers for the telephone switchboard operator. At 11.40 he ventures out on the streets around the station – the only foot patrol on duty. He passes many parked cars. He does a PNC check to find out the owner of an isolated new Mini in a pub car-park and whether it has been stolen. At 12.15 he gives a ticket to a parked Volvo because of its expired tax disc. As he is writing the ticket a prosperous looking man who turns out to be the Volvo's owner comes up. GO says, 'I've started so I've got to finish.' (This, he explains to me, is because he must account for each ticket.) The owner says the car has been in the garage, but GO replies that the garage will have to explain. He seems unclear on this point, and the man as if sensing this uncertainty says, 'Well, *I* don't know.' He tells GO that he used to issue such tickets himself, implying that he's been a police officer. GO discusses the situation on police pay, and the owner gives his opinion: 'More pay, reduced crime rate, more bobbies.' He mentions that he owns a tackle shop. GO gives the man the ticket and moves on.

He asks me afterwards if I realize what a lot of 'blagging' (bull) there is in his job. I reply, 'You blagging him or him blagging you?'

'Oh no, blagging him,' he says. 'When you give them a ticket or something, you have to be nice to them.'

One bloke he knocked off for an offence asked him if he wanted a lift. (Some further light was shed on the Volvo incident later in the shift.)

As we walk GO explains his philosophy and general impression of the job after three months. He doesn't knock people off for everything, while some police are really hard. For example, he took action against a man who was found 'quitting' a vehicle with the engine running after the man refused to give him his name and address. The man's stroppy attitude decided it; on the other hand, if an offender was going to work, GO wouldn't knock him off. In the cadets you learn a lot about the police service, he says, but the work itself is hard to learn.

He has no complaints about pay or paperwork. He has to complete his pocket-book before the end of the shift for checking. A 'purge' on pocket-books started two weeks ago after a detective was caught out over a discrepancy in his pocket-book. GO complains about sergeants' contradictory instructions; for example, today he returned to the station to obtain a crime number for a crime report, in line with one sergeant's general instructions to complete crime reports before the end of the shift, but the patrol sergeant sent him out again, saying, 'What if an incident happened on your beat?' But he thought the station wasn't far from his beat, if an incident were to occur. One sergeant tended to nag probationers but not the full constables, a distinction he seemed to think unfair; another sergeant was OK, someone you have a good laugh with. But a third sergeant was almost 'two-faced', and GO disliked him; he was a good policeman and had to keep you up to the mark, but GO seemed unsure about the sergeant's attitude. At a unit social, the sergeant stayed with 'the gaffer' (the Inspector) and didn't talk to the 'pro-cons'.

At 12.45 p.m. GO walks up to a parked Ford Capri, saying he has seen the car before in some connection. Two men are examining the offside wing, part of which has been sheared off apparently in an accident but not noticed previously because of the snow. The owner is not present but is known to the two men, both local residents. One of these owns a second car which is parked next to the Capri and has a yellow scratch above the offside lights. It is suggested that a tall van damaged both vehicles during the night. GO accepts this account and says he will do a report. The owner of the second car is given an HORT-1 (a form requiring him to produce his driving documents within a short period). He accepts this and shows GO his licence. While this discussion is going on, Control asks GO for his location. (There is no further message, and it emerges later that the call was intended to find out if GO was able to walk to a particular location for a particular task. But as a result the task was passed to someone else.) GO tells me that he's started 'knocking people off' (booking them) for having only one light. It seems a silly offence; the drivers always say, 'It was working when I started', but GO realized without any prompting that it had to be dealt with. He spots a car with no amber cover to its lamps but says, 'I should knock him off. But I can't always stop them.'

At 12.50 p.m. he finds a car with an overdue excise licence and decides to take action. A smartly dressed young black man walks across the road to the car.

'Know there's no tax on this car?' asks GO.

The black man walks round and on to the pavement, looks at the window and says 'You're bright', but without looking at GO directly. He goes round to the driver's side, gets in and starts the engine.

GO says, 'He's not going to drive off, is he? Because I've got his ticket. I hope so.' There is a momentary pause before he bends down and says, 'Don't run off, because I've got this ticket.'

Then he completes it. The man is still revving the engine, and GO puts the ticket through the window. Saying nothing, the man picks it up and then leaves it on the seat; as he attempts to drive off, the car is impeded by snow.

Afterwards GO says the car is probably not registered in his name. 'I'm not biased,' he says. He indicates that blacks do not bother about the formalities connected with car ownership. He repeats an earlier comment that blacks have too expensive cars, and connects the man with a house near to the car, where he says Jamaican men and prostitutes live. These men are pimps, he says. Black pimps dress flash, he states. GO goes on to describe how his mate – a policeman – and a friend were dancing with two girls in a local hotel when a black man approached the girls and asked them if they wanted to be prostitutes. 'You'd be angry if someone approached your girlfriend, wouldn't you, and said that? You'd want to punch them, wouldn't you?' During our conversation GO also complains about the radio and says he experienced a radio failure in the town centre. He could have been attacked by four hundred 'niggers', he says, and couldn't have called for assistance.

We return to the section station at 1 p.m. for GO to change into wellingtons. GO asks the station PC if he knows a man of the name given by the Volvo owner. 'Yes,' replies the PC, 'but he is not an ex-copper; he knows them, that's all.' The PC mentions a business owned by the Volvo owner but doesn't, I notice, refer to the tackle shop mentioned by the man. The sergeant on duty has never heard of a policeman of that description in twenty years. GO is then told to buy some wallpaper adhesive for a senior officer who is decorating the station bar. He meets BJ and asks for a lift to the main station. GO mentions the prostitutes' address, and BJ tells a story about arresting a 'buck nigger' in a bath-robe. He and two other PCs were chasing a prostitute and trying to arrest her. She fled into the house, and a black man tried to bar entry so he was arrested for 'obstructing the police'. It seemed that a lot of energy was needed to get him in the car. BJ drops GO off to buy the adhesive, and then GO walks back to the station, as the end of his shift approaches.

FIRST-RESPONSE CAR DUTY — 10 P.M. TO 6 A.M.

The patrol sergeant and the Inspector discuss the duties list. The Inspector says he will put a particular PC with a first-response driver. He's a good man who might gee the driver up. At 10.15 p.m. I accompany another driver, DL, and his partner, JR, to a house where a young woman complains about having seen one of the neighbour's children breaking her windows. The two PCs visit the neighbour's house where the mother complains in turn about the first family. The young woman, she says, is a prostitute and has shown the mother's children pornography. As the two policemen leave the house, another neighbour and his wife accost them respectfully and complain about the young woman's family. DL insists, 'There's got to be two prostitutes for a brothel to exist. She can take as many boyfriends as she likes.'

There is then a call to a fire. The car arrives at the house at 10.35 p.m. The top window is emitting smoke. The policemen enter to find the family downstairs. The family, it emerges, is already known to the police. There is an older couple, a young couple and some children. The older woman accuses her husband of setting fire to the house to 'get the children out'. The husband, who appears to be drunk, starts to shout incoherently. DL pushes him into a chair. DL asks the young man if he has seen the older man light a fire. 'No,' he replies. He thinks the old man started it by accident after going upstairs to sleep in a cupboard; answering DL's questions promptly and coherently, he describes the sequence of events in which the man ascended the stairs and the fire was subsequently discovered. His girlfriend appears distressed. Fire officers have arrived, along with a panda car and DL disappears up the stairs where the fire officers have also gone. It later emerges that he has checked serial numbers on some stereo equipment in the son's room. JR chuckles, 'Well, you've got to take your opportunities.'

Towards 11 p.m. they leave the house. For a while DL follows a car with a line of apparently young black people wearing West-Indian-style hats at the back; he asks for a PNC check, and it proves negative. DL spots a young man 'hanging round' some shops and stops the car. JR calls the man over for a word. The man, who gladly gives his name and address, is apparently waiting for a late bus. DL returns to the station for a fresh radio. Here a sergeant says that he will write up a report on the fire himself.

At 11.15 p.m. DL and JR leave the station to return to the second of the two houses visited earlier. The second householder has complained to the station about the previous visit. He tells the policeman that the boyfriend of the young woman next door has just assaulted him with a weapon. He had to use a dustbin lid to defend himself and was obliged to withdraw into his own home. DL and JR are not impressed. The man says he has seen the local RBO about the family next door but received no satisfaction. He goes on to say that he will make a formal complaint against the two policemen for not doing anything. They leave the house as the third local resident in this dispute arrives again. The complaint they've just received is then put to the couple next door. The young man against whom the allegation has just been made is shivering by the fire. How can he have attacked the man next door? he asks. JR assures him that he won't do anything about it. The policemen leave, joking between themselves that the dissatisfied householder will complain they went in the house and 'knocked' the alleged 'prostitute'. DL remarks amiably to JR that he is surprised at JR's last remark because JR is usually silent.

At 11.35 p.m. they return to the town centre. A call comes from Control to look out for a 'non-stop RTA' (a driver having failed to stop after a road traffic accident). In the town centre a walker PC is seen directing a sports car to stop. As it does so, DL drives by and brings his car to a halt. The driver is co-operative, and says he has been drinking, when asked by JR. He is taken into the police car to be breathalysed, a job which is given to the inexperienced foot patrol officer. DL is also in the car. The foot patroller says by way of preamble, 'You have been involved in a non-stop RTA.' The man is obviously nonplussed by this statement. DL takes over, takes the breathalyser kit and administers the test after a quick statement. The test proves positive, and the man is arrested and cautioned. The car then moves off to the station with the prisoner, and here the walker deals with the second test required by law.

A general alert has gone out to surround the local football ground where intruders have been reported. At 00.05 a.m. DL drives up a street adjoining the ground and waits by the wall separating the street from the Home End. As the car drives up, a young man is seen leaning against the wall of the ground. I hear one of the officers say, 'I bet he's something to do with it.' The young man is asked to stay till the matter is cleared up. He obeys, saying nothing very much, clearly very drunk. JR goes to assist other officers in a second car which appears to be entering the stadium further down the street.

As DL continues waiting, he and I discuss his work. He gets less money but more satisfaction in the police than in his former job. He wants definitely to join CID though there's a lot of paperwork involved. 'Most coppers are in it for this sort of thing' (meaning catching criminals), he says. DL has in fact no radio at this point, having been unable to find a suitable replacement.

When the drunk young man slips down on to the pavement and lies there, DL comes over and tells him to stand up. When the man still shows reluctance, DL arrests him for being drunk and incapable. The man is then put in the car but protests that if the police hadn't stopped him he would have walked home by now. He tells us he has an ulcer. DL then relents, and he is allowed to sit on the edge of the car seat with the door open. I stand by him. Eventually he gets up because apparently he doesn't want to sit in that position, owing to his stomach problem. Nothing is happening. DL takes the young man's name and the address to which he is going, and tells him to go home. He walks off slowly – to his sister's, he's told us.

DL laughs when he spots a foot patrol officer speaking with the man further down the street. Then another foot patrol officer and another constable appear and tell us it is all over, two arrests having been made and one person still being sought.

DL complains about the problem of the defective radio. He then drives along the probable route of the drunk man he's just spoken to, but concludes he has gone home. At the station, DL soon learns that one of the men arrested has the same surname as the man earlier 'detained'. As he rushes from the station, the station sergeant says, 'As long as you're *sure*.' DL drives to the address the man gave him. The door is opened by the man we know. 'Can we come in?' asks DL. The man is silent, and DL quickly walks through the gap in the doorway. As I follow, the man recognizes me and protests. DL tells him the reason for our visit. The man protests loudly again, but DL grabs him by the hair and tells him to be quiet. It is about 12.40 a.m. He is taken to the car, and DL drives to the station. There is no caution.

DL says to the man, 'You hopped over the wall. I saw you come over the wall.'

'I didn't,' says the man.

'You did,' said DL; 'you've taught me a lesson.' He uses the man's first name at the end of this remark, which seems to refer to his earlier forbearance in not making an arrest at the outset.

We arrive at the station at about 1 a.m. With the man in custody, DL, JR and a panda driver return fairly promptly to the house where the arrest has been made. They ask the woman living there if they can search, and she agrees. She sits chatting to JR while the panda driver searches the downstairs front room; meanwhile DL and I go down into the cellar, but nothing is found. Then DL checks the upstairs bedrooms. Two children are sleeping in the back room and a baby in the front where the mother has been sleeping. There are no carpets on the floor; quietly but efficiently DL looks under the beds, finds a loose floorboard and then shifts it to look beneath, discovering nothing. DL returns down the stairs and checks the outhouses at the back. With no result, DL returns to the station and questions the man. In the course of the next hour or so it emerges that the man will 'cough' for previous 'breaks' at the football ground but not for this one; his two friends however are prepared to talk about this night's incident. Eventually the night duty detectives are called in.

There is a discussion involving the station sergeant and a further detective about the appropriate choice of charge. The detective thinks they should be charged with being 'found on enclosed premises' (Vagrancy Act 1824); this charge could be amended later if necessary. This opinion is conveyed later to the station sergeant, who thinks perhaps there could be alternative charges: 'burglary with intent to steal' (Theft Act 1968) or 'found on enclosed premises'. The sergeant reasons, in pondering this question, that the football stand is not a building within the meaning of the burglary provision of the Theft Act, because it is open-topped. He telephones the senior officer on duty. In response to a question over the phone, he replies 'Oh, yes, it's a good 'un. They've got form.' The senior officer advises that the charge from the Vagrancy Act be used, suggesting that the powers that be can amend it later.

The detective appears to play no further part. After the arrests and some discussion of interrogation arose, he laughed and said, 'Kick them once if they cough and twice if they don't.' He jokes at one point, 'If I walk to the station, I might get picked up by DL.'

On at least two occasions during this period JR and DL say they saw the man arrested by DL come over the wall. When they are asked about this point by the sergeant, there is laughter. On one occasion the detective is present while they make remarks to this effect to one another.

When it is finally reported that the men have 'coughed it', the sergeant refers ironically to the 'psychology' of interrogation. 'They see it on telly in *The Sweeney* – the nice one and the nasty one – but it still works. It appears that one of the men wouldn't confess to DL because he called the man's kids 'bastards'; another PC offered the man a cigarette, and he 'coughed it'.

The sergeant talks to me about the Judges' Rules. He says that following a case in 1976 the police don't have to caution till evidence sufficient for a court is gained. Formerly, he says, you cautioned on arrest. It has also been ruled that statements gained through the police using lies are OK. 'What else can you do,' asks the sergeant, 'apart from giving them a beating?'

At 2.35 a.m. a break is taken. I learn incidentally that JR has to do a report on a 'criminal injury' to DL – a cut to the face which fell within the terms of the wounding offence under section 20 of the Offences Against the Persons Act 1861. Presumably this report is for the purpose of an application for statutory compensation. I also learn that the breathalysed driver has come through negative on his second test. He did in fact offer to give his name and address to the other party at the accident but the latter abused him; thus intimidated he drove off. An officer remarks defensively that he wouldn't have been arrested if he had given his name and address. The Inspector makes a visit to the station and comments on a recent 'good night'. He liked the variety of the charges – four burglars, two breathalyser offenders.

In the station office two officers in the supervisory ranks discuss corruption and dubious police procedures. The first supervisor says he has seen the files in the Challenor case. 'I thought I was "practically minded",' he comments, implying that this scale of manipulation was different. He says that a man would find a radio on his car seat and go to the station to ask to make his own confession. The drinking clubs are mentioned, as a source of free drink for officers. The second supervisor laughs as he recalls a raid when he was a member of the Drug Squad. He caught one man with the hash and thought, 'I'm sticking to him.' Then the sergeant picked up the hash, split it up and said, 'Here's your bit', to each of the gang. But they all pleaded guilty.

I note that DL reports to JR that the other first-response car driver (mentioned by the Inspector) wants to swap his partner for JR – perhaps an indication of the 'geeing up' the Inspector thought necessary.

PATROL SERGEANT'S DUTY – 6 A.M. TO 2 P.M.
I arrive at 8.30 a.m. and ask the Inspector to allot me to a patrol sergeant. He chooses HP because he says HP is the more experienced of the two. At 9 a.m. HP sees a PC about his paperwork. The PC is told off for very poor work in a crime file; the names are

wrong, words are illegible, irrelevant matter has been included, Christian names have been introduced at the wrong point. HP explains that the sergeant charges a person, not the PC. Another mistake is that the file deals with the wrong question. What has to be proved is the identity of the IP (injured party), not who is not the IP. The PC looks concerned at this criticism. HP raises his voice for a few minutes and then lowers it as he goes into the details and talks about what has to be done to amend the file. During the reprimand I leave the two in the patrol sergeant's room. I meet the Inspector and explain that I've left the room because of the reprimand. He discourses on the fall in recruitment standards since his day. HP joins us as we speak and confirms this experience.

Around 9.30 HP takes breakfast and explains that the patrol sergeant is responsible for checking files, especially the officer's statement. But it could be the nearest sergeant who does it, e.g. the station sergeant, or a sergeant involved in the particular incident. In his former force one subdivisional section comprised one sergeant and four or five PCs; you saw the Inspector only once a day. This was in contrast to the current position here (with up to five sergeants and 18 PCs per shift). On the whole he feels the ranks are closing up a bit. 'It's difficult, sometimes, you have to forget you're one of the lads.'

Around 10.30 HP leaves the station on patrol in a brand new car. He gives a lift to one of the RBOs. At 10.40 HP notices a particular man walking along the street and wonders if there's a warrant out for him. He stops the car. The man – thin, middle-aged – acquiesces as HP checks with Control whether there is such a warrant. Control confirms his supposition, and the man is placed in the car and taken to the station, after HP has dropped the RBO nearby. The warrant concerns defaults on payments imposed by a court, possibly including those to do with rent or rates. The man asks HP if he can have all the payments dealt with by one court. HP doesn't know. Everything is very matter-of-fact; no difficulty between the policeman and the arrestee. At 11 a.m. HP arrives at the station and phones the station where the warrant was issued. A senior officer apparently wants some hardware. HP suggests that inquiries be made at a store which another senior officer is currently visiting.

He then drives to a school to interview a headteacher about a school concert. He speaks to the deputy head, looks at the hall, asks about the numbers due to attend and is quite satisfied. It is now about 11.15 a.m. He tells me his educational history; he left sixth-form studies in mid-course, after some conflict with the headteacher.

At 11.35 a.m. HP visits a house in order to interview a girl who has applied for a croupier's licence. But she is absent. 'She's quite a girl', says HP. After a quick visit to the bank, he is back at the station ten minutes later. He takes the car back to the garage and talks with the mechanics about a fault. It turns out that the car has been wrongly assigned to the particular station. He enters the station office and is shown a new set of batteries (presumably for the radio). He examines them and works out how to put them in the charger. After about half an hour he moves into his office and does some paperwork for an hour and a quarter to the end of the shift. At one point during the shift he tells me about the recent disciplining of a probationer. Really it was lack of self-discipline, he says. The charge was neglect of duty, as the PC was spending up to an hour in a night-club. The men were with us on this one, HP feels. I noticed that the Inspector gave a friendly 'hallo' to the disciplined PC when they met in the office.

Résumé

Having completed our outline of the formal elements of the system and offered some examples of it at work, we are now in a position to begin the work of interpretation, and of testing the various hypotheses. These are the central tasks of Chapter 3.

Notes

1 Numbers in a unit may vary over time. We found 15 PCs (12 male and 3 female) in the unit chosen for case study. (The supervisors on the subdivision included 1 female sergeant and subsequently 1 female Inspector.)
2 The quantity of resources, both personal and material, varies between forces, as do the details of organization. However, some features make for a degree of standardization, as our research on force policy revealed. The force establishment, listing ranks and posts, will be set partly by reference to schemes and formulas considered at national level by joint working bodies; these reflect the results of inquiry and analysis, and refer to quantitative needs arising from the crime rate, road mileage, commercial property and so on. Hence local establishments can be understood partly in terms of the standard application of factors arising from national discussions. In addition forces may conduct research on their locally perceived establishment needs. Another major factor will be financial, at both the local and national levels. Hence organizational differences, as well as similarities, need to be kept in view in assessing the significance of these formal elements of policing (cf. Hough, 1980,

pp. 18–21; Brogden, 1982, pp. 97–120; Chartered Institute of Public Finance and Accountancy, annual police statistics).

3 Command-and-control systems, which were being introduced at the time of our research, are reviewed in Manwaring-White, (1983, p. 71). See also, Pounder and Anderson (n.d.).

4 The Mock Auctions Act 1961 proscribes certain dubious practices in the sale of goods by competitive bidding.

CHAPTER THREE

Decoding the Message

A NOCTURNAL RHYTHM

The rhythm of shiftwork manifests itself in certain temporal patterns. For, example, the early part of the morning shift may entail drivers making visits to overnight 'breaks' which involve the completion of a crime report and the checking of the immediate area in order to see whether a Scenes of Crime forensic investigation is required. Much of the daytime period is comparatively quiet in terms of calls, however, and the officers may be able to pursue existing inquiries or to seek work on their own account. In the evenings and nights, calls are received to deal with violent disputes and burglaries, and checks on night travellers are made; it is this time which produces arrests. As the early hours advance, quietness supervenes again. One is reminded of the traditional night watch from which modern policing emerged in the nineteenth century. Security in the hours of darkness remains an important point of attention for a public force designed to remedy the deficiencies of citizen self-protection (Emsley, 1983, p. 61). This concentration of certain types of important activity in the night hours gives an extra edge to the proposition that policework is often veiled from public view. In the morning the remnants of the night's misdoings become the subject of report and inquiry, and so the cycle moves on. Our task must be to construct a connected account encompassing all these various phases and suggesting some of the consequences stemming from such differences. The next sections try to develop our immediate impressions.

DIVERSITY

A glance at the work of the unit suggests the diversity of subjects which an officer may be called upon to deal with. At one end of the spectrum we may note the presence of trivial chores, for example, concerning petty cash; or there may be a requirement for a driver simply to transport another officer. Going up the scale of serious-ness, we found incidents ranging from traffic offences and a call to attend an injured dog, to an ambulance escort, a search for a missing person, a complaint of burglary and the arrest of suspects. Within a certain range of non-specialized tasks (for example we did not see drivers undertaking fraud inquiries) there is a broad band of unit tasks in which much of police relevance is included. This phenomenon also manifests itself in the variations of urgency and perspective which can occur during the span of a single shift. FN, for example, fitted in attending at an attempted bank 'snatch' between two visits to succour an injured dog; DL performed street checks, visited disputing neighbours and made an arrest for illegal entry within the space of one shift.

FRAGMENTATION OF WORK

Unit policework seems formed out of a myriad of incidents each of which may well be unrelated to the next one, or to any other. A quick call here, a few words, an entry in a report or pocket-book: these together constitute a fragmented texture of events. For example, the men with the pram, stopped by EM, flitted in the narrative and flitted out almost as quickly as they appeared. Typically several unconnected members of the public, often widely separated in space, enter the officer's field of operation during a shift. The relevance of each contact also seems limited, so that completion of the business in hand appears the principal objective of the officer; there is often little development or articulation of contacts opening up new ground or casting fresh light on what has gone before. Many of the people who engage in interaction with officers can be viewed in consequence as types possessing a limited repertoire of relevant attributes: 'non-stop RTA suspect', 'possible witness of a missing person' and so on.

A general fragmentary quality thus applies not only to the incidents but to the perception of individuals who play their brief parts and step from the spotlight of police attention. A proportion of contacts are inconclusive, as exemplified by FN's failure to contact the ambulance he had been asked to escort, or by his transport of another officer to make an unsuccessful house call. HP likewise could not proceed with a licence application by a croupier for a similar reason. More dramatic examples of such inconve-niences were found elsewhere in our observations when alarms required immediate attendance but proved to be faulty or when hoax calls were received – a suspicion which, in one of our earlier cases, was not far from the mind of EM, the officer concerned. Important calls may not produce a successful conclusion; CK's search for the missing boy was without result, as was FN's drive in search of a robbery suspect. The deployment of unit resources in this fashion means that officers run up frequently against obstacles, or the relevance of demands is found to peter out (cf. Ekblom and Heal, 1982, pp. 43–5).

DESULTORINESS AND TRIVIALITY

Another related feature of the unit's work is an apparent desultoriness or lack of structure, most evident in our examples where minor matters seem to take a long time to reach a conclusion or when a long stretch of time is spent 'on patrol' without any obvious result (cf. Holdaway, 1983, p. 146). For example, BJ's visit to the home of a USI complainant was apparently motivated by the need to obtain a birth certificate, but there was no urgency in his approach nor in that of the CID officer who advised him. HP took some time to examine the new batteries which had been allocated to the radio system. Continuous patrolling appears in the shift patterns of EM and FN where it was sustained despite the lack of evident results; in reply to a question on this point, FN's alternative to patrolling at rush-hours was to park the car – arguably an equally unfocused tactic.

In addition to the desultoriness of some work, there is a proportion of trivial chores, as revealed in the foot patroller's tea-making and the panda drivers' morning 'bacon run'. These can be extended by virtue of a surprising preciosity, for example over the petty cash payment mentioned earlier. Triviality represents in part a concrete answer to desultory phases when there seems to be nothing going on and a lot of time to spin out (cf. Cain, 1971, p. 69).

The Organizational Demand for 'Call Readiness'

The qualities of fragmentation, inconclusiveness and desultoriness stem not so much from the characteristics of the officers or their collective norms as from the organizational demands of 'call-readiness'. Fragmentation is linked to the need to conduct interactions with half an eye on the next call, to be able to bring an incident to a close with reasonable dispatch and to move on without leaving embarrassing loose ends (cf. Ekblom and Heal, 1982, p. 42). The call system takes command over the individual's dispositions and instantly imposes its own priorities. The relevance of each contact is thus restricted to a narrow band of immediate concerns. In the same way inconclusiveness can be associated with the way messages are handled and dispatched. Any

call for assistance from the public which has a prima-facie substance and relevance to policework is passed on; yet there is
necessarily a proportion of such work which is inconclusive
because there proves to be nothing of substance, people cannot be
found, addresses are incorrect and so on, or because the relevance
of the matter to the police turns out to be different from what
initial reports suggested.

Behind the inconclusiveness of the work therefore lies the
organizational system of receiving and dispatching calls which
ensures that some, at least, of such work is fruitless or less relevant
than it at first appeared. Furthermore, to engage, for example, in
frequent bouts of complex self-generated work may infringe the
prerogatives of the controlling system of dispatching calls. Patrolling without result thus continually ensures readiness to meet the
requirements of the call system, even if calls are for long periods
absent. Triviality in terms of minor chores allows the officer
freedom to postpone whatever routine job is being undertaken in
favour of a more significant task, should the need arise. Far from
being a simple evasion of responsibility, performing trivial work
represents a response to the functioning and requirements of the
call system. This logic sustains routines like the 'bacon run' which
in other respects appear demeaning to the police self-image (and
wasteful of an expensive public resource).

The power which the call system holds over the pattern of unit
work is forcefully illustrated by those incidents where a collective
unit response is evident, when unit members are drawn together to
work as one. Such examples of group work typically arose as a
result of emergency calls: the report of a 'non-stop' driver, a
domestic dispute, or a search for an escaping thief. In such cases
there is no evidence of desultoriness or reluctance to do more than
one's individual task. Rather it would appear that the collective
response of the unit members is made possible and is prompted by
the 'call-readiness' which the routine functioning of the system
demands and promotes. In these incidents the apparently 'laid-
back' nature of normal policework is swiftly displaced, suggesting
that we have to look further than the occupational self-interest of
the PCs themselves to find an adequate explanation; it is rather the
structural nature of their organizational tasks which conditions
their response.

Nor is this simply a question of rank-and-file quest for excitement (cf. Smith and Gray, 1983, p. 53). It is the supervisory rank
of controller which is responsible for allocating more than one
available car to incidents when necessary. We see, for example,
how the controller overrides a minor call to direct the PC to a

major one, in this case a bank 'snatch'. In this connection we should note that BJ identified the van patrol as the place for excitement, rather than referring to the demands of unit work. Operating together as a large collective team is not necessarily the result of an over-enthusiastic misuse of the communication technology but precisely the apotheosis of its logic, since it appears to guarantee the full use of 'spare' resources (despite the possibility, as one supervisor in interview recognized, of inflaming some situations).

These organizational influences and the responses to which they give rise have been set in the context of a tendency for unit work to dissipate – a result of dispatching what is frequently not relevant or what proves to be less relevant on inspection. However, it would be unfair to exclude elements of continuity which we can also discern; we should pay some attention to why these appear and to which features of incidents seem to encourage continuity, because of a perception of their enhanced relevance.

Continuity and Legal Work

There are some incidents that stand out as part of a pattern, either pre-established by the demands of an earlier incident (like the taking of a complainant's statement) or carrying within them an agenda of action and inquiry (like an arrest). Typically these continuous and connected events involve what we might call legal work, i.e. they are concerned with interpreting and applying definitions of law. The arrests involving EM and DL which we recounted were marked by this suspension of minor, routine contacts and showed instead a thorough pattern of action, from inquiry to arrest to custody, and so on. In DL's case we saw a strong interest not only in catching a 'criminal' but in taking a full part in the interrogation process – an enthusiasm that seemed to fit well with his interest in joining the CID. Such a pattern of continued action is not merely characteristic of 'crime work'; it is also present in the less contentious work associated with missing-person inquiries, as we saw in the case of CK.[1] While such incidents do not necessarily involve straightforward legal action they do, as the examples show, raise questions about the safety of juveniles involved and may therefore be conducted in the light of a possible agenda of offences (Baker and Dodge, 1977, p. 308). The legal aspects to such 'welfare work' are highlighted by the case of unlawful sexual intercourse dealt with by BJ; the object of his visit was a birth certificate to complete his file, not merely to offer sympathy and support for the family. In the case of a missing child, he gave way at the mention of the social worker, thus accepting the primacy of social-work agencies as the legal guardians of child welfare, once a missing person had been located. The boundaries of agency responsibility in such cases thus emphasize the police responsibility for dealing with a range of offences.

In addition to these serious calls on the unit's attention, in terms of crime and personal welfare, legal matters are implicit concerns more generally. Traffic, animals and licensing represent the more mundane subjects for police attention, for which significant legal provisions exist, though these did not necessarily give rise to sustained attention in our examples. Legal work in the context of the unit means a series of actions, including the interpretation of situations, the making of inquiries, the invocation of powers, the taking of statements, the process of reporting or charging suspects, the compilation of a case file for decision and the formal witnessing of events in court. As we saw, these actions may be separated in time, and so at any one point a number of cases may be ongoing at different stages of development. BJ's file, for example, was well advanced by the time we learn about it, but other cases were just beginning, and some may not come to fruition or are subjected to delays (as CK remarks). However, the lines of continuity are clear.

The incidents which give rise to a continuity of police response, which seem to represent integrated episodes with their own sustained significance, tend therefore to carry some actual or potential relation to legal work, concerned with upholding the law where there is a significant risk of a possible breach, or carrying through the formal business of dealing with an offender. This common feature of legal relevance unifies the otherwise disparate subjects to which significant police attention is given; unit work becomes more clearly visible as the ongoing practice of distributing and rationing scarce legal resources in response to prima-facie demands. Elements of continuity represent the concrete achievement of a significant degree of relevance founded in the law, which forms the coherent basis for the diversity, etc. immediately observable.

Addressing a Disparate and 'Unknown' Public

While we have so far sought to distil a legal substance from the disparate elements of unit work, we should also examine more closely how the public is addressed through the pattern of work and in what ways it may be able (or unable) to influence unit operations. We have already pointed to a certain fragmentation of public contact, giving rise to an impression of how individuals seem type-cast by their limited contacts. It remains for us to relate our impressions in more detail to the structure of unit work which is beginning to emerge through our account. The first category of the public that requires attention is composed of those who call upon police assistance: the 'elective' public, in contrast to the 'non-elective' citizens whom the police themselves contact. Those who use the telephone to call for police assistance represent obvious examples: the elderly woman visited by EM and the young woman visited by DL.[2] But they also point up another significant feature of the relationship between public and police. Whereas both duly received a police visit in response to their complaints, the relevance of their calls for assistance was differently assessed – an attempted burglary in one case, an inconclusive neighbours' dispute in the other. In other words, the police determine how they should respond, irrespective, it would seem, of the strength of feeling. And this assessment has to do with the relevance of what they are told at the scene to their allotted tasks and responsibilities.

The filtering of public requests through the framework of police relevance prevents the dissolution of police action into literally 'what the public wants'. The power of the police to dispose of their own resources is perhaps indirectly acknowledged by such tokens of gratitude as we saw offered by the elderly woman and, prior to this, by the moped's owner. Here we witness some kind of exchange and mutual satisfaction, where the relevance of incidents to the officer and the complainant coincides more or less precisely. On the other hand, the doubtful relevance of other reported incidents produces only a brief inquiry, an impression of indifference followed by disengagement. Disputes, as we saw, tend to fall into the latter pattern; indeed, we see how in the example the original caller, having made a complaint against a neighbour, received a visit from the police following a counter-complaint against her boyfriend or cohabitee. In such cases, police action is shown to be far from a simple result of public suggestion. The public therefore tends to be cast into the slots and roles created by the legal system and by the representative pattern of police judgements. The various other individuals who cross the paths of police officers fall into similar categories. The arrestees – young males in our examples – would appear to become objects of procedures designed to make them confess to alleged offences as quickly as possible; a witness is likewise seen as providing a legal instrument for this purpose in the shape of a statement.

Some of those independently approached by the police – the 'non-elective' public – carry with them similar legal connotations.

Men pushing a pram and a young man by a bus stop became the object of night checks; once assessed, they were dismissed from attention. This 'non-elective' public is the subject of attention from patrol officers in public places, rather than in the homes and buildings from which calls for assistance are made. Being on the streets, or travelling through, opens up the possibility of receiving police attention in their search for offences; vehicles are one typical starting-point, whether for GO, the foot patroller, or DL, the first-response car driver. However, many vehicle offences in themselves form an indefinite area of attention, for which some discretion in enforcement is viewed as legitimate. In the example of GO, we see how he explained the use of discretion in terms of responding to a 'stroppy' attitude and how this partly manifested itself in his diplomatic manner when dealing with the plausible white Volvo owner, in contrast to his concealed hostility to the brusque black driver. Relations with the 'non-elective' public in this case are therefore framed within police criteria which – paradoxically – rely explicitly on their perceptions of the police–public relation in any given instance as the test of whether action is to be pursued. In this sense, minor offences become an axis around which police–public relations are amplified, for good or ill. The co-operative offender, like the undoubted victim, can thus entertain a positive relation with the police by virtue of the discretion to adjudge legal relevance, just as the non-co-operative offender and the 'doubtful' victim suffer the reverse, by virtue of the same discretion.

Relatively absent from the contacts generated by unit officers however are the local informants who might assist legal work in either a preventative or a detective fashion. Police drivers in particular must rely on the fleeting contacts made during the course of their assigned tasks; the exchange of favours which may arise in this context would appear to be limited to an odd cup of tea. There is no chain of 'spots' offering shelter and refreshment for officers on the treadmill of call-related tasks. BJ's relationship with the shopkeeper – receiving coffee in exchange for listening to the informant's concerns – is an exception here, which is perhaps attributable to his experience as an RBO. The temptations and rewards of the 'spot' remain much more the preserve of the officer on foot, like GO, as the Volvo owner's mention of his tackle shop perhaps obliquely suggests. This sketch of the police–public relation, in the case of unit work, reinforces our sense of the impact of organizational and legal structures, speeding the unit through legally relevant encounters which may be initiated by the public but are in no sense organized or directed by it. The cultivation of contacts and the development of trust, as well as the possibility of corrupt influence, are neatly sidestepped by the dynamics of unit organization.

So far we have tried to delineate a picture of unit work against the background of the formal elements identified at the outset. We have subjected this picture to an immanent critique, moving from impressions and suggestions to construct a sketch of some central structural features revealed in the description. Our next task must be to develop these topics further and to introduce some fresh material so as to complete a rounded account of unit work. In particular, interviews with four supervisors and seven PCs will be used to provide illustrative quotations. We begin with the question of organization and examine how the various features combine together to influence unit operations.

A Structure of Work

The organizational and occupational aspects of unit policing may be tentatively divided into four: the relation among the types of work performed; the forms of supervision; the forces moulding the 'human relations' of the unit; and the question of management. We propose to postpone discussion of the last of these until later in the chapter, when we have looked at the legal aspects of the unit's work and at its relations with the public, which together impinge on the whole issue of the place of units in the broader organization, and thus on the question of management.

DIFFERENT GRADES OF WORK

Differences in the scope and nature of the tasks performed by unit officers are revealed in the description that we have given, showing for example the restricted nature of the tasks expected of the inexperienced foot patroller, in comparison with other officers. GO's patrol involved a scrutiny of stationary vehicles in which self-evident illegalities were searched out; complex inquiries and witness statements were not required for this task; his relative immobility prevented him from extending his scope of work too far and relieved him of the necessity to respond to the variety of calls which are serviced by officers in vehicles. At the opposite end of this spectrum we find DL, whose duties were consistent with the wide brief which his mobility allowed. Serious emergencies – such as a house fire and a reported burglary in process – were assigned to this highly mobile officer, who also helped stop a moving vehicle and dealt with a contentious neighbours' dispute. A wide range of duties is also expected of the panda drivers, whose work included attention to 'suspicious' travellers, missing persons, disputes, accidents and complaints of crime.

The existence of structured differences in competence and seniority in the unit was revealed in various ways. DL, for example, in one case took over the breathalyser procedure when the foot patroller appeared to go about it clumsily. The expectations placed upon a first-response car officer are perhaps indicated by the former's confident decision later to make an arrest despite the lack of a credible independent witness but rather to rely in effect on plausible circumstantial evidence; he moreover took an active personal role in the interviewing of suspects. An interesting contrast in terms of the typical circumstances of arrest lies with the foot patrollers who are routinely called upon to deal with shoplifting suspects reported by store detectives in the city centre. Judgement is here regarded as less onerous, since the security staff will usually have observed goods being taken and will have detained the suspect attempting to leave the store. Accordingly, the inexperienced officer is more or less presented with a suspect and more importantly a witness. Contrast this apparently self-evident situation with the reliance on circumstantial evidence observed in our previous example. Such points suggest that we should set these differences in the context of a system of allocating available personnel to given roles.

Inspectors, who allocate their available personnel to the roles, require first the running of the unit base and then the deployment of mobiles. They tend to put the most competent experienced officers in the most mobile roles. Top-grade drivers with competence and experience are needed for the first-response cars, which represent the most effective mobile resource at the unit's disposal and the resource designed for the most demanding incidents. Panda cars are then driven by less experienced officers with the standard driving qualification. Again, panda cars are more capable than the walking officer of meeting a wide variety of demands, so it makes sense to give the job of 'walker' to officers of less experience and competence than those assigned to car driving. Finally, given the presence of at least two sergeants dedicated to station duties (controller and station sergeant), the job of station constable is deemed most suitable for those whose work needs to be corrected by supervisors with the greatest ease. An additional reason for putting the most competent and experienced in cars is that they will be able to give prompt assistance to other mobile officers, including the walkers.

All this means that the system's priorities dictate that walking roles will be the last category to be filled by deployment of available resources. As we have seen, differences in competence and experience will be distributed to the detriment of the walking role (cf. Jones, 1980). Units necessarily contain the least experienced officers in the force, as we suggested in Chapter 2 and these will tend to be deployed to station duties and walking roles. The allocation of officers to their posts, with officers of greater experience and competence allocated to the most mobile roles, thus follows from assumptions about the differential urgency and difficulty of the demands imposed upon the system, together with the nature of the personnel, with their different levels of competence, allocated to the unit. Foot patrol is structurally the last priority of the system of allocation to roles, because enhanced mobility is an essential condition for attending incidents where the greatest competence is thought to be required. 'The walkers are generally the ones to be sort of cast on one side,' as one supervisor put it.

The common-sense assumption that the more experienced members possess a greater competence (though driving tests add a more objective dimension to the deployment) is pertinent to junior officers in a very significant sense. The experienced officers constitute a focus of exemplary expertise which transcends the simulations of competence projected by the official training system. Immediate observation of a senior colleague presents a crucial channel for the perpetuation of common sense, practical competence.

> When you're working nights, the best thing to do is to hide up in a dark alleyway and, when you see somebody walking past with a parcel or something, stop them, ask them where they're going ... You can say that to somebody, but when it comes to doing it, the best way to learn about it is to watch somebody do it.

To some extent this influence is acknowledged officially by the system of 'tutor constables'. Its informal significance is enhanced by the absence of any obvious form of guidance or source of reference based on rational-technical norms. Instead of such an impersonal standard, the example of senior colleagues represents the norms of acceptable practice founded on official consent or, to express it more critically, a lack of effective objection. Through such means 'practical' policing competence is continually reproduced, as the testimony of supervisors themselves bears out: 'The best training that I can recall is the on-the-job training, being attached to senior men ... and being guided by my sergeants and the Inspectors.'

While our examples did not give a great deal of attention to supervisors (of whom there may be five or six per unit), there were some signs even here that supervisors are required to perform work over and beyond the task of supervision. HP, for example, made visits in connection with a request for a croupier's licence and with a stage performance; such work lies within the voluminous category of 'general duties' (in police jargon) and is not covered by the PCs on the unit (Baker and Dodge, 1977). Over and above this, supervisors may, as HP indicates, be prepared to arrest on their own account. Even the Inspector (during FN's patrol) was reported making an arrest. The involvement of supervisors in work which demands similar patterns of application to those required of PCs integrates them to some extent into the work of the unit; they can be seen as performing 'real work'. One PC put forward such an approving view of a unit Inspector: 'He's very practical ... He's not averse to getting outside his car and doing a job himself ... I would say he's very good in that respect.'

We have also observed the relative separation of officers from their specialist colleagues. Particular specialists like the dog handler or a CID officer may be engaged in brief contacts, but there is no continuous co-operation with specialists. Incidents like night-time arrests may require the attendance of night duty detectives, but the work of the unit is usually conducted within a framework of group self-sufficiency. Contacts with those outside the unit tend to be tangential or based on the routines of paper report. At the same time, co-operation with other units is necessarily precluded by the system of shiftworking. The relative absence of external contacts produces a consequent isolation of working practices within the unit and a corresponding opportunity for any similarities in ways of working to be amplified throughout the group without counterbalancing influences from outside. However, specialist influence is not absent from the unit, precisely because the supervisors themselves owe their promotions to a history of specialist involvements. One put it like this: 'There seem to be far more specialist men [sic] than unit men promoted.'

If the supervisors can display in such cases specialist competence (for example, in accident investigation), the hierarchy of competence within the unit can then be made manifest, and their authority may be correspondingly increased: 'The most satisfying aspect of my job in recent months has been the detection of that "double fatal" road accident ... The blokes [sic] on the unit found it very, very satisfying.'

The pyramid of ascribed competence in the unit is thus constructed in terms which relate to the specialist sections of the organization. And this specialism, in its various forms, presents itself as a source of support and advice for the PC. As one expressed it: 'Each [of the sergeants] shines . . . a little bit more on one [aspect] than another. We've got an ex-traffic bobby . . . a drugs and crime . . . they've all got . . . specialities.'

The result of associating the senior positions with specialist competence is to reproduce the process by which specialism becomes the avenue to promotion. Rewarded positions in the organization are perceptibly linked to a specialist background, and ambitious officers are thus led towards following in the tracks of their seniors. This is not merely a subjective orientation; it has its effect on the work of the unit by allowing or encouraging 'proto-specialism' – particular interests which fit some of the requirements of specialist competence, in so far as these can be expressed within the restricted format of unit work: 'Different officers have different potential . . . One of my jobs is to try and help him on his way for going in the CID, if he wants to.'

To the extent that this influence successfully prioritizes specialist work it reinforces awareness of a scale of relevance throughout the work of the unit. The 'better type' of work has specialist connotations, while mundane work does not possess such prestige. We see how influence operates if we look back at the comments of the Inspector who openly expressed satisfaction with the pattern of arrests on a particular night. Good work as evaluated by supervisors fits in outline the prescriptions of specialist forms, such as arrests for serious traffic offences or burglary. One supervisor mentioned that the Inspector wanted the unit to be better than others. Queried as to what 'better' meant, the supervisor replied: 'More efficient? . . . More arrests if you like, a better quality of arrest, you know. Not a lot of drunks; more arrests for crime.'

The intervention of supervisory officers in support of their PCs assists the realization of this upward curve of competence. In unpredictable, unexpectedly difficult situations the offering of a reserve of effective assistance by supervisory officers can promote their influence as exemplars of competence and reinforce the authority of their positions. Where a questionable degree of violence has been deployed, for example: 'I've got to use my sort of expertise and guile and try and . . . smooth it over.'

If something outside the usual boundaries of police relevance occurs, then a supervisor can be called in. If parents are reported missing late at night, for example, the question of the welfare of the child arises, requiring the advice of a supervisor who knows the relevant legal powers and procedures. Given the potential range of unit work the importance of supervisory assistance is built into the structure of unit operations. The following remark from a PC exemplifies the point: 'The sergeants in this unit get involved with the troops in most of the jobs they do.'

The inconclusiveness of much unit work, combined with a pressure to impose on jobs criteria relevant to the police, produces a common negative categorization. The term 'rubbish' is used to denote irrelevant demands, which carry in this context a burden of frustration:

> 'Rubbish' is used to indicate the things that you're going to do every day ... Messages for one thing is something that all panda drivers learn to hate ... Four or five court warnings or caution warnings ... minor crime, petty offences ... You have to realize that it's ... far from everyday or rubbish to the people that it's happening to.

> Well, it is rubbish, it's not policework ... You go to calls where they've rung up the nines [999 emergency call] and, oh God, you know, bloody lost-and-found dogs, it's ... rubbish ... I think the public need educating to understanding the use of the treble nines.

This sense of frustration or boredom, though by no means unreflective, extends beyond the rank-and-file perception to the supervisory level, which shares this systematically based perspective on relevance. 'In the day you're busy, but a lot of it is rubbish. I use "rubbish" ... instead of "routine", you know ... People locked out of cars, property inquiries and things like that.'[3]

Over against the category of 'rubbish' are marked out the topics of crucial relevance to police which, in calling upon their official duties and powers, form satisfying as well as coherent episodes in the cycle of unit operation. The prevention and detection of crime, as general objectives of the police, put them in direct touch with the prestigious structures of legality.

The most pertinent kinds of legal work therefore represent a form of satisfaction in a pattern of work that shows fragmentariness and inconclusiveness. Utilizing constabulary powers in relation to the traditionally accepted functions of the police transcends the mundane demands of much unit work:

> [As a personal priority] I look to crime and think of the prevention and then detection.

> [The most satisfying part of the work is to induce a confession.]

He says, 'All right, Officer, I did it.' ... You've sort of overpowered them intellectually.

The most satisfying job to me is to take a report of a crime and ... to show at the end of the day that the crime has been detected.

Patterns of work therefore are influenced by the recognized hierarchy of competence in the unit and the consequent deployments. Notions of 'good work' are based on the organizational significance of central functions, as opposed to matters perceived as more mundane.

SUPERVISION AND DISCIPLINE

We have seen indirectly some of the specific supervisory forms which operate in the unit. Throughout there emerged from time to time the disembodied voice of the controller sergeant; there was the supervisory process implied in paperwork; further, direct supervision was observed in the station, less obviously in the subdivisional territory at large. An examination of each of these in turn should reveal their specific impact on operations.

Radio communication is used in unit work within the framework of a central control which assigns tasks to individuals and facilitates co-ordination of unit resources where necessary. A controller cognizant with the circumstances and locations of typical tasks and in routine contact with officers on the shift is in a position to draw inferences about the operations of unit members, and to make inquiries where necessary.[4] As one supervisor suggested: 'You know within reason they're on their beats ... When, you do call them up you expect a true [report] with their location ... You have a cup of tea here and they might [go] for a pint there, but if you call and they answer they'll do the jobs.'

In addition, the Inspector must be informed by the controller about all incidents – a further possible check on lapses of diligence. The supervisory implications of the radio control system are related to the extent to which the pattern of work shows a fragmentary quality, a characteristic we have noted. The greater the frequency of successive individual assignments, for example, the greater the opportunity to exercise supervision by the continual referral of calls to the individual officer; similarly collective work during an incident puts the officers under the monitoring eye of the controller. The records of the central control, particularly in such circumstances, are also a resource for later inquiries by supervisors. However, a large number of simultaneous items may be less easy to monitor at the time. A similar result emerges from the opposite contingency; the *lower* the frequency of assignments the more this form of supervision diminishes in importance. Since the radio control is not used as a deliberate form of regular supervision unconnected with any tasks, the supervisory impact of radio control is accordingly limited by the amount of input to the system and the task-related function which it is given.

Some evidence of the possibilities of supervision by means of radio control is given by instances where there is some form of independent feedback to the radio controller as a result of an assignment. In the case of EM, a call was made about a piece of equipment supposedly left behind after the original visit; in the case of DL the way an incident had been handled was the subject of a subsequent message passed to the controller; similarly FN, having failed to make a call, was requested to return to the location. Few though such instances may be, they indicate the possible ways in which the assignment of tasks possesses built-in supervisory implications, and the fact that most such assignments are clearly attended by officers is consistent with this interpretation.[5]

The few instances recounted here when a PC apparently evaded the demands of the call system do not present as clear-cut a picture as might appear at first glance. Reports, in one case of a 'stolen car', in the other of a man 'thieving in a car', were the subject of a *postponed* response by the same officer (EM). In the first the officer also proffered a misleading account of his movements to the controller. Yet what is seemingly at issue is the relevance of the report within the normal codes of dispatch work; without the essential administrative reference points of a car number or a proper contact location the calls are put one step back in the queue when weighed against more substantial demands on the officer's time. The misleading account offered by the PC fits the administrative logic of a 'paper' narrative required by the senior echelons of the force (cf. Chatterton, 1979). It is not clear that the supervisory logic of the call system has been altogether evaded; rather it has been rearranged or transposed to fit the immediate contingencies of the PC's work, in which relevance is assessed in terms consistent with major organizational goals.

Not all the unit members are equally subject to the demands of the call system. The subdivisional first-response car drivers are held in reserve for the more serious emergencies; otherwise they are expected to perform tasks generated from their own patrolling and observations. In our example DL's PNC check on the travelling car appeared to have no basis in any call; if something discrepant had emerged from the PNC inquiry, then DL would probably have made a stop. The work of the driver is thus framed by expectations of additional tasks generated proactively, but these remain limited in range and depth, confined to scrutinizing the immediate environment for apparent deviations. The same type of scanning of the immediate environment takes place on foot patrol, only here the zone of operation is restricted somewhat to stationary vehicles. Like the first-response car driver, the foot patroller is obliged to show some signs of self-generated productivity, since there is a limit to the type of radio calls to which the patroller can respond effectively: 'I work for myself all the time. When something goes over the radio to do, I do it, but otherwise I go looking for offences.'

The proactive operation of patrol entails a more systematic search for offences than the continuous patrol which we have identified as part of the desultory pattern of unit work. Rather the former involves a located inspection of likely sites, keeping the eyes open – exemplified by the foot patrol of GO, during which several stationary vehicles were scrutinized. For these officers the paper report assumes a larger significance as a form of productivity.

The centrality of paperwork as a means of supervision is illustrated by the conduct of the experienced patrol sergeant HP. He spent time with a PC insisting on a definite standard of coherent paperwork in line with legal requirements of proof and relevance; this instance was linked to his acceptance of responsibility for the unit's paperwork and in particular for the officer's statement – a key legal document. Thus he spent time later in the shift performing this task of reading unit paperwork. His attention to paperwork here contrasts strikingly with his apparent lack of interest on this occasion in establishing exactly what the unit officers were doing or in supervising them in the performance of their allotted tasks. The comments of HP on disciplining a PC for neglect of duty do not, on the other hand, suggest that he was unconcerned with such questions; rather it seems that paperwork can form a major and routine object of supervision in an 'active' unit. The significance of records is brought out further in GO's reference to a 'purge' on pocket-books; supervision in this form emphasizes the organizational pertinence of unit work by providing a resource for higher supervisory levels to monitor and investigate what has been accomplished. Both the Inspector and the Superintendent will read paper reports submitted by a unit.

As one supervisor expressed it: 'Through paperwork I think I influence quite a lot the way they work, the way they deal with matters.'

Q. 'You're reading between the lines, in fact?'

'Oh yes ... The minute I walk away [from a supervisee] he knocks somebody off for an offence. The only way I know what he's really doing is by what he's putting on paper. And that's when I can get at them.'

Crime reports, accident books and process files submitted for consideration as to further action constitute a routine flow of documentation reflecting the volume and variety of unit work, overshadowing the humble pocket-book in which evidence is recorded. Entries in station books may also be required, representing another record of attention; we have already seen examples of the use of the 'violence-in-marriage' book and the occurrence book. The volume of records and reports, in so far as it signifies the amount of activity required to produce them, constitutes a resource for supervision. The more significant the volume, the more supervision through this medium is possible. In this respect paperwork can serve a similar supervisory function to radio control, particularly for those officers who are expected to submit relatively frequent reports.

Direct supervision represents the third category which concerns us here. Some PCs are more subject to direct oversight than others – for example, the station PCs, one of whom will be the station sergeant's junior partner in responding to station visitors and dealing with prisoners, searching and looking after property. In addition, station PCs manning telephones liaise with the controller over messages from various sources including the public. But walking officers and those in vehicles will not be directly supervised unless they are engaged in joint work or if they call for assistance. In the former case it is likely that a supervisor, probably the patrol sergeant, is in effect undertaking 'on-the-job' training, showing the probationer how to talk with the public, make an arrest and so on.[6] As one patrol sergeant put it: 'The most important part of my role is the training of probationer constables.'

Patrol sergeants will not, however, directly oversee the routine work of those officers who they deem competent, typically referring in practice to the drivers as such. As another sergeant said: 'I've got to have confidence in some of the PCs which then enables me to concentrate more on officers that need more supervision, such as probationers.'

Supervision of a direct form takes place in relation to drivers when they call for assistance. Unusual difficulties may arise, for example, when there emerges the possibility of placing a child in care; on such subjects the patrol sergeant is likely to be called in to resolve matters, since the functional and legal boundaries of social welfare agencies are necessarily touched.

The three forms of supervision – by radio control, paper report and direct oversight – can be combined in various ways. If there is a large volume of messages from the public, giving rise to a series of dispatches which the controller can monitor, and if these incidents, combined with patrol encounters, generate a large volume of paper reports, then supervision can be made that much more intensive and better informed. Direct oversight gains in importance to the extent that the given tasks are seen as presenting difficulties to the officers concerned. On the other hand, a low volume of public messages and a shortage of matters to report will not give the same opportunities for effective supervision. An impression of competence reduces the urgency of direct supervision. In these ways the system of supervision is dependent for its effectiveness partly on the input to it; but the typifications of competence also play a part, as in the case of direct supervision. Each section of the unit is subject to a different combination of supervisory forms; foot patrollers may have to accept a significant proportion of both paperwork and direct supervision; panda drivers are subject to routine calls through radio control and are required to submit reports; subdivisional first-response drivers must respond to emergency calls and submit a respectable quantity of paper, concentrating on the more serious legal violations. Supervision thus is never a uniform process but one dependent on the specific question of its forms in relation to the inputs passed through the system.

We have so far examined the supervision processes within the unit but have yet to look at the question of discipline in the sense of responses to overstepping the boundaries of discretion. Infringement of legal proprieties, as we shall instance in more detail later, are not the object of supervisors' suspicion. Indeed, there is a sense in which they are seen to accept certain norms and to promote them indirectly within the unit. The construction and mediation of a consensual working norm can be seen indicatively in the reported conversation between supervisors heard during DL's shift; how 'practically minded' an officer can legitimately be is thus the subject of a careful and refined presentation in which both officers visibly gravitate towards an acceptable mean. Similarly the comments of the station sergeant on the law and practice relating to suspects reveal the 'realism' of the supervisory perspective, and its objective basis in legal structure. Even the Inspector is seen by a WPC (encountered on FN's shift) as an officer who shares the experience of a contentious arrest. To the extent that supervisors actively share in the construction of a working norm the whole question of a response to improprieties is put into a different perspective. It would seem to follow that only accidentally, or by some failure to respond to signals suggesting the working norm, might PCs fall outside the acceptable boundaries.

The same question can to some extent be posed in respect of the diligence of officers in carrying out their tasks. Once again the working norms of the supervisors themselves play a part in creating norms of diligence, the assumption being that if acceptable standards of productivity are maintained then minor breaches of work discipline will be tolerated: 'I don't go knocking people off for having a cup of tea when they shouldn't, but as I say I've got my own standards.'

Precisely because the supervisors are involved in the work of the unit, their standards would seem necessarily to influence – and reflect – those of the PCs.[7] The reports of a PC (BJ) and a sergeant (HP) bring out the significance of this process by which disciplinary intervention is consensually based. Both showed an interest in the maintenance of a standard of diligence, and HP referred explicitly to the necessity for acceptability in applying disciplinary measures. A reputation for self-disciplined individual competence permits the taking of opportunities for combining business with pleasure. Through the 'blag' unit officers can informally express displeasure at the conduct or attitude of individuals. Disciplinary action must therefore be set in the context of the 'human relations' of the unit, which we should now concretely address.

HUMAN RELATIONS

The question of 'human relations' in the unit translates itself into 'morale', i.e. the maintenance of a required attentiveness and application based on shared confidence and enthusiasm.[8] The closed boundaries of the unit necessarily throw a great deal of the onus for maintaining morale on the internal relations of the members, since the unit's relative isolation through extended periods, including night-time working, conditions a certain dependence on group morale.

Because comparisons between the burdens of different workers are possible over time, those working within the unit are likely to look towards a 'fair' distribution of work corresponding to the role allotted to each. The allocation of calls through a central system permits the comparison of workloads, as does the use of paper reports as a means of productivity. The allocation of responsibilities by area, for example, between panda cars, also makes possible a comparison of the relative burden of each officer. To the extent also that the call system and the nature of patrolling produce a construction of work into discernible units, the system of central allocation and assignment encourages an emphasis on the equalization of workloads, by circulating personnel if necessary. By centralizing unit work, the system creates conditions for positive morale and unit solidarity if standard tasks are perceived by the rank and file as well distributed. Moveover there exists the necessity of co-ordination in response to serious incidents. These may involve calling together available mobile resources to give assistance; they present an opportunity for mutual aid to be rendered and for the values associated with such help to become a factor in unit solidarity. Major incidents of crime, missing persons and accidents become the means by which a mutuality among the unit can be allowed to grow and to influence the subsequent attitudes of officers towards one another:

Q. 'Do you think there's quite close shifts here?'

'Certainly. Very much so. You are relying on the other members of the shift because if you're out in the streets and you're getting any bother you have to rely on them to come and help you out.'

The centralization of tangible rewards may also be influential. For example, leave arrangements fall to the Inspector to administer. Here again is the possibility of a disposition towards ensuring equalization and the encouragement of group morale through the use of generous leave arrangements. Another routine reward is the provision of convenient meal arrangements; here group socialization becomes a possibility when officers are simply divided into two groups for consecutive meal breaks. The spontaneous possibilities of culturally elaborating the interrelations of the members can be seen in the regular card-games, often involving large groups, which were observed at such times.

Group socialization at off-duty times observes the same boundaries of unit affiliation, not necessarily to the satisfaction of some, like this PC: 'I think it happens on all the shifts, you know. Several people I've spoken to don't like coming up to the bar here because they find it very cliquey.'

These influences – of group isolation, equity, co-ordination and rewards – make possible the existence of the 'comradeship' which an officer such as BJ can regard as characteristic of unit work. But this valued integration of the group is dependent on the 'benign' operation of several factors as reinforcers of one another and therefore relies on supervisors to recognize and apply the logical tendencies of the system.

The 'human relations' of the unit can thus become the explicit object of supervisory surveillance and intervention in order to maximize enthusiasm and thereby efficiency. Such an approach draws on the inspiration of 'man management' advocated by theoretical texts, adding a distinctive dimension to the supervisory process as a whole: 'I'm very conscious of the welfare of the men [*sic*] that are doing the job . . . their morale . . . If you've got a good atmosphere the blokes [*sic*] will work.'

The welfare measures at the Inspector's disposal fit into such a conscious policy, as a sergeant agrees: 'He's quite concerned about the welfare of the blokes [*sic*]. That's one thing that really I find him quite good for . . . time off when they need it.'

Surveillance goes beyond physical checks – confirming a presence or absence at a time and place – to include personal knowledge, strengths, weaknesses and dispositions: 'It's the *man* [*sic*] that you supervise, not the position.'

Problems of physical supervision which appear on the surface need to be set alongside the possibilities of this more intensive type of supervisory gaze. A closely observed terrain of personal particulars is brought into more general focus by becoming the confidential property of the supervisors, as explained by an Inspector: 'I share confidences with my sergeants about the men [*sic*] on the unit. I never do it the other way round.'

Once these particulars have been assessed they form part of an individual profile which can be used as a resource for tasks such as deployment. For example, in the case of the first-response cars, an active and outgoing individual can be deliberately deployed with a more patient and thoughtful partner; a male first-response car driver with an allegedly dispiriting succession of female partners can be given a regular male partner instead. Jaundiced panda drivers can be circulated to other areas in order to pep them up. In each case subsequent results can be assessed in individual terms. Part of this style of supervision lies in the maintenance of 'approachability', encouraging contact from PCs or the expression of their views, thereby enabling a greater span of individual particulars to be subjected to supervisory knowledge. 'Reasonableness' hence becomes an important quality in supervisory work, denoting the attempt to construct consensual norms.

> Everybody shares a very worthwhile relationship with the Inspector, I think . . . They feel that they can go to him with any problem that they've got.

> [The Inspector] is always reasonable.

This sense of a personal relationship between individuals is set within the context of implicit occupational expectations: 'I think he's fair to everybody, yes. I think, he's got to be, hasn't he?'

Harnessing the formal means of supervision and the integrative forces affecting the unit and adding a focus on individual welfare and morale constitute a potent combination of supervisory influences. As PCs put it: 'With a unit like this, which is a very close unit, very . . . hard-working they'll stick very close together'; 'it's a good team in this unit.' Failure to take advantage of these potentialities spells organizational disaster. As one supervisor said: 'You can get a bad Inspector . . . who can bloody ruin a shift.'

How the crucial role of Inspector fits into the *wider* organization we shall leave till the legal work performed by the unit and its relations with the public have been discussed.

Legal Work

LEGAL DOMAINS AND FORMS

The ways in which the unit performs its legal tasks must be understood in the context of the fragmentary pattern of work already identified. Given the variety of calls and demands upon the officers, there is a related variety to be expected in the types of legal relevance which characterize situations attended by officers. This variety gives rise to an agenda of attention and interest in which some legally relevant topics attract greater interest than others. How such an agenda works in practice can be seen in some of our examples. We should remember first of all that some of the matters brought to police attention may on inspection prove to be more relevant to the civil than to the criminal law. CK, for example, responded to a report of a stolen car only to discover what appeared to be a civil dispute, a report of which simply went into the occurrence book – a record of residual incidents. Moreover, the same incident may be approached from both a civil and a criminal law perspective. EM's awareness of this double legal relevance is represented by his advice to a couple in dispute concerning separation. It seems that where civil proceedings have some general social salience as a remedy then officers may resort to referring to them as one solution to the problem under review.

A range of matters brought to police attention thus carry legal relevance, but not necessarily in terms which are interpreted as relevant to the police; incidents located within the territory of civil law by the officers in attendance can be seen as of reduced relevance. Debts, nuisances, domestic disputes and neighbour disputes can be regarded as falling into this zone, one of ambiguity and limited police relevance (cf. Reiss, 1971, p. 77). Matters of dispute can also border on the territories of other enforcement agencies and social agencies of various kinds, which may be seen as the proper bodies for referral. In addition, there may be options to take private proceedings against offenders – for example, in cases of common assault; reference to such options can be encouraged by an official declaration in police standing orders, as we found in this particular force. Another dimension is thus added to the complexities of relations between civil and criminal law.

The complexity of the law relating to policework does not stop here. There is also the question of distinctions within the criminal law as to the form of offence definition, the nature of the evidence required and so on. Perhaps the simplest from this point of view are those offences for which good evidence can be produced readily by the observations of the police; on patrol with GO we saw how a ticket was issued in response to a simple violation observed by the officer himself. Quite different are those occasions when more complex judgements are required on the basis of specific offence definitions and in relation to more than one possible witness; the question of exactly which offence has been committed appears among our examples in the case of discussions about the proper charge for those arrested in DL's shift.

The general legal duty of the police, which is expressed for unit officers in terms of their wide brief to respond to all types of relevant events, contains therefore a wide range of potential legal avenues and corresponding legal problems. This is not simply a question of there being many laws, but of structural differences in the type of laws which impinge on unit work. In the case of vehicle offences already referred to, we may link their form to the general pattern of administrative law and regulation in which the complainant is effectively the state itself, represented by its agent in this regard, the police. Contrast this administrative form with the more complex and arguably more confused terrain of disputes with their typical interaction of civil, criminal and – where public agencies such as housing departments are involved – public law domains.[9] Whereas in the latter type of case police action may be seen as superfluous, because of the legal alternatives in play, the administrative form of offence, often readily witnessed, implies a problem of selectivity at the level of the more frequent and trivial offences. To overcome this problem, attitudes to the police are utilized as a rough guide to decision-making, a point exemplified by GO's remarks; 'stroppiness' to the police officer – an indication of public antagonism – invites enforcement.

The form of the offence also becomes significant in cases where the law imposes a requirement on the police themselves to judge whether, for example, a breach of the peace might be committed.

Whereas with a vehicle offence the facts required are reasonably straightforward and objective, here an officer is asked to construe the known facts – notwithstanding that in both cases the offence is witnessed by the police themselves. The significant discretion accorded to the police by the law of public order has the effect of spreading and multiplying sources of discretionary judgement among members of the force, irrespective of the rank structure. Public order is therefore – unlike some legal topics previously discussed – seen as unequivocally relevant to police, and behaviour in public places is scrutinized on this basis, but it can become controversial within the unit in those situations where influential judgements by supervisors are made which contradict those of the unit PCs.

Concrete examples of such situations emerged during our observational period when individuals were spoken to about possible offences, and where their supporters intervened, producing an argument in the streets between the police and members of the public. In such situations public order law becomes a reference point for PCs in difficulties; on the other hand, supervisory intervention may introduce a countervailing influence wishing to avoid further controversial arrests. Our evidence would indicate the significance of the involvement in such episodes of definite groups – the disreputable poor (dismissively termed 'toe rags') and young blacks – whose contacts with police receive fuller discussion at a later point. However, the conclusion to which we should now direct our argument concerns the relevance of public order law as a support for unit decisions, as a resource to be called upon in the course of normal work, rather than as a preventative measure with an independent significance.

Whereas at the outset we discussed the objective external constraints imposed or suggested by the various legal domains, we are presented, in the case of public order law, with a further structural variant emphasizing a subjective element in the factors influencing police decisions, and one that can be reduced to a pragmatic resource when required. Our examples enable us to look more closely at the elements which combine to influence decision-making in cases that require some definite interpretive work.

PRACTICAL JUDGEMENT AND RELEVANCE
One determinant of the use of discretionary judgement is the 'key' in which events are presented. 'High-key' presentations from the public, i.e. consistent circumstantial accounts open to singular and decisive confirmation, tend to draw acceptance from unit officers, while 'low-key' presentations with no corresponding consistency

or support are disbelieved. The elderly woman's presentation of her victimization was particularly effective in this sense because it offered to EM the right kind of consistency and circumstantial backing, while the details – such as the opening of the meter doors – showed attention to the conditions of proving singular events (in other words there is no reason why the doors should not be closed other than the occurrence of an exceptional event, while the interest of meters to a thief provides a plausible motive for such an action). But this does not necessarily mean that less clear accounts will not be provisionally accepted. Where matters of no great consequence are at issue, judgement becomes less critical. Thus in a similar reported case the disappearance of the kettle, though provisionally accepted by CK, appeared rather less interesting to him, suggesting that we need to look not only at the 'key' of the presentation but at the typical relevance of the subject-matter. Bona-fide domestic burglaries, for example, represent significant subjects of interest to which careful attention is paid.

In the case of the complaint of assault made in the neighbours' dispute dealt with by DL, the low-key circumstantial atmosphere and the existence of a prior motive to make a complaint led the officers to dismiss the specific allegations. Further evidence (not quoted here) suggested that the other officer, JR, had experienced a series of contacts with the complainant – hence his sceptical passivity. Here a low-key presentation was important. But relevance may override the key of the presentation, restraining or impelling action accordingly. The prospect of an arrest for burglary, for example, sustained DL's attention to circumstances which at the current time lacked grounds for definite conclusions but were open to further inquiry. The influence of relevance is seen in EM's responses to another domestic dispute compared with the complaint of illegal entry to a car; while there was every sign of circumstantial distress and of a section 42 assault offence, (Offences against the Person Act 1861), EM typified the domestic incident as marginally relevant to the police because he could not arrest. Yet the allegation against the boy in the second case led to a full-scale alert and immediate arrest. We can go some way towards an explanation for this apparent discrepancy by paying attention to the wider legal structure in which such incidents occur; in a case of burglary or breaking into a car, a court conviction can be sustained by independent witnesses or by police evidence; in the case of a neighbours' or domestic dispute, it is possible that a complaint will be withdrawn at some stage, particularly when, as in section 42 prosecutions, the consent of the victim is deemed necessary for the proceedings to take place (cf. Reiss, 1971, p. 80; Lidstone, Hogg and Sutcliffe, 1980, p. 97). In the absence of definite counter-indications, the typification of such disputes as inconclusive or unproductive precipitates withdrawal.[10]

This point about the legal structure does not rule out the other social elements which may enter into the process: for example, the dependence of especially working-class women on the support of a male income and their lack of family savings, which may lead to their persisting in a violent relationship; or the problems of the council housing allocation system for those living in stressful circumstances, which may influence attitudes in disputes.[11] Rather we can see that these elements impinge on police attitudes through their *legal* consequences and are relatively hidden from view by the primacy given by the police to legal considerations, and why they may be replaced by cynical rejections of the passions involved. Being described by police as 'pigs' or as the makers of mischievous allegations is the fate of those who do not fall into the neater or more prestigious compartments of the criminal justice system. As in the cases of public order incident already referred to, legal judgements are informed by, or reflected in, attitudes to the disreputable segments of a population; legality becomes the prism for social censoriousness. In these detailed examples we have seen how the unit officer makes common-sense empirical inquiries and judgements based on an agenda of police relevance, but one which is significantly influenced by the legal forms contextualizing particular options.

To check the character and importance of legal work within the scope of unit policing a survey of our observational materials on PCs' duties was performed. This revealed that, of 140 public contact events observed, 88 (63 per cent) were offence-related. In calculating these, for example, missing-person and absconder inquiries were not considered to be offence-related. The offence-related events comprised: 6 arrests; 2 traffic tickets; 3 offence warnings; 16 ocasions when crime complaints were accepted; and 61 miscellaneous 'inquiries', including checks, visits, messages, statement-taking, or other work connected with an actual or possible offence. Such findings indicate a small core of important actions related to events actually perceived as offences, together with a large 'tail' of mundane preliminaries or ex-post-facto activity. This varied but high volume of offence-related events tend to support the idea that an agenda of legal relevance is a significant feature of much unit work.[12]

PROCEDURAL FORMS

Having so far considered substantive aspects of the law as they relate to actual judgements 'in the field', we should not overlook another layer of complexity added by the procedural requirements imposed on the police in their dealings with suspects and especially in relation to custody and interrogation. The course of the arrests described in our examples allows us some opportunity to illustrate how complex and ambiguous these procedural requirements can appear in the context of events. In the manner of the arrests we should note the extent to which consent plays a part, a consent which however is evidently dependent on the determination of the police request. In one case, a car was halted and the breathalyser procedure was accepted; in two other cases, entry to premises was secured, and, in one, a search was conducted with the occupier's agreement. Yet in both these cases there was clearly an element of coercion; the mother's protest about her boy being taken away was ignored, and, in the second case, the man's objection on recognizing the researcher was stilled by an aggressive act. Nor was formal cautioning on arrest particularly evident. In such cases it would appear that the police do not approach their task in the guise of legal officials, rather they prefer to resort to informal methods where possible, even in instances when they may have powers to act.

A significant result of this informality is the blurring of exactly which powers and duties the police have in such situations. Since the police do not communicate about their powers and purposes, members of the public can regard what they do only in terms of an arbitrary power which it is safer to assume is legal than not (cf. Ericson, 1982, p. 160). What appears as informality on the police's part also contains a mystificatory element which multiplies the potential power of the police. One officer (in a case not reported here) when speaking to a colleague referred in the presence of the person concerned to their prisoner having been given 'conjugals' at a particular time; this confidential reference to rights on arrest – in other words, to cautioning – epitomizes the obscurity attached to procedural rights. Moreover the whole question of the status and relevance of procedural rights is made more complex and uncertain by comments such as those of the station sergeant in our examples. Thus, precisely the officer most responsible for ensuring procedural propriety is persuaded of the qualified status of the rules and their doubtful legal force; if this is the case for supervisory officers, how can it be otherwise for the rank and file? The definitional problems implicit in particular rules can thus be exploited, as we found when EM denied that a juvenile in the charge room was being 'interviewed', an activity that by a guileful redefinition presumably takes place only in the 'interview room'. In such ways those who claim to 'know their rights' can be disconcerted. A pragmatic focus reveals itself more sharply in the introduction of very doubtful evidence in order to extract a confession from a suspect, a ruse apparent in the case of the 'breakers' and confirmed by the sergeant's remarks. Once again mystification becomes a device for the attainment of police ends (Holdaway, 1983, p. 96). In addition in this case we observe the maintenance of an intimidatory atmosphere in which suspects were enveloped, another stimulus to confusion and anxiety; again the sergeant and the CID officer talked in terms which accord a degree of relevance or acceptability to such practices.

Attitudes like these are far from the exclusive possession of the rank and file. 'Practically minded' police officers, in the description of one supervisor, are evidently to be found in the senior ranks, and the openness with which such attitudes are discussed ensures that the rank and file have ample opportunity to imbibe them. One officer of supervisory rank explains how PCs are informally educated in these ways of thinking.

> Without wishing to ... get involved in any great argument, police do tell lies ... I wouldn't want anything to do with a policeman who [arrested] somebody in the streets for doing nothing and who go and tell blatant lies. I think it's like you put the icing on the cake afterwards, just to make sure it's eaten ... It's like a parent in a family, educating their children by process of nature, do you see what I mean? 'Well, son, you need this ... oh it's got to be a bit stronger than that', you know, and this goes on. But as long as it doesn't get out of hand and you realize the pitfalls then I think it's an unfortunate practice, that we have to do it, but an acceptable [one] in my own mind.

The particular example of conversation between supervisors about 'practical' policing cited in our discussion of supervision is also pertinent here. Beneath these attitudes and their corresponding practices we can discern the conditions which make them possible. The absence of tightly defined procedural rules – and penalties for their breach – allows the development of a pragmatic occupational ethos; moreover the absence of non-police supervision and of legal representation for the suspect further excludes this private theatre from more than formal external examination. In this sense the attitudes portrayed here possess an objective legitimacy. When a PC (such as DL) searches a house for stolen articles, having been admitted because of a fire, there is arguably little to which formal objection can be made, even if the fact of such a search were to be made known. 'Due process' has neither the material nor the conceptual force which might challenge such practices.

In summary, legal work is conducted within a fixed agenda of police relevance, constructed in relation to objective legal structures and influences, and undertaken in a pragmatic spirit not inconsistent with the legal realities of procedure for dealing with suspects.[13]

The Democratic Relation

The unit's relations with the public have to be understood in the context of the complex organizational and legal forms already described. Characteristic of these relations was a dependence on the typification or categorization brought to bear by the police upon an encounter. The role of the public in initiating such encounters leads us to refer to an elective public which, principally by means of calls to the station, presents to the police raw material for subsequent scrutiny and action. However, this initial presentation tends to exhaust the active role of the public; once an officer becomes acquainted with the matters concerned, police action depends on an assessment of police relevance. Those who are subsequently approached by the police, and those who are initially approached by officers on patrol, do not in principle enjoy even the limited potential to dispose of police resources which the elective public can claim. Somewhat detached from these elective and non-elective publics stand the more systematic contacts sometimes maintained with 'spots', where refreshment and gossip signify a special mutuality of interest between individuals and the police. External to all these are the latent publics who neither call on the police nor otherwise receive police attention. Such a categorization of relations with the public proceeds directly from the organizational analysis we have conducted, but we should not overlook the broader social basis on which this categorization is superimposed, particularly as it concerns the distinctions of age, class, race and sex which help constitute the general social order.

Table 3.1 shows a classification of PCs' contacts with individuals according to age, race, sex and type of contact (elective or non-elective), in addition specifying the characteristics of those arrested (who are also included in the non-elective public). This table includes apparent 'spots', here classified according to the immediate circumstances of the contact.

Table 3.1 Public Contacts by Unit Beat PCs in the Period of Observation

Number of contacts

Types of person(s)	Elective Adult Offence-related	Elective Adult Other	Elective Juvenile Offence-related	Elective Juvenile Other	Elective Total Offence-related	Elective Total Other	Non-elective Adult Offence-related	Non-elective Adult Other	Non-elective Juvenile Offence-related	Non-elective Juvenile Other	Non-elective Total Offence-related	Non-elective Total Other
(1) Males												
Black	2	1	0	0	2	1	3	3	2(1)	1	5	4
White	20	10	0	0	20	10	17(4)	14	11(1)	2	28	16
(2) Females												
Black	1	1	0	0	1	1	2	0	0	0	2	0
White	19	9	0	0	19	9	14	7	0	0	14	7
(3) Non-individualized groups												
Black	0	0	0	0	0	0	0	1	0	0	0	1
White	0	0	0	1	0	1	0	0	3	1	3	1
(4) Unclassified individuals and groups	2	5	0	0	2	5	4	5	1	0	5	5
	0	1	0	0	0	1	1	3	1	0	2	3

Notes

1 The numbers of contacts refer to individual members of the public, not to contact *events*, which may involve more than one individual.

2 Arrest figures appear in brackets. 'Arrests' refer to observed events personally involving the officer 'shadowed' at the time.

3 Five uncategorized contacts, comprising two white males, two white females and one white non-individualized group, were excluded from all calculations.

4 'Juveniles' and race are subjective categories based on field observations.

5 Non-individualized groups and unclassified individuals and groups refer to contacts about which information is in some respect incomplete because, for example, the actual contact was not observed directly, or members of the group were not individually counted.

6 Totals for percentage contacts by sex, race and age were calculated as follows: sex (1) and (2); race (1), (2) and (3); age (1), (2), (3) and (4). Thus there were 86 male (33 elective + 53 non-elective); 53 female (30 + 23); 17 black (5 + 12); 128 white (59 + 69); 145 adult (71 + 74); 23 juvenile (1 + 22); other contacts amounting to 65 (28 + 37). Of all 168 contacts, 103 (44 elective + 59 non-elective) were offence-related.

THE ELECTIVE PUBLIC

The elective public constitutes potentially the most significant agent of unit police deployment (Reiss, 1971, p. 11). Given material access to a telephone, an individual caller can readily call on police assistance, provided the message passes the initial tests of relevance imposed by central control. This ease of contact facilitates routine complaints to the police; however, it also increases the chance of mundane or irrelevant matters coming to official attention and receiving relatively short shrift accordingly. In addition to the legitimate complainant with a genuine police-related problem, there are the ranks of mischievous, unlocatable, or repetitious callers. It is likely therefore that the most reciprocal and warm relations with the public will be sustained with legitimate complaints who have a clear personal interest in the presence of the police. Thus a complaint of burglary (given its high relevance to police) received from a woman alone (with the connotations of a missing protection) can give rise to a serious degree of attention, responded to, on the other side, by a grateful offer of refreshment. At this consensual extreme, relations with the public offer satisfaction for both sides, even if this amounts to just a cup of tea, a chat and a filed crime report. But the boundaries of relevance, not public wishes, have an overriding power, as we see in those cases where women complain of domestic assaults; what is critical to police response is the structure of relevance they impose on such cases.

Where there is a situation of immediate conflict how the police respond does not depend on the caller complainant but on a police assessment which may mean that the caller is subject to police action. The more numerous and contentious those involved prove to be, the less likely it is that a resolution seen as impartial and adequate by all parties can be arrived at; indeed, an independent police view is likely to be adopted, focused on the most apparent legal indicators, such as injuries or damage.

We must also look at the composition of the elective public. There is no reason to assume that the elective public is necessarily representative of all the population, and from Table 3.1 we can point to the relative absence of youth (only 1 per cent of elective contacts). By contrast women in general appear prominently in the elective public – 48 per cent of elective contacts. The precise meaning of such a distinction is less clear, but it does suggest that the police's relation with the public is differentially structured with respect to major social categories. The significance of the frequency of contacts with blacks (8 per cent of elective contacts) may become clearer when we examine non-elective contacts – a point that applies to all those percentages. However, other evidence pinpointed the specific infrequency of contact with Asians generally. Their routine absence, despite a significant presence in the local population, is reflected in police perception, as one supervisor put it: 'Asians are sort of a very close knit community ... We get very, very little trouble with the Asian community, but if we do get it, it's always invariably a *major* incident.' In this case it would appear that a self-contained section of the community can insulate itself from police attention provided that it is not subject to external complaints and that it avoids patrollers' interventions.

THE NON-ELECTIVE PUBLIC
When we turn to consider the non-elective public – those approached by police or subject to complaint – it is interesting to note the contrast; this category contains a high proportion of males (70 per cent), youths (23 per cent) and blacks (15 per cent). Black males as a sub-group had a high proportion of non-elective contacts (75 per cent of their contacts, compared with 59 per cent for white males), though the total for blacks is very low. On similarly low figures, 96 per cent of contacts with youth were non-elective, and they accounted for 33 per cent of arrests. In the case of patrol contacts, police approaches are frequently oriented to checking suspicions, while the same is often true of those about whom a complaint has been made. The extent to which such encounters are characterized by a pragmatic brusqueness or a problematical use of discretion has already been discussed in relation to legal work. The possibilities of engaging in significant negotiation or exchange depend on the nature of the issue on which police attention is concentrated, with offences perceived as minor offering the most scope for negotiation and more serious ones the least.

Comparing offence-related contacts with other contacts may help to shed light on the relations of the police with particular groups. For all contacts combined, 61 per cent were offence-related. The pattern is common to the elective and non-elective categories (both 61 per cent). Looking at the information on classified individuals we find a similar pattern in nearly every cell, *including* non-elective males (62 per cent). There is little difference here between black and white males in the non-elective category (56 per cent and 64 per cent respectively). But there is a higher percentage of offence-related contacts in the non-elective juvenile category (81 per cent); the high percentage of arrests in this category is consistent with such a result. Hence youth apparently remains an especially problematical category for police relations with the democratic public.

The possibilities of large-scale public confrontation arising from hostile individual encounters are most significant in relation to marginal populations – the 'toe rag' disreputables and young black males. The former are defined by the interlocking of stigma, poverty and persistent police contact:

> People who ... don't look after their houses and are dirty are generally not very helpful towards us, you know. They've got no respect for themselves, they've no respect for anybody, have they?

> Obviously, you get a lot more crime up on [my panda area] by the very nature of ... the way people live; if there's unemployment, etc., it's going to hit them before it hits the people that live on [a more affluent area].

> [On the area where I worked] they don't like the police, it's no use beating about the bush ... You do tend to keep going back to the same people, the same faces ... Where I'd arrested a lad before, for a similar offence, and ... went back to him again for another and he denied it ... I knew he'd done it ... Wasn't a lot of proof there, but the way you handle him, the way you talk to him, in the end, he ... admitted it.

The identification of a significant underclass, familiar from ecological studies (cf. Gill, 1977; Brogden, 1982), thus seems to follow from the routine operation of the general unit system. It is not simply an artefact of special police measures or deployments (cf. Mawby, 1979). Rather the intensity of police attention runs in loose tandem with the 'solutions' chosen by males of the underclass in particular in an attempt to resolve their problems and with the reactions those 'solutions' produce among their contacts, including local residents, generating a cycle of complaints to the police, investigations and stereotypical suspicion. A collective response to this can occasionally erupt, involving the risk of violent conflict. As one supervisor put it, referring to a particular street:

> I know that they are as thick as thieves, to coin a phrase, up there, they are very cliquish. They've got a lot of *esprit de corps* in their own way, and then if they see one of their friends or neighbours going to get lifted or arrested or anything like that, they are going to stick together.

That relations with young blacks could suffer from cognate difficulties is confirmed by comments from officers:

It's always difficult to speak to them with a uniform on. In fact sometimes it's impossible, because ... they do resent the uniform.

The fact that a policeman has gone [to a party after a complaint about noise] is resented ... more often from West Indians than it is from whites.

While officers tend to be sensitive to the pragmatic need to handle such contacts with care, this does not alter their basic disposition to proceed as normal:

The minute they start gibing me with harassments and, you know, bigotry ... I put them very diplomatically and very patiently in the picture. I don't give a damn what colour they are, as far as I'm concerned they're a person ... Obviously I'll go to all lengths to try and stop warfare between black and white, any racial conflict, but that won't stop me nicking a coloured person, if I have to, and it won't stop me talking to them, and it won't stop me stopping them, and inquiring ... They're no different than anyone else

This 'business-as-usual' disposition removes attention from the objective mechanisms by which perceptions of 'harassment' can grow and places emphasis instead on subjective goodwill.[14] The focus of the legal system on the individual, combined with the emphasis on routine productivity implicit in unit beat policing, produces a difficulty in posing broader questions about the general composition of unit work as it affects different sections of the community (Jefferson and Grimshaw, 1984b). The non-elective public has no recognized means of articulating directly any resulting disquiet; it can only submit to the categorizations and judgements of the officers concerned, or resist in large-scale confrontations.[15]

SYSTEMATIC CONTACT

If there is at least some evidence that the unit police officer can make systematic contact with members of the public, it applies most significantly to those on foot patrol, rather than to those in vehicles, who remain subject to the pre-eminent demands of radio control. Our observations yielded one 'spot' for a driver and two (one of them 'in the making') for foot patrollers. A friendly chat and a cup of tea are more likely to occur in the former case, following an exchange useful to both sides but one which by its nature is unlikely to give rise to recurrent contact. Foot patrol on the other hand provides some opportunities for systematic contact based on the delicate proprieties surrounding gossip and refreshment which constitute the consensual framework for an officer's 'spot' (cf. Cain, 1973, p. 37). The most naturally pertinent of these are individuals who have a static 'watching' role in premises neighbouring the street – store detectives, people keeping a night watch, shopkeepers. While providing a social leavening to isolated police roles, such 'spots' can also become the means for complaints or advice about police-related problems to be aired and for information useful to the police to be received.

Ironically these roles are the least priority for deployment by unit beat supervisors. Indeed, the relevance of such 'spots' to the foot patroller – and their irrelevance to other officers – suggests that the concept of the 'bobby on the beat' has to be seen as possessing an underside quite different in appearance; it is not so much what the 'bobby' does 'on the beat' that is important (as management studies confirm; cf. Clarke and Hough, 1984), but the opportunities such patrol gives for sustained contact with the public 'off the beat'. What is problematical for the organization is the extent to which such contacts represent an opportunity for undue influence to be exerted over the activities of police officers in return for favours, or, as in the case of the PC disciplined by HP, lead to indolence. The 'gain' to the police organization, in terms of systematic consensual relations with the public, is balanced against the potential 'loss' of impartiality or diligence.

In the context of foot patrol, how this issue presents itself depends on the locality worked. But, given deployment favouring town centres, it is likely that the issue of 'spots' is related to the presence of various commercial and retail undertakings operating in a town centre. It is not surprising to see an enterprise with a potential security problem entering into a close relationship with the officers working in that area – for example, a large store whose detectives are routinely visited by police. It may be questionable to what extent this close relationship involves fundamental 'situational' crime prevention, highlighting instead the importance of a flow of shiplifting arrests for foot patrollers. The recurrent and consensual relations with a section of the public observed here present some problems for an organization intent on impartially upholding the law; yet they are limited by the absence of routine 'spots' for the patrollers in vehicles. In this sense the unit beat system has reduced its problematical dependence on a selective portion of the public, at the expense of not significantly engaging in systematic recurrent contacts at all.

The public directly concerned with unit work can, then, be divided into three broad groupings: the elective public, asking for assistance but dependent on police judgement; the non-elective public, subjected to police intervention; and people at the residual 'spots', who share a more recurrent relation with the police. In addition there are latent publics *not* involved in police activity. These groupings are socially constituted in ways that remain unanalysed by the organization; nor can they be readily assessed or evaluated, given the imperatives of the organizational forms within the unit, since response is in principle activated by the controller system and individuated according to the legal judgement of the officers concerned. The public remains largely an unanalysed material substance traversed by the autonomous activity of unit officers.

The Wider Organizational Setting: Management

In reviewing the question of management in relation to unit work, we have to look first at the position of the unit Inspector. There are clear organizational mechanisms by which the Inspector can achieve eminence within the unit: through, for example, impressive displays of competence and the allocation of rewards. But by virtue of the shift system the Inspector is isolated practically from other officers of his own and of superior rank. Apart from encounters with the officers in charge of the consecutive reliefs, contacts with other Inspectors will normally be limited to joint attendance at the Superintendent's subdivisional senior officers' conference; contact with senior officers will be confined to the subdivisional Superintendent. Moreover the system of shiftwork itself reduces the direct link between the Superintendent and a unit Inspector, making the latter responsible for most major decisions, especially at night, when, as we have seen, important work can arise. Only a serious incident such as a train crash is likely to be seen by an experienced Inspector as necessitating calling out the Superintendent. Contact between the Superintendent and the unit Inspector represents therefore the thread on which hangs most of the senior supervisory and management relationship with the unit. Since direct supervision of the Inspector is likely to be confined to very major incidents, the means by which this relationship is maintained will tend to focus on the paperwork submitted through the Inspector to the Superintendent and on general conversation at subdivisional conferences and elsewhere. A narrow isthmus of supervision thus separates the operational units from the managerial echelons of the force. Moreover since the Superintendent's direct contacts with unit members are likely to be infrequent, the significance of this straitened band of supervision is accordingly increased. One sergeant remarked of the Chief Inspector and the Superintendent: 'Their responsibilities are so remote, aren't they?'

Managerial influence in this context is likely to centre on the most important incidents encountered by the unit and on notable trends in the paperwork it submits. Much of the work is generated in response to incidents or messages, and there is consequently reduced scope for advance specification of types of work to be undertaken. However, with the balance of resources at his or her disposal a Superintendent should be able to monitor and predict the outcomes of particular kinds of work and to indicate proper priorities and procedures in dealing with specific or concrete individual problems; thus in an oblique manner the implicit priorities of a Superintendent should in theory be discernible in the pattern and distribution of work by unit officers. The character and volume of legal process work, the emphasis on crime detection (as opposed to reporting routine traffic offences), the prevention of public disorder – all these are topics on which broad priorities could be set out and communicated to officers through the unit Inspector. The depth and impact of the Superintendent's influence will however be dependent on the extent to which the gap between the officers and the Superintendent can be bridged; hence the significance of the role of the Inspector. The test of that influence lies in the success of efforts to specify particular priorities which in some way challenge or modify the 'natural agenda' of unit work. Advice to spend more time in talking with disputants, or to avoid public contention involving large groups of police, for example, would draw into question aspects of this 'natural' process; and no certain resolution could be predicted, given the discretion of officers to pursue legal matters if they see fit. The complex issues raised by any such hypothetical specifications are more concretely illustrated by the accounts from unit supervisors which suggest how 'policy' in this context becomes a focus for what are in reality highly particular cross-pressures and influences, from above and below. First, we have a case where an Inspector explains the subtleties of a 'policy' suggestion from above.

If my Chief Superintendent ... hears something ... albeit it's not an official recommendation from headquarters, and he thinks it's an important enough ... guide ...

Q. Would he have to comply with it?

A. Well, you do really, although there's no disgrace on you and there's no disciplinary offences committed if you don't. It's good sense, I mean, the one incident which was brought up by [the Superintendent] at the last meeting I had with him was assault on police ... I agree with [the Superintendent] when he said there are far too many 'assault on police' charges being preferred for very, very trivial incidents ... If a PC is pushed and he arrests a man I've got to go up there and try and sort it out and try and dissuade him from pressing a charge of assault on police ... if he's, say, arrested for section 5 [Public Order Act 1936] ... well, I wouldn't dissuade the officer, I'd bloody tell him he wasn't going to do it ... The mere fact that he did assault a policeman during the course of his arrest would be introduced in evidence to support the more serious charge of the section 5.

The chain of management on this particular issue, affecting the legal discretion of all concerned, is evidently conditional on a less than straightforward process of personal influence from the Chief Superintendent downwards, which eventuates, in this case, in the supervisor's brusque insistence to the PC on a recommended course of action. Citing an alternative way in which the officer's original purpose could be expressed (through the insertion of evidence in a case file) provides a means by which the intervention can be justified, in the absence of a disciplinary sanction.

The chain of managerial intervention operates frequently through a sequence of advice couched in terms which are addressed to the officer 'on the ground' and therefore recognize 'exceptional circumstances':

The Chief Constable wasn't very happy with the way the RBOs were working on this division ... Since then I know that the Superintendents have been to several meetings with the Deputy Chief Constable and the Chief Constable ... That is the most significant sort of policy change. I can't use an RBO now unless I've got good and justifiable cause.

The supervisor here is aware of an advisory process above him which impinges on him in terms of a rule with a significant qualifying condition. How that qualification is defined in practice becomes a matter on which clearly the supervisor himself has some bearing and potential influence. The possibility of defining and producing a 'good and justifiable cause' is in fact borne out to some extent by our observations of RBO work.

Another instance reflects perhaps more clearly the context of a unit supervisor's operational decision-making which relates to the oblique awareness of managerial priorities as well as to the 'natural reflexes' of unit officers in contentious situations. Here the speaker is a sergeant, describing a public-order incident involving young black men:

> This was really against the grain, where if he had been a white youth that was behaving in the way he did he would have been locked up and charged with no trouble at all . . . That [namely, *not* to arrest] was my decision, yes, for which I was criticized of course, not by . . . any other supervising officer but by the lads [*sic*] themselves. [It was] to smooth down what could have been an extremely volatile situation . . . The situation was such that I didn't really have a chance to think of what the policy would be in the heat of the moment, but it was my decision . . . On reflection it would have been considered policy by certain senior officers on this subdivision.
>
> We were trying to effect the arrest of a coloured man in the street when we were surrounded by thirty other coloured men, and a number of them were excited and one in particular was waving a pop bottle in what certainly could have been described as a threatening manner. But there were only six of us. I'd no doubt that had we decided to arrest him eventually he would have come to the police station. He would have got there eventually . . . I don't know how many casualties would have been alongside but we would have won. But there would have . . . been . . . a pitched battle in the middle of the road.

Apart from the pertinence of the racial issue in this account, an impression emerges that the supervisor is caught between a half-clear perception of 'policy' on the subdivision, on the one hand, and the 'natural urge' of the unit, on the other hand to invoke their legal powers and display their collective force in the context of a no doubt mundane pattern of normal work. A 'pitched battle' with members of a sensitive population may be anathema to some senior officers; to unit members it seems to represent a less awesome prospect.

The concept of police 'management', in the sense of a rational-technical specification of means and ends, hardly comes to terms with the indirect, qualified and discretionary features of the relationships between the ranks that are described in the various instances set out here in some detail. Rather we must suggest that the goals of the organization, in so far as they are set by the higher ranks in the force, are subject to a number of conditions before they can be achieved in practice. These concern the legal discretion of officers and the pragmatic ends and agendas which they routinely construct. To specify the 'best outcome' in a given situation presumes the applicability of some rational-technical canon of excellence which can be readily expounded for the attention of junior officers; yet conflicts like the one just described suggest that such a canon does not exist. Thus, for example, the doctrine that 'public tranquillity' is the overriding objective of the police, later propounded by Lord Scarman, Sir Kenneth Newman and others, represents, on this evidence, a pronouncement in a vacuum, rather than an advance on sure ground (cf. Scarman, 1982). Such declarations would seem likely, on this evidence, to sink into the pragmatic quicksand of 'operational matters' rather than to build the foundations of a philosophy of policing.

Testing Hypotheses

On the basis of the above examination of unit beat work, we are now in a position to conclude our interpretation by seeing how well our rival hypotheses withstand the test of confronting our data.

Hypotheses Stemming from Existing Problematics

The general theoretical schools which we have identified present different perspectives on the material discussed so far. The most accessible of these is perhaps the 'machine' model, which corresponds closely to the formal system as described at the outset. Here the technical and organizational resources of the unit are seen as unproblematically allowing an appropriate response to a variety of demands. Indeed, the form of unit policing perhaps owes much to this mechanical conception, emphasizing speed, efficiency and service; any problems are attributed by this model to a failure of communication – the wheels, as it were, do not always engage with the right gear. If this is the hypothesis of the 'machine' model then in some ways it is shown to be a useful one, since we have observed a level of compliance from unit officers, and noted how messages are often dutifully received, and so on. And where in particular there is no message, the contacts between the centre and the operating edge of the system do break down, as the 'machine' model would have suggested. Yet a critical assessment of the evidence relating to the hypothesis must also point to the inherent problem of such a machine: the inefficiency of mechanical responsiveness in the context of a varied set of demands with a decidedly mixed relevance to police. Hence the desultory and fragmentary quality of the work experience, and the officers' search for coherence through a practical legal orientation involving the deployment of independent judgement, the particular outcome we witnessed, lies outside the competence of the 'machine' model to predict. It is this sense of the importance of the officers' own perceptions and responses that constitutes the merit of the 'subcultural' approach, our second major hypothesis.

The 'subcultural' viewpoint picks up the significance of officers' working norms and their basis in common-sense perceptions. We saw how incidents were interpreted in practical ways which produced, for example, categories of credible and less credible complainants and divided work into 'rubbish' and 'good arrests'. Standards of diligence were adjusted in practical ways to produce acceptable results, as were the procedural forms imposed on police investigations. Yet once again a crucial dimension of the hypothesis about a rank-and-file 'subculture' opposed to that of management fails to come to terms with the evidence. Here it is the failure to mark out a firm dividing line between the 'subculture' and the 'official culture' of senior officers, thus drawing into question the notion of subculture and suggesting instead that we are observing an integral *police* culture. Senior and supervisory officers offer role models to junior officers, indicating the acceptable norms of practical policework. With the 'machine' model's proponents, we must assert that supervision does not routinely fail, as the subculturalist hypothesis tends to imply. Rather, it seems that supervisors have various means at their disposal to mould and shape the outlook of practical police officers. Similarly it seems that the law remains a focus of the officers' attention, even if in a practical form, rather than disappearing beneath subcultural norms. In these ways the subcultural conception forms an inadequate guide to an understanding of unit policing.

What then of the 'environmental' model? This urges us to produce an all-embracing conception of unit police work, encompassing relations with diverse publics, with a complex legal system and with senior management. In many ways this is the most generally productive of the established conceptions; it permits an analysis of public contacts both elective and non-elective, promotes an understanding of the legal domains and forms surrounding practical unit policework, and reminds us of the possibilities of influence by the Superintendent and those in higher positions. We have seen how these suggestions have proved fruitful in analysing our evidence. But a note of caution is also necessary about the general drift of an 'environmental' approach; it should not lead us to overestimate external influences, a point which emerges in connection with the attenuated management influence on operations. Even more strikingly we have noticed the significant subordination of the public to the structure of relevance adopted by the police. This reflection tends to reaffirm the self-sustaining power of the organization itself. Only *in extremis* would the 'machine' – as we may call it once again – succumb to external pressure. The dynamics of unit policing once in place are not readily diverted. We need also to recall the underlying discrepancies and gaps which characterize the operations of unit policing; these negative forces – in matters of public contact for example – are as significant for any critical assessment as the positive ones which environmental theories are well placed to account for.

How relevant has the class-functionalist perspective proved when considering our material? In testing this, we have to examine how far police activity has manifested discriminatory features in respect of class (and, by extension, race). Were discrimination to be influential, we might have expected a clearly and simply biased pattern of contacts; in the elective category, for example, shopkeepers and middle-class residential populations would have been prominently served. However, in practice, contacts in this category included a range of social groups, amongst which there were groups considered to suffer oppression, for example, women in domestic disputes. Clearly then the class-functionalist position cannot account for the full range and diversity of police contacts.

If these hypotheses are inadequate in the various ways mentioned, how successful are our hypotheses, which essentially expect unit behaviour to be explicable in terms of the three structures – law, work and democracy – with the legal structure the key to an understanding of the relation between them in connection with any particular piece of unit behaviour?

Hypotheses Stemming from our Reconceptualized Problematic

In thinking through the relationship between the various determinants of unit work, subdivisional unit work is best understood in terms of a set of organizational features conducing where possible towards legally oriented work which, paradoxically, excludes *both* the public and external management from substantial influence except in relation to incidents where particular countervailing powers are brought to bear. Thus, despite the reactive character of much unit work, the public is not a major *determinant* of unit activity. This is so for three reasons: the patchwork nature of the contacts sustained; organizational (and occupational) pressures towards defining relevant unit work in terms of the legal duties and powers involved; and the formidable organizational structure of controls, interests and influences informing the question of what constitutes relevant unit work.

Public contact with the police is generally brief but, more significantly randomized and individualized, a patchwork of non-recurrent encounters that depends alternatively on specific initiatives of officers and callers, whether on patrol or going to a call. Random, individual encounters and single specific initiatives for contact thus constitute the democratic public for unit officers. There is nothing resembling a direct representative audience for unit officers, who deal largely with individuals, and small inchoate groups. The elective public can indeed enjoy a power to dispose of and benefit from police attendance, thereby contributing to its pattern of activity, but can do little more. Compliant victims are usually only too happy to accede to the police adopting a legalistic view; disputants have little option if a resolution of difficulties is not immediately forthcoming. The public which sees itself as marginal to the call system – juveniles, minorities – does not generally play an elective role at all. The community of citizens thus enjoys little sustained, organized contact with police capable of exercising a power over their operations, or of influencing significantly their objectives; 'spots' can exert power over only a limited section of unit work. At the same time the impact of the unit police on the public rests broadly on an accumulation of random, individual, highly specific encounters, the significance of which is accordingly uneven.

The underlying importance of legal definitions in unit work is determined initially by the standard requirement to filter the demands of the public for service according to criteria of relevance. In addition there is an intrinsic element of inconclusiveness and fruitlessness about response to public calls which heightens the salience of work that allows the authoritative use of legal powers to effect concise conclusions. But though there are opportunities for work which satisfies other highly valued criteria (emergency welfare offers one such possibility), the exercise of police powers in law enforcement – when such opportunities occur – represents the most commonly valued goal for unit officers, because it enables them to fulfil the distinctive capacities accorded to them in law; to fulfil organizational criteria of relevance; to exercise the only distinctive skills they possess as measured by training requirements; and to combat the inherent frustrations of much of their work. The exercise of such powers brings decisively into play their individual legal discretion informed by their practical common-sense perceptions – a major autonomous antidote to the 'treadmill' character of the routine round of call response work, and its frustrations, ambiguities and unproductiveness. A 'good' arrest represents a compensation for the frustrations of mundane work on the unit and a sign of personal success, which may point an officer towards specialist work in the future. The technical resources of the unit are thus linked together to respond to initial demands from the public, which are then focused on specific matters of police relevance by the intervention of the controller and the subsequent interpretations by officers. The distribution of adjudged competence in the unit produces a corresponding distribution of officers to mobile roles, in which urgent calls receive the attention adjudged most competent. Yet this emphasis on mobility and rapid response continually comes up against the critical problem of relevance.

Immediate supervisors have a number of methods of achieving their aims using the resources of radio control, paper report and direct oversight. They are assisted in this by certain organizational features which enable them to act as a role model: the differential competence of unit members and the practical 'on-the-job' nature of most probationer training. Realistic demands by supervisors for productivity, supported by readiness to teach and assist their constables, and alertness to supervisory methods can be effective in establishing a measure of control over unit work. The existence of common supervisory goals and co-operation in securing their achievement produces an effective supervisory team; an Inspector can, for example, expect co-operation from sergeants who are well qualified and themselves have expectations of upward mobility in the force. The consent of junior officers is acquired by ensuring that uniform demands are made on officers of equal competence. Deployment of officers to the various beats in circulation, and balanced assignments of work, contribute to the same effect. Focus on human relations and welfare tightens supervisory control. If the supervisors possess impressive competence relevant to unit workers they will be able to exact like standards from their subordinates. If they can concretely resolve particular unpredictable difficulties for subordinates, their stock will be enhanced; decisiveness in demanding and quickly moving operational situations will also increase respect. An Inspector, by taking command at difficult incidents, can become a trouble-shooter and, effectively, a pacifier of potential complainants. Standards of substantive performance are determined by the effect of supervisors' influence, which can be focused in various ways. Acceptable competence is determined empirically (rather than by rational-technical norms), by results that are satisfactory and do not give rise to substantial objection. Any controls exercised by complaints and by the courts in respect of legal work – marginal though they may be – can thus be mediated through the influence of supervisors, what they deem acceptable policework. Through these various channels supervisory influence can be considerable.

In sum, the centrality of the call system through which work of apparent relevance to policework is made available to unit members, and the inherent frustrations of much of the resulting work, combine to heighten the importance of legal process work and, in its absence, interactive skills designated to expedite transactions effectively. Patrol is a secondary mode of unit performance, subject to the first. The organizational features, such as training and personnel intake, making for the fundamental importance of the examples of working competence exhibited by experienced officers and supervisors represent a second set of significant determinations on unit functions. In so far as these latter features complement the former, and there are significant organizational factors (e.g. the need for an empirical index of achievement) conducing towards this end, the result will be a unit oriented to expeditiously handled and trouble-free transactions and a significant volume of legal process work. In so far as they are not complementary – for example, by insistence on non-legal purposes – the result will be a loss of motivation and a drop in co-operation. An effective intervention by external management is possible only to the degree that it is adapted to these basic conditions. The relative marginality of management, in operational terms, is an important feature of unit work.

So, whilst the public is rendered critical to the whole system through its role in call initiation, the design of organizational resources to respond ensures the prominence of legal definitions and ultimately of specific legal process work. The centrality of this feature of the organizational context of unit work determines that leadership examples (the importance of which to unit working results from further organizational features), to be comprehensively influential, must conform to a legally oriented competence. It is assisted in this by the empirical approach to competence in which working styles acceptable to the practical operation of the law displace abstract rational-technical norms.

When compared with the 'fixed points' system which it replaced (cf. Chatterton, 1979), unit beat policing displays a distinctive commitment to the innovatory technical impetus held to be characteristic of modern bureaucracies. Motorization and personal radios allow a considerable degree of acceleration in securing police response and linking together the individual members of the unit. In this way the input of messages can be increased and output thus enlarged in a manner that can be monitored and assessed. The importance of speed is highlighted by the allocation of the most competent members to the most mobile roles. Yet we have rehearsed at length the problems of relevance which such a system constantly generates. Meanwhile other police techniques – including public contact and advice, crime prevention and long-term detection – are consequently diminished in significance and exported to the more specialist sections of the force. The resort to technology is thus consistent with a reforming bureaucratic impulse which utilizes advanced technical means to produce a more controlled, impersonal and routinized performance. But as we have seen there is a self-defeating superfluity to this use of technology, which encourages the assertion of independence, where possible, through coherent legal work. It is this police reaction to the system which perhaps threatens in the long term to undermine it as much as the criticisms by proponents of 'community policing'.

In closing it may be worthwhile referring to the comment of the station sergeant on the sorry state of modern policing: the virtual absence of preventive policing. It did not take an elaborate analysis for him to come to this conclusion; yet with our materials we can see that the basis for his remarks is a substantial one. The system requires an *effective reaction* to incidents, the more critical, the better, since in such crises the system purportedly demonstrates its promptness in quelling immediate perceived dangers. What it cannot do, as the unrelieved *longueurs* of mobile patrol also demonstrate, is provide an effective preventive service, since its priorities point in exactly the opposite direction. In addition to substantiating this now commonly held wisdom about unit work, we hope to have revealed the organizational logic by which such effects are produced; they emerge not as functions of the individual dispositions of officers but as consequences of the organizational conditions in which they operate, the implications of which the officers then elaborate in the ways that we have observed.

In Chapter 9 we will address the theoretical and political implications of this and of the other aspects of policing we shall be examining. The first of these, which we turn to in Part III, is the resident beat system.

Notes

1 Punch (1979a, p. 148) points up a continuum between 'law enforcement' and 'social welfare' in policework, despite his strong presumption about the importance of social welfare work in policework.

2 Black (1970, p. 736) reported research showing the importance of telephone contact.

3 On 'rubbish', see, for example, Smith and Gray (1983, p. 62). Punch (1979a, p. 135) similarly refers to the sceptical view taken by officers of 'social welfare' or peace-keeping tasks.

4 Clearly there is the possibility of variability in organizational procedures and effects. The Metropolitan Police system was described by Smith and Gray as 'industrial democracy' with no significant supervisory input (1983, p. 29); on the other hand, Manwaring-White (1983, p. 72) notes the Met.'s project of introducing a new command-and-control system. This project may have implications for the supervisory significance of radio control in the Met. Scott and Percy (1983, p. 141) describe message-processing systems as low-status and inefficient. Manning (1980) reviews a system in which dispatchers and patrollers are unknown to one another, unlike the situation studied here. It is difficult however to conclude *in general* that supervision, as he implies, will routinely fail. The question of the influence of 'background' knowledge is not given the attention it deserves in a further comparison of British and United States systems, in Manning (1983). Tifft (1978, p. 98) suggests that radio dispatch precludes direct supervision but generally yields immediate service.

5 Contrast this apparent diligence with the account of Van Maanen (1983, p. 282).

6 Van Maanen (1983, p. 277) indicates a very different picture.

7 Van Maanen (1983, p. 302) shows how norms of diligence and 'practical policing' are conveyed to officers by sergeants.

8 'Human relations' is here a compendium term used to refer to the field of work-group relations within the organization – classically represented by Mayo (1945). See also Harvard Business Review (1979); for a very different, critical approach to the historical extension of social surveillance, see Foucault (1979).

9 On the legal domains in play in domestic disputes, see, for example, Raisbeck (1976); and Parker (1985).

10 Faragher (1985), reporting an observational study, points out that it is the *police* who informally influence women's willingness to pursue remedies against violence, an objective rendered difficult by the legal system generally. Chatterton (1983), in an important study of police discretion in relation to violence, does not comment on the relevance of such particular legal domains to the police, despite its pertinence to the argument.

11 The housing problems of battered women are described by Binney, Harkell and Nixon (1981).

12 Other studies tend to suggest that these findings are not untypical.

Considering patrol dispatches (as distinct from contacts of any kind), Reiss (1971, pp. 71–3) found 58 per cent of calls were defined as crime by the citizens making them, but only 17 per cent were regarded by the police as crimes (including 'auto violations' and disputes). Thus, the prima-facie relevance of incidents was offence-related, but the police took a different view after examination. Wilson (1968, p. 18) records that 10.3 per cent of citizen complaints radioed to vehicles involved 'law enforcement', 30.1 per cent 'order maintenance', 22.1 per cent information gathering (about alleged crime) and 37.5 per cent service calls (including missing persons or property, medical and other emergencies, and so on). A substantial proportion of such complaints was thus offence-related. Hough (1980, p. 13) classified incidents attended by patrols as 36 per cent crime, 19 per cent public order, 31 per cent 'social service' (including domestic disputes) and 14 per cent accidents. For a further detailed listing of 'incident' calls, see Ekblom and Heal (1982, p. 81).

13 McBarnet (1981) has strongly emphasized the absence of effective procedural rules, an argument which is apparently endorsed by Holdaway (1983, p. 100). However, he stresses the role of police strategies in maintaining control, distinguishing them from the functioning of law. Yet we have argued that such strategies occupy positions within the legal system as a whole, smoothing the path of criminal justice administration. With the Police and Criminal Evidence Act 1984 this terrain is remapped by new powers and duties in ways that do not alter the fundamental positioning of the police as the discretionary gatekeepers of the system. On 'improving' evidence, or 'gilding the lily', see Smith and Gray (1983, p. 224).

14 Police prejudice against black people is described by, for example, Holdaway (1983); the use of derogatory terms, present in our examples, seems endemic.

15 Reiner (1985b, pp. 127–9) reviews evidence suggesting 'differentiation' in the use of police powers, highlighting the salience of youth, the lower class, black people and males as categories subject to intervention. The broader implications of these differences may be unresolved, but here they raise issues about the structural relations of police with such social categories.

PART III

The Resident Beat System

CHAPTER FOUR

Working the Patch

The Formal System

As with our examination of unit work, we commence with an outline of the formal elements in order to render the subsequent narrative more comprehensible and to remind ourselves of the basic resources and lines of connection which collectively make up the determinate context out of which the nature of resident beat policing emerges.

PERSONNEL

The system of resident beat-work includes the fourteen RBOs, an assigned detective constable (DC), a collator, the RBO sergeant and the subdivisional Superintendent. They system is conceived, broadly, as a 'specialist' function: front-line community-relations work. Experienced personnel are thus recruited into the system by a selective process from a field of volunteers. Officers may be approached direct if felt to possess the right qualities. Being highly regarded by the force – officially 'the corner-stone of force policy' – the system is officially regarded as a 'step up', a prized element in the acquisition of an appropriately balanced career profile, and a platform from which promotion may be successfully sought. Consequently, for the bright and ambitious it is a temporary placement, a chance to broaden experience; for others, however, it can be a relatively permanent placement, if they so wish, provided work performance is satisfactory. But, in so far as it is a 'prized' job location and a platform for promotion, it tends both to attract and to be filled by the former. In general, then, the resident beat system can be regarded as a temporary placement, from the viewpoint of the RBOs themselves. The DC position does not offer quite the same prestige and will be filled by a volunteer expressing interest; but it offers little in terms of career advancement, especially if the incumbent intends to remain in the

CID. Similarly, the collator's job has no special status, usually being filled by mid- or late-career volunteers wanting, for a variety of reasons, an indoor position, either temporarily or permanently. Since it is definitively not a 'dumping-ground' for miscreants, transfers away from the system are usually voluntary – on promotion or to further career development; though, precisely because it is highly regarded, involuntary transfer is a possibility for those who may have volunteered imprudently or who have been unwisely selected. The sergeant position is similarly selected; whether the occupant uses it as a springboard or remains in post for a relatively long period is, again, largely a matter of individual preference, subject to satisfactory job performance.

There is no prior training before entering post, with only occasional days' training whilst in post. In general, officers are expected to learn the new demands of the job through 'on-the-job' trial and error, through imitation of colleagues and by seeking advice.[1]

TIME

The work period arrangements for resident beat officers are 'discretionary'. That is, RBOs work their 'beats', for which they are responsible on an individual basis, according to a self-chosen weekly work schedule. They choose their hours of work ostensibly to suit what they consider to be the policing demands of their area. Certain limitations are occasionally imposed (by the subdivisional Deputy, who vets the proposed weekly work schedule in advance) to ensure that some variation in cover is maintained and that two adjacent shifts are not 'uncovered' at the same time; but, subject to these occasional limitations, hours of duty are discretionary and may even be 'split': for example, a four-hour tour in the morning followed by a four-hour tour in the evening. Duties will normally be undertaken in uniform, though plain clothes can be employed on occasion, with permission, for a particular expressed purpose. The detective constable works hours in accordance with the CID shift schedule, whilst the collators and the sergeant usually work days, with evening working counting for overtime.

SPACE AND RESOURCES

RBOs work from two main offices, one provided for the PCs, one for the sergeant, collator and detective constable. Other office space is provided in the section stations for four others whose 'patches' are covered by these stations. Since they are regarded fundamentally as foot patrol officers, cars are not provided for their use. They may use their own bicycles and, for that matter, their own cars. If beats are a long way from the station, or if a whole series of inquiries at dispersed locations is necessary, the use of cars might be accepted as a more economical use of precious work hours, but no mileage allowance is available.

COMMUNICATIONS

Each officer has a personal radio on a permanent basis, which is linked to the unit control system. Whilst officers can be called up on the radio, especially if unit resources are stretched, they are not subject to radio control calls as a matter of routine. However, they must sign on and off with radio control and can be used by the unit. In these instances, the commands of a superior ranking officer cannot be set aside. The collators and the DC are not subject to supernumerary unit demands; nor is the sergeant.

SUPERVISION

Routine supervision of the RBOs and the collator is the responsibility of the RBO sergeant, who has powers of oversight (directly through patrol observation; indirectly through the evaluation of paperwork submissions), advice, command and discipline. He or she is also responsible for completing annual staff appraisals and for ensuring that certain visits – to schools and police pensioners, for example – are regularly made through the institution of a self-recording 'visits book'. A DC, though 'outranked' by the RBO sergeant, is regarded as subject to CID supervision. Since this role is advisory with respect to crime matters, the supervision of crime reports and files largely falls to him or her.

The Superintendent is the ultimate authority who can deal with matters directly or work through the sergeant, and if necessary transfer officers. He or she also requires the submission of monthly self-reports by the RBOs: a diary of activities undertaken and results achieved.

RÉSUMÉ OF DUTIES

The general job specification of the RBO refers to a general responsibility for a beat or area. In terms of discrete functions this involves foot patrol work, community-relations work, gathering 'intelligence' for the collator, following up assigned 'beat crime', dealing with minor complaints and nuisances, delivering messages, submitting reports of crime, crime files (with respect to 'beat crimes' dealt with), process reports and miscellaneous paperwork concerning 'community' matters, and completing visit-book entries and monthly self-reports.

A specifically assigned detective constable has an advisory responsibility with respect to RBO crime-work, including responsibility for liaison with the CID. The DC operates as a 'specialist manager', cementing the co-operation expected between detective expertise and uniform participation in criminal investigation. In terms of discrete functions, the DC receives the beat-crime reports assigned to the RBOs by the CID, allocates these to the appropriate beat officer, advises on crime inquiries, offers guidance about the completion of crime files, deals with his or her own crime files and assists in presentations at court.

The collator's general job specification refers to the collation and dissemination of criminal intelligence and the maintenance of records. This entails receiving and recording information, updating and 'weeding' records and files, issuing 'intelligence' bulletins and promoting the use of the system.

The RBO sergeant is generally responsible for supervision of the PCs. In terms of discrete functions, the job involves overseeing patrol, supervising paperwork, ensuring visit-book records are updated, offering advice and passing on that offered by the Superintendent, issuing commands, appraising staff, dealing with minor disciplinary matters, reporting serious breaches, assigning special tasks and undertaking community relations work, both independently and on behalf of the Superintendent.

The Superintendent's role is partly advisory and partly supervisory. Concretely, he or she selects and transfers officers, reviews monthly reports, conducts staff appraisals, advises, commands, oversees, deals with referred discipline matters, refers serious disciplinary matters to the Chief Superintendent and conducts his or her own community-relations work.

A GROUP OF CONSTABLES

RBOs, like unit-beat and all police officers, are constables – a common status which cuts across all distinctions of rank and specialist function. Since their areas may differ, however, we cannot specify the use of their constabulary powers in advance of empirical inquiry, nor, in consquence, the capacity of 'law', the courts and citizens to constrain action.

RELATIONS WITH THE PUBLIC

In a similar vein, it is impossible to predict from the formal remit precisely what form contacts with the public will take, in advance of empirical inquiry, nor in consequence the role of the public as a determinant of police action.

The System Working

Having outlined the formal position of resident beat-work with regard to the organization, the law and the public, we can commence an examination of the system working. A useful start may be to offer vignettes of RBO life. We have constructed eight 'life-in-the-days' of RBOs, from observations made of eight of the fourteen RBOs observed. The aim is to offer a comprehensive selection of the *range* of RBO working, including, especially, those persons and 'days' which demonstrate most sharply differences between such ways of working.

Patrol work	(8 a.m. to 4 p.m.)	AB
Patrol work	(10 a.m. to 6 p.m.)	BC
Patrol work	(10 a.m. to 6 p.m.)	CD
Patrol work	(9 a.m. to 5 p.m.)	DE
Patrol work	(8 a.m. to 4 p.m.)	EF
Patrol work	(9 a.m. to 5 p.m.)	FG
Patrol work	(10 a.m. to 6 p.m.)	GH
Patrol work	(2 p.m. to 10 p.m.)	HI

These observational accounts were selected from twenty-nine such periods of normal working, occurring from October to January. The twenty-nine periods covered three duties from 8 a.m. to 4 p.m., eight from 9 a.m. to 5 p.m., seven from 10 a.m. to 6 p.m., nine from 2 p.m. to 10 p.m., one from 3 p.m. to 11 p.m. and one from 6 p.m. to 2 a.m. The whole of the shift was usually not observed, through choice, since meal breaks often neatly divided shifts into discrete halves, or because officers had assigned part of their shift-time to a variety of routine administrative tasks, or because hours of duty were unexpectedly changed. Calling 8 a.m. to 4 p.m., 9 a.m. to 5 p.m. and 10 a.m. to 6 p.m. shifts 'earlies' and the rest 'lates' means that the observation periods break down in the ratio 18 'earlies' to 11 'lates'.

In addition sessions were spent with the collator, the detective constable and the sergeant, as well as with another sergeant (not part of RBO strength) permanently placed in a local black youth club, and the Superintendent. Eight further sessions were spent with various RBOs on non-routine activities: pornographic book-shop raid (1); night van (1); prostitute patrol (1); RBO meetings (2); public order duties including town patrol (1); a 'demo' (1), and a football match (1).

AB

I arrive at the subdivisional station at 8 a.m. for an 8 a.m. to 4 p.m. shift with AB. Before setting off on patrol he tells me he has a file –

a case involving numerous motoring offences – and the updating of his pocket-book to complete. By 9.30 a.m. we are off. We arrive at our first port of call at 9.50. We are told of some thefts of the previous night – a bag and swimsuits taken from a swimming coach, and cigarettes and lighter from the caretaker's unlocked office – which are duly recorded in AB's pocket-book, the basis from which the subsequent crime report will be completed. The caretaker is not at work till the afternoon so will have to be contacted later for further essential details needed to complete the crime report.

After listening to the story, AB asks the swimming coach whether he suspected anyone. He said that three black kids had constantly to be 'shooed off' the premises for 'hanging around' whilst not using the facilities. AB asked if one was tall; being told this was so, AB confessed he had been watching the cycle sheds in the hope of catching those responsible for a series of bike thefts and had noticed three black youths loitering. (I had spent a fruitless evening in a parked car with AB, keeping watch, and we had observed three black youths apparently 'hanging around'.)

The swimming coach replied by saying that his swim squad had had their cycles pinched from the cycle sheds; he also mentioned he'd had a track suit stolen on the same night as his bag. AB brushed aside the mention of the track suit, presumably because no complaint had been filed, and urged the swimming coach to warn other baths about the theft of his swimming bag.

By 10.30 a.m. we are back out patrolling. As we walk, AB tells me a little about the residents on his patch: 'A queer lives there'; 'A publican councillor, whose wife has left him, lives there'; and so on. We call at a building site for a social chat, about AB's hobby, shooting, with his brother-in-law; and then at a butcher's, for a smoke and another chat. Asked by the butcher if he is busy, AB replies non-committally: 'Yes and no. I've got stuff on, but there's no rush for it.' We carry on and visit a garage, to discuss AB's car with a mechanic, and then another, where we sit for a rest (AB's bad knee is playing up) and a smoke. Whilst we rest a long-haired youth passes by. AB tells me he is on the dole, lives with a girl also on the dole, does freelance car repairs and runs two untaxed cars. (Later we pass one of these cars. AB justifies his lack of action by saying he could 'do' him any time and that anyway he has no tickets with him. As it happens, it is close to lunch time.)

We continue our patrol. AB apologizes for the lack of 'action', but says it is sometimes like this, though it can be very busy; for example, at holiday time there is a stack of 'special attentions' (vacant properties which, having been notified as such to the police, require regular, preferably daily checking – a job which falls to the RBO). However, he continues, even without outstanding paperwork (epitomizing, we may note, 'busyness' for AB), there is always something to do such as look out for out-of-date tax discs(!), stop cars and issue HORT-1s and so on. Patrolling, for AB, seems to be about 'being seen'; 'knowing people' is important, less in order to use them as possible informants and more because the ice has then been broken, making it easier *generally* when making inquiries.

A radio call to AB, for me to phone the Chief Inspector some time, then follows. We stop at an off-licence that AB knows and ask to use their phone. AB phones in, but the Chief Inspector is not around. At 12.30, AB gets the bus to his home for lunch, and we agree to meet up at 2.10 p.m. at the subdivisional lock-up station.

BC

I arrive late, at 10.30 a.m., at a section station situated at one end of the subdivision, for a 10 a.m. to 6 p.m. shift with BC. He is drinking tea and reading the papers and invites me to join him. Afterwards, at 10.45, he begins to sort out his work for the morning, by going through his 'basket'. This contains 'unoccupied premises' and 'minor complaint' forms. Two of the latter, those involving kids annoying residents by being noisy and playing football, are put on one side, since they entail evening visits; the addresses of the other two – one concerning criminal damage to a door, the other an indecent phone call – are taken down, and are to be part of our morning's work. Yesterday's visits to 'unoccupied premises' are recorded on the appropriate space on the form, and BC's pocket-book is then completed.

By 11.15 a.m. we are ready to set off on patrol, at which point the duty shift Inspector pays a call. The ensuing conversation contains a mixture of supervisory advice about appearance (I.: 'Your hair looks scruffy over the collar of the uniform.' BC [joking]: 'I'm trying to look young'. I.: 'It doesn't work') and about an indecency file BC is completing (I: 'He's got to go to court to be bound over') and jocular comment – directed at the WPC staffing the office – about the 'page 3' girls in a *Sun* centre spread ostentatiously being read during this.

At 11.30 a.m. we are off on patrol. We pass an old woman on the doorstep. BC asks after her health. After a 'general chat' BC declares 'We'll have to go', smiles and says to me, 'We'll never get rid of her otherwise.' On leaving he says to her he'll pop in some time; he tells me she is a regular 'tea spot', picked up in the early days when he would deliberately be in certain places at specific times so as to get to know certain residents.

We go off to a council estate to see the woman about the criminal damage complaint. She is not in. We are then approached by a shopkeeper about some keys left in his shop by a lady. If we see her, can we tell her they are at the police station? BC eulogizes to me about the 'closeness of the community'. He also confides to me that when first on the 'patch' he tried to do something about parking (down narrow streets); but, because this antagonized residents, he no longer bothers – it is 'reasonable'. He also confesses he could 'knock off' all the shops, should he be so minded, for having blinds too low. But he doesn't, of course, because 'policing in this country is friendly' and 'people appreciate it if you give them a rollicking instead of knocking them off'.

BC is not apparently in agreement with force policy on school visits. He prefers simply to get to know the kids and visits schools only if some specific nuisance is being committed by kids from the school that the school itself cannot handle. (He mentions 'coloured' kids from the local school jumping out in front of cars and making them stop suddenly, by way of example.) In any event, he feels that force policy really implies only getting to know the kids. His one secondary-school head is not keen on police going in lecturing. The yobs around here are 'decent yobs – if you know what I mean', which means there is less *need* to go in schools.

Our next port of call: a stately home. The curator mentions some vandalism that they have not bothered to report. BC tells the curator to phone the police station if there is any more. He does not check the damage.

The complaint about the indecent phone call is next on the list; but the woman in question is not in. BC discusses the matter with the housekeeper, concluding that their usual advice is to go ex-directory if calls become persistent. The chauffeur there offers us the milk money (£2) to get a drink. BC declines. I take it as a joke, though BC later recounts the incident as an example of the temptations 'up here'. He sees it as an attempted bribe by the chauffeur, who would replace the money himself. I remain unconvinced. Apparently, the head of household is a 'self-made man'; such men, according to BC, are 'as good as gold' with the police.

After the visit, we walk back through fields, for BC to have a smoke off the road. BC confesses this is his summer hideaway for a quick smoke and a sit down. He later mentions the need – not always recognized by 'lip-happy' youngsters – to trust people before 'you let on about perks of the job'. I take this as a compliment.

We return to a section station at 1.50 for lunch. Fifteen minutes later, after the soup is cooked, BC signs off for lunch with Control.

CD

I arrive at the subdivisional station for a 10 a.m. to 6 p.m. shift with CD, who is on the telephone. After the phone call CD has to see the Superintendent about a replacement to cover the other half of the beat CD has recently taken over.[2] So it is 10.30 before we leave the station to undertake the thirty-minute walk to CD's patch. Because of the distance involved, CD tends to prepare beforehand and to draw up a list of definite calls, since there is no possibility of 'slipping back' to the station for some forgotten item.

The first call is to an old lady in a large detached house. She has been suffering at the hands of some local children who have been making her life a misery by playing 'knock down ginger' and, more seriously, throwing stones and breaking her windows. Having apprehended the lads involved, CD is reporting back. We are invited in and offered coffee. CD explains that the lads have admitted the incidents, that they are being 'fact-reported', after which the likely outcome is a caution. CD wonders whether this is 'acceptable' to the old lady. The old lady thinks compensation for the windows might be more 'educative', but seems willing to accept the caution once CD explains that it is up to her should she wish to pursue a civil remedy.

A social chat follows easily, with CD being shown the old lady's antiques, in which CD expresses interest. The old lady, on Christian-name terms, seems to like CD (a pattern that is to be repeated throughout the morning). Given that CD is a relative newcomer to the patch, this is an impressive beginning.

Next port of call, around midday, is a house on a local council estate, the home of a principal organizer of the estate's tenants' association. The call seems purely a social one, perhaps for my benefit, though it has started to snow by this time. We have more coffee.

We soon leave, and CD visits, at around 12.30 p.m., an old lady who has recently had a mastectomy. CD is genuinely worried about her, believing she needs social-work assistance but is too proud to ask. The call is intended to get the old lady's permission for a social worker – whom CD has already 'lined up' – to call. The whole exercise is conducted with tact and competence; and this time the offered coffee is refused.

Back out into the snow and on to the house of a local prostitute (time: 12.40 p.m.) to check whether she has made out a transfer application. The tenants association wants her out, and she has agreed to request a transfer. Since CD has put a report in to the Superintendent about it, and a further report was due yesterday, CD is anxious to finalize the matter. However, once again the prostitute is out. So we go on up to the housing office to check whether they have received a transfer application. Apparently they have, which means CD can now put in the report. A discussion follows as to where the prostitute might go, during which time CD learns where she was previously offered (and turned down) properties.

On the way to the housing office, a lady stops to ask the way. Despite the snow, CD displays no irritation on being stopped and carefully looks her destination up on a map. Failing to find the wanted place, CD then sends the lady to the housing office. It is now 1.30 p.m. and snowing hard – time for lunch. We turn round and head back for the station, where we arrive, cold and wet, for a 2.15 p.m. lunch break.

DE

At 1 p.m. DE and I leave the subdivisional station for a school visit. We arrive at 1.15 to await the film which is to be brought by the community-relations sergeant – the public liaison department being the resource/support in a visit like this. By 1.30 the film has still not arrived, and DE is getting anxious, not surprisingly, at the prospect of having to talk to the entire third year without a film. It is a difficult situation; I cannot help but feel for him. The school, apparently, has no standby plans.

By 1.45 delaying tactics are no longer possible, and DE is invited to address the third year. He starts with a general outline of his job and the purpose of the visit – to *prevent* his having to meet them as criminals. Most crime starts as 'kids' silly pranks', he continues, which everybody here has committed and to which the film, were we able to see it, attests. He also stresses the role of groups in criminality – a consequence of group membership leading to individuals failing to think for themselves. They owe it to themselves, since they are legally responsible for their own criminal actions, to think for themselves.

He then invites questions. Some of the questions enable him to make a general exhortatory point; he repeats them for the group to hear and answers in some detail. He answers more specific questions individually and quietly, in a voice it is impossible for the whole group to hear. His general manner throughout, despite his earlier anxiety, is confident and easy, and his general tone is 'liberal', for example: 'Yes, there are some malpractices, but I'm as opposed to them – which are comparatively rare these days – as you are.' With no help from the school staff, who don't even manage to keep the chattering down to a tolerable level for him, he manages competently, pedagogically speaking – except, as mentioned above, when he replies quietly to particular questions in a way which eliminates many from the dialogue; he misses the point of only one question. He seems to warm to the task and is obviously enjoying it; he is able to inject a note of humour too.

DE's general set of positions embraces the following ideas. Crime grows out of silly pranks which it is his job to *help* prevent. Assault by police is to be deplored, but most such accusations are false, and people arrested who do not show respect (who are abusive, and so on) deserve all they get. Historically, the police were members of a community protecting the sleeping village and were still only citizens-in-uniform with few special powers. He states a personal opposition to capital punishment: he would rather stop the murder than hang the murderer. He feels that the policeman's most difficult assignment is informing relatives of a death in the family; the most terrifying moment is walking down the street as a policeman for the first time – because of the responsibility. To the numerous questions about the height and educational requirements necessary for joining the police, he tosses off quick answers in his obvious impatience to get back to the wider public-relations objective.

By 2.30 p.m. it is over, though many stay behind to ask individual questions. As if on cue, the community-relations sergeant then arrives with the film, complaining that he had to chase to another division for the film because, at £250 a time, management decided it was too costly for divisions to possess their own films. To the question as to 'how it has gone', DE replies that he had the 'usual stuff' about 'police beating up people' and so on, but that he is glad because it made the whole thing more lively.

At 2.35 p.m. it is time to join a group (two classes) of first years who saw another film – one called *Seven Green Bottles* – a few weeks back. This is to be the follow-up session. The film, a realistically shot colour film, was about seven cockney youngsters who truant, commit vandalism and thieve from cars, parking meters, gas meters and market stalls. The general theme is one of increasing seriousness of offence and, concomitantly, the ensuing punishment and consequences. As the seven slide down the gradient of seriousness, fewer and fewer remain, as at each stage youngsters drop out of the gang, having 'learned the lesson'. The first lad drops out when his mum warns him off becoming an 'old lag' like his dad; the second after being given a stern warning, an official caution, by a Chief Inspector. The third dies in a fatal (stolen) car accident, and the fourth drops out when his mother, chastened by the death, takes him back from the council home he was in. The fifth lad is dropped out when he is sent to an assessment centre, from which he escapes, and is left 'on the run'. The sixth is taken away, after robbing someone, for failing to buy a stolen radio, and the final youth is portrayed 'on the run', to the accompanying theme music: 'You are what you do, you are what you are.' In general, the film emphasized a number of points:

(1) Minor delinquency leads to major criminality, unless firm steps are taken early.
(2) Officers behave correctly, but they are only human. (An officer threatens to 'wallop' one of them if the lad kicks him.)
(3) There is no honour among thieves. The youths are pictured arguing and blaming each other.
(4) The leader–led thesis, with the former characterized as vicious, unfeeling, pathological bullies.

DE introduces the session by talking about being a resident beat officer and helping, and about them reaching the age of personal responsibility. In this context, the film is intended to make them think. This is followed by questions by both the community-relations (CR) sergeant and DE on the film: 'Do they remember so-and-so?' 'What do they think of that?' This is very directed, especially by the CR sergeant, who is pedagogically inferior to DE. He wants to drag out from the children the moral of each bit of the film and get them to 'agree' with it, for example: 'Did you notice that though there were seven they all did what one said? They stopped thinking for themselves and followed the leader? Do you have a gang you play with? You do, don't you?' And so on.

While the sergeant stresses the leader–led thesis, DE's theory seems to be slightly different: 'When you're in a gang, you stop thinking and act moronically, don't you? You go bananas.' Other themes strongly pressed are the importance of *thinking* about what you do because it always has *effects* on others (for example, silly pranks can have the effect of instilling fear in the elderly), and *personal responsibility*. The sergeant in particular is constantly worried about 'getting off the point'. DE's style is more varied and casual, emphasizing the need to imagine themselves in the position of victim.

The kids are generally interested, though usually they answer only specific, factual questions about the film. Towards the end, when the CR sergeant is called away, a spate of hands go up to ask questions, perhaps suggesting that focusing the lesson through the film is a mistake from their point of view. After the lesson, many stay behind to talk to DE.

During the post-mortem discussion, the CR sergeant expresses a view that it has all been a waste of time since the film was 'too old' for them and the kids didn't 'get' the points. (The former point is doubtless valid, in so far as the film has dealt with experiences which are possibly beyond most of those present; as for the latter, he is probably expecting too much from first-year children.)

At 3.40 p.m. we leave the school and return to the subdivisional station for coffee. At 4 p.m. I leave.

EF

I arrive at the subdivisional station at 8 a.m. for an 8 a.m. to 6 p.m. shift with EF, who arrives twenty minutes later. He announces that he has to go through his drawer to sort out what he is to do today, and that he must see another RBO who is due in at 9 a.m. Since the former takes very little time, the latter seems the more urgent task. Whilst waiting he writes up his pocket-book – his diary with a fuller record when offence-related incidents occur. Here, things are written out in full question-and-answer style; unlike elsewhere, which is written in a very perfunctory style. He also shows me a paper on the case for amending the law on indecent exposure and indecent assault, which has been prepared by a local community worker (as a discussion document for his local Labour Party), and for which EF provided the necessary legal advice.

At 9.15 a.m., having seen briefly the other RBO he was waiting for (about a social, not a police, matter), we set off in EF's car. He parks the car at the edge of his patch and commences patrol.

At 9.35 we call in at a motor-cycle scrapyard about a bike for yet another RBO. Ten minutes later we are visiting another scrapyard, but don't stop as the boss is out. At 9.50 we are in the civic amenities yard. EF successfully requests an invitation to tea. Whilst drinking tea, we have a radio call from Control to phone the switchboard of a local firm making and distributing lorries and tractors; EF says we will be visiting there shortly in any case.

We are soon off. The next stop, at 10 a.m., is a café which EF says he has not visited before since it is off his patch. I can only assume he is 'sussing' it out as a possible 'tea spot'. EF asks the owner if he is having trouble with local youths. The owner replies, 'No', because apparently he had no pin-tables. On leaving, EF remarks to me that the owner is the 'unfriendly' sort. Asked to elaborate, he says 'just a feeling'. To me, the man seems no more than usually reticent for a first-time visit. Perhaps the lack of an offer of tea, or perhaps the quietness of the man – EF preferring the talkative kind – has swayed EF's judgement.

Next stop at 10.05, is the garage. Offered tea, EF turns to me to ask 'if we have time'. I leave it to him. He accepts. Once again, the chat, as with all visits so far, is purely social without any crime-related information being proffered or requested. And as with the café, strictly speaking the garage is not on his patch.

Back on our way, we pass a day centre at 10.25. EF says he's never visited this before and so he decides to introduce himself. Entering, we meet a part-time warden, another old woman and an old man having tea. We are offered some, the part-time warden interjecting smartly to say, 'That's what they've come for.' EF denies this, not surprisingly since we have had two mugfuls in thirty minutes (which are beginning to do things to my stomach). In the course of the conversation we learn how an old man became disgustingly drunk and was seen loading a van with boxes of new shoes one night; he immediately becomes the prime suspect of the women for the 'offence' of removing the flowerpots from outside the next-door flats when EF mentions these have a habit of going missing. We learn that a relative of the subdivisional station typist goes to the centre, and we learn that EF knows the dog-handler son of one of the inmates; but this is the extent of 'police-related' matters, the rest, as before, being all social.

On patrol again and at 10.40 we get a radio call about a woman who has seen some kids at the back of her neighbour's lounge. EF is told to check it out. When he does, the woman is not in, and the neighbour's house appears intact.

We continue and visit a bedridden old woman 'to see if she is all right' and has food in the house. She expresses gratitude at the visit and says she feels all right now EF has been. EF checks the food cupboard to see if food is available, and we leave with EF exclaiming, 'Well, what can you do?' My unspoken answer is to wonder what he was hoping to do, since the woman is visited by the meals-on-wheels service, the social services, a good neighbour and a son; and my suspicion is that this extreme solicitousness is partly for my benefit.

Passing a butcher's, we enter and speak to an Indian, a young man EF once 'nicked' for thieving and who is now up on an 'affray' charge. EF has advised him (on the law) in the past and offers him (legal) advice now, if he needs it. After we have left, EF tells me he thinks the man is likeable, but a 'bit of a lad' and 'a militant' – the meaning of which I don't pursue.

Next stop is the lorry and tractor firm. The earlier radio call about the firm turns out to be a request from a switchboard operator for EF to use the PNC to check a car number. She has apparently witnessed a hit-and-run crash and, having taken the car number and make and informed the police, wishes now simply to check her observations. Her curiosity satisfied – she was right – we move on to the personnel manager's office, with EF 'complaining' to me that he knows the PNC isn't supposed to be used like that but . . . with the implication being, 'If that's what the public wants, what can you do?'

The purpose of the visit to the personnel manager's office is to see what progress has been made in connection with some stolen tyres. The personnel manager suspects the gateman because without his co-operation he finds it difficult to see how the large tractor tyres got out; the gateman is also suspected because he has a £200 fine for drunken driving to pay off. During this discussion the manager also relates an incident about one of their 'best workers' who was caught pinching and whom they dismissed, but without also contacting the police. EF thinks they are making a rod for their own backs, because if others are prosecuted in the future for similar offences they might see it as discriminatory. The personnel manager is apologetic but adamant that it was an isolated incident.

We leave and call in at the bus depot to see, socially, a superintendent, who EF had not seen for a while. Whilst there, he gives a little legal advice about the bus company's legal position once a juvenile has pinched money from a conductor.

At 12.40 p.m. we call in at the shop of the mother of a family BS has known for some time, ostensibly as legal adviser over crime-related matters. However, he is also visiting as emotional counsellor, since the crime-related matters are complicated, involving sexual assaults on her children (one an incestuous near-rape of her daughter which the mother is unaware of), and because the family is deemed 'funny'. The previous RBO has warned EF off them because he unwittingly became a 'father-figure' to the boy in the absence of his real father. EF is allegedly trying not to get too involved. The chat is social – unsurprisingly, because the previous night when he spoke to her it was very serious and legally oriented – and endorses my growing suspicion that EF is having a blitz on his contacts for my benefit (though it may be that my view is jaundiced on account of a stomach upset by too much tea).

We move on, and attempt to call on an old lady informant, who, unfortunately, is out. EF sings her praises; her father was a police sergeant and she 'loves the police'.

At 1 p.m. we are accosted by an old man who wishes to apologize for his rudeness of the other night. Apparently, EF visited his house because local kids had been giving him and his wife trouble. He came in drunk whilst EF was talking to his wife and was a 'bit loud'. This morning he apologizes continually and says what a grand job the police are doing. He smells of drink. EF thinks he is 'a bit of a nutter', though he has a real problem with kids putting fire-crackers through his letter box and igniting the curtains. I ask whether he is a drunkard; EF believes it likely.

At 1.15 we make two quick 'shopping' visits: to see if the beams EF has bought from a contractor are still intact in an old house due for demolition; and to an antique shop to 'keep an eye on' the corner unit he is after.

Finally we head back to the car, after I have mentioned at 1.20 that I need some lunch. EF's reply, that he sometimes doesn't bother when out on his patch, seems incongruous in comparison with his 1½-hour meal break that I witnessed the day before; but it is in tune with my feeling, growing all morning, that he has been going all out to impress – first with the number of his contacts, now with his limitless stamina.

FG

I arrive at the subdivisional station at 9.30 a.m. for a 9 a.m. to 5 p.m. shift with FG and look around for him. I find him at the front door complaining about having been landed with door security (a new function instituted temporarily after a mainland bombing initiative by the IRA). He says that this particular shift 'always uses RBOs for this job', despite the large number of walkers. Though sympathetic when he discovers four shift officers are off sick, he still feels it always falls to him or to another RBO. In view of my presence, all the supervisory staff, up to the Chief Inspector, make noises about a replacement, but no shift officers are available. So another RBO is called in at 10 a.m. Due to work demands he is not able to arrive until 11.10.

During the time on security duty we talk. For example, FG constantly makes sarcastic noises about the number of shift men wandering around and says that RBOs should not be used in this fashion, since they should be on their patch as often as possible. He says that he constantly goes round his patch in semi-plain clothes (that is, anorak instead of police topcoat), because many people find the uniform off-putting; though, in his case, people on his patch now know him so well that a uniform is no longer necessary as a visible deterrent. Nor was his alternative clothing effective any longer as a disguise in which to catch the kids playing football in the streets.

During this period, an Asian man enters the station to 'produce' his driving documents. Apparently he has lost his insurance papers. He plans to get a photocopy from his brokers but he needs a couple of days to do this because of work commitments. The PC on the desk says he will be reported for failing to produce. The Asian man persists with his explanations. The PC reiterates his reply. After the Asian man has walked out, looking disgusted, FG, clearly critical of this PC's brusque manner, says to me, 'This job's about knowing how to talk to people – some have got it, some haven't ... PC should have explained to the Asian he had till midnight to produce and then invited him to go up and get a photocopy now.'

On the question of prevention, FG claims that time on the patch is 'preventive' because, when he was away on his holidays (he doesn't specify how long a time period this was), the period produced six crime reports when it 'should have produced only two to four'. (FG is referring here to 'beat-crime' reports – namely, those handed back to RBOs by the CID, of which twelve to fifteen per month would be normal according to FG – as opposed to the total number of crimes dealt with on a patch, which is more like forty or so per month.) He also claims he can confirm the value of preventive work from his own records, which demonstrate that the 'niggly little stuff', the minor complaints (for example, football in the streets), can be prevented by talking to both parties. FG jokes about the last time he made an arrest; he says, 'His parents had to be present [meaning the arrestee was a juvenile]; now he's drawing his old-age pension.' He also thinks that being paid to walk around a patch is a skive, as it allows you to develop numerous contacts (for various bargains) and gives you time to do things like shopping on 'the firm's time'. 'Policemen should never have to do things on their own time', according to FG.

His own beat has few problems: some 'flashing' in the park, but not much crime, nor damage, nor complaints. The major frustration is not being allowed to get on with the job because of duties like the present one, or court duties, football matches, or even 'community-relations' meetings, all of which 'keep you from the patch'.

At 11.10 a.m. we at last set off on patrol, through the park and round the patch. A radio call from Control tells us to meet an Indian man at a particular house about a case of criminal damage. FG tells me, 'That's a "pro's" house'; he says to Control that we'll be there in a few minutes. Meanwhile, we call in on the treasurer of the local residents' association for a book on accounts FG has lent her. (FG, an ex-accountant, is the honorary auditor.) But for the radio message, he would doubtless have stayed for coffee.

We meet the Indians – the landlord and his friend – at the house. All the windows have been broken, though there has been no attempt to break in. The Indian landlord apparently let the house to a Jamaican who, because he was retiring to Jamaica, stopped paying the rent just before Christmas. Then a neighbour rang the landlord about the criminal damage; the latter came to board up the windows and report the matter to the police. FG asks whether the landlord knows about a girl living there; he doesn't, and thinks she must have been living with the Jamaican tenant. Out in the garden, FG talks to the next-door neighbour about the incident. She says a Jamaican girl, whom she did not recognize, 'did' (i.e. smashed] the front windows; a white man broke the back ones in a separate incident. Back inside, FG adds up the damage, takes details from the landlord, mentions the sub-letting of the flat to a girl who was a prostitute (with a strong implication that he must or should have known), picks up and keeps various letters and documents addressed to now departed occupants and then asks the landlord to phone when an exact estimate of the damage is available, since the insurance people will check with him.

During all this, the phone rings. The landlord answers it, but hands the phone to FG, who pretends to be moving into the house. The caller asks after 'Midnight'.

We leave the house. On the way back, FG laughs at the landlord's pretence or naïveté about the prostitute living there. He implies that it serves the landlord right for letting to such people, but sympathizes with him to the extent that he was unwittingly caught in the middle of what was a domestic 'tiff' (though in the crime report he later completes, he suggests that people who don't like 'pros' living in the area were responsible). FG refrains from putting in his pocket the letters he has kept because he says they are 'contaminating'; more generally, he expresses general disgust at the state of the house.

We return to the station for 12.45 p.m. and ask whether anyone knows 'Midnight'. One RBO (EF) offers a name; another (DE) replies 'Nonsense' and offers another. FG informs the collator, who is leaving the room, that the prostitute no longer lives there. He seems uninterested. The RBO (DE) who offered a second name for 'Midnight' seizes on the letters that FG took from the house. One is addressed to a man he has 'wanted to get' for ages. DE assumes as a result he was 'poncing off' his own daughter. FG says that you can't 'get' a man for having bills addressed to himself. The picture becomes more confused as study of the letters seized reveals that the 'pro' FG thought was living there wasn't. Nobody seems to know the man who rented the house, though a man with a similar name is a known ponce.

Between 1 and 2.20 p.m. we have lunch and play cards. At 2.20 FG completes the crime reports for the criminal damage. At 2.50 FG is in the station office when a panda driver asks after a man whose son is wanted for questioning. FG says he is a police interpreter on his patch. After the latter phones the panda driver, FG takes over the call.

At 3 p.m. we leave once more to patrol the patch. We are stopped by two lads with a kitten for which they are trying to find a home. FG tells them the police can't help but, if they can't find a home for it by four o'clock, to bring it to the police station where he will keep it. We arrive at the shopping centre at 3.15. FG suggests tea, for which we go to an Indian couple's shop. After a social chat, we leave at 3.45 and return to the station. I leave.

GH

I arrive at the subdivisional station at 10 a.m. for a 10 a.m. to 6 p.m. shift with GH, who is not there. Nobody knows of my visit. Rumour has it that the RBOs are at court. An arrested demonstrator has come to trial, and crowd trouble is thought to be a possibility.

At 10.30 GH enters the office, having been with the social services for two days as part of a new training initiative. He has not been informed of my visit. He fills in an accident book, recording a road accident. We talk generally. GH says he now knows people well, though originally he was pushed around nightly. He tells me of a fight which stopped when he arrived, whereas the panda driver dealing with it was having 'a pig of a time'. GH sent the fighters home and had them together the next morning over a cup of tea. Now both are the best of friends.

He mentions that he is an eccentric, who likes to cycle round with his cape just to get noticed. ' "Look at that prat over there," some will say; but they've seen me' – a theme he stresses constantly.

GH thinks most of his best work is done in pubs because most of his informants are there. It helps with 'yobs' since it gains their respect, and with 'domestics'. If you know who has been in the pub from opening to closing time you can anticipate them. However, he says that according to standing orders RBOs are not supposed to enter pubs unless necessary.

To assist his job he uses his car and calling cards, both at his own expense. Everyone on his patch fights to give him cups of tea, he tells me; and two families (one black) in particular he knows really well. Though he has 'put one of the lads away', he doesn't persecute. They appreciate that.

He stresses the importance of contact with the kids and schools. Though he doesn't bother with street football, he is having a purge on pavement cycling. If caught, he 'sentences' them to one hour at the cycle training park (and pays for them!). He doesn't know whether he is 'supposed' to do things like that in the job, but the kids enjoy it.

He says he is enjoying his job though he adds, 'You have to make yourself enjoy it.' The best time is from 4 till 12 p.m. Nobody used to work it after dark. By working hard initially, he says he's made life easy for himself now. 'They' ring him at home now; indeed, he doesn't need to patrol his patch because the calls he gets keep him fully informed. He concludes that he works his patch as well as it has ever been done, adding that it is worse than DE's: 'He's only got one or two ['bad'] roads on his.'

Between 11 and 11.30 a.m. GH has to go to another sub-divisional station to witness the counting for the Police Federation election, for which he is divisional rep. Whilst I am waiting for him, another RBO, DE, joins me. I mention GH's final remark about his patch being worse than DE's. His reply is that GH is 'a bullshitter. If his is so bad, he ought to be on it more.' DE also thinks GH is 'mouthy and dumb'. When I say that he might be the next divisional Police Federation 'rep', DE says he hopes not: 'I wouldn't have him representing my interests. He looks after number one.' He implies that others dislike GH.

At 11.30 GH returns and we set off in his car around the perimeter of his patch. Then we park the car and walk, entering shops for quick chats and information gathering. During this GH mentions the perks: free tea, hair cuts and so on.

A woman asks us to return to the newsagent's. She is worried about working there alone in the early morning without her husband, who is ill. Specifically she mentions a car parked outside in the early morning. GH says he'll pass on the information and get someone to call. After we have left, he tells me he'll enter it into the briefing book and 'someone' would come: 'Anything for a cup of coffee.' He also talks of the possibility of preventing a robbery (a reference to the parked car), adding, 'The kids are daft enough around here.'

We enter an infants' school and speak to a teacher about the project they have done about GH's previous visit. As we walk through the playground, children rush up to hold his hand. He wonders afterwards if I was surprised at his reception. He believes

they will speak of his visit for hours afterwards. He says he has to
do it though sometimes he would prefer not to hold some of their
'scruffy' hands. Earlier, he mentioned that most of them probably had one parent 'inside' (in prison).

We continue on our way and meet an old man. GH tells me
that this road we are in was virtually 'no-go' for police when he
started, with people prepared 'to jeer and throw things'. But, as
he says, 'I worked at it, and gradually they came round to my way
of thinking.' The old man says some lads were burying something
in a garden the other night. We move on to a betting-shop. There
we learn of a break-in a few nights before at the Co-operative
store. GH thinks the two pieces of information might be connected. We move on to the Co-op. The manager informs us that a
number of lads were hanging around on the night of the break-in,
two of whom were those the old man told us were burying stuff in
a garden. One of the three was later seen by an anonymous
informant selling cheap cigarettes outside a pub.

When we leave the Co-op GH is clearly elated: 'See what I
mean? A few minutes' chat here and there and we may clear up
this break.' Earlier, on learning of the digging, he said he would
keep the information to himself 'for the time being' and see what
would turn up. Later, he would tell the collator.

Now he thinks he has enough to bring the lads in 'on suspicion', though 'proving it is another thing'. One of the lads,
apparently, is on bail awaiting committal for another offence GH
has already 'bagged' him for. He says we'll return after lunch and
dig around for evidence. I wonder about doing that without permission. He replies, 'None of these will mind us digging their
gardens.'

We go to a café. GH mentions that the owner regards him as a
friend; he also speaks of himself as giving nothing away but
'getting everything' from the man. The basis of this inequality
seems to be the fact that, as GH says, he could knock the man off
for not having a gambling licence for his pinball machines
(though he isn't sure whether the man knows he is law-breaking);
but he chooses not to because he is an invaluable informant.

We stop for lunch between 1.20 and 2 p.m., and then proceed
to the subdivisional lock-up station to sign statements about an
immoral-earnings case. Afterwards, at 2.15, we visit the traffic
control room. This is intended only for traffic observation, but
the equipment is used to observe football crowds, and so on, it is
admitted. GH seems oblivious to the civil-liberties aspects of
this. At 3.15 we move on to a second-hand dealer's, basically to
keep out of the rain. One of the dealers is reasonably co-

operative, but another refuses to talk about the lads suspected of the Co-op break-in.

Other items to emerge during the afternoon are GH's membership of all the clubs on his patch; the fact that he has started a community association and 'taught them how to hold meetings'; and that he is a member of a fraternal society of some sort.

We return to the station at 4 p.m. for a phone call about a car that failed to stop for a crossing lady. GH 'will bring him in and do him', he says. Whilst at the station, he mentions the Co-op break-in to a DC who is co-ordinating information on one of the lads (a persistent young thief, allegedly). Apparently, he already knows about everything, bar the digging. The DC is going to bring him in tomorrow and charge him with it so that, when he goes to court on Monday (for another charge), they can mention it and then insist on a custodial remand.

HI

I arrive at the subdivisional station at 2.20 p.m. for a 2 p.m. to 10 p.m. shift with HI. We set off on the twenty-minute walk to the patch. He immediately announces he has to see the Superintendent of another subdivision at 3.30, though he doesn't know what it's about. A first-response car stops to give us a lift and drops us at the social services office. A probationer is spending a few days there, as had another RBO (EF), apparently. Both HI and the social services see customers/clients as joint problems. Cases are discussed openly using consonant conceptual frames. HI is asked whether a particular boy has been reported missing from home. HI says to check with two subdivisional stations, since one of the boy's parents lives on one subdivision and the other on a different one. He tells me the social services are good to him; they let him have access to their files, which is good for tracing addresses and so on. We have coffee and leave at 3.20.

We go to the local community centre to see the caretaker about the theft of a pedal cycle. It is a follow-up inquiry, but there's no news. HI is anxious to get away as the man is 'a bit of a talker'. We continue to an old people's home at 3.30. HI uses the matron's phone to call the Superintendent to say he's just got the message about the appointment and 'would 4 p.m. be OK' since he needs to get a lift first? He then phones the subdivisional station for a panda. Whilst waiting for one to arrive, he talks to a butcher who is having trouble with someone shitting on his doorstep at night. The 'someone' is apparently a man who has accused the butcher of having an affair with his wife. HI would like to catch the man, but cannot justify 'waiting around half the night' to do so.

The panda arrives and takes us to the appointment for 3.50. On the phone to the Superintendent HI has learned that their meeting is about a complaint HI sustained when arresting a 'queer'. Apparently he and CD arrested the man for importuning, but he punched HI, winding him. CD jumped on his back, giving HI time to recover, but the man got away none the less. As HI and CD gave chase, the man fell and broke his nose. Subsequently he complained that the broken nose was the police's fault.

Having been returned to the patch by the panda driver, HI tells me of his meeting. The Superintendent is a 'funny bloke', 'one of the old school', because he expects you to stand at attention with your hat on. The complaint has been marked up for 'no further action' because the complainant – an 'obnoxious business man' – refused to complain in writing. In court, the man was acquitted on the charge of 'importuning' but had to find his own costs. HI is considering bringing a summons against him for malicious complaint, though since the man has not complained in writing there is no point.

We call on a house to follow up a HORT-1 call (failure to produce the necessary driving documents). The man is out, and the mother is anxious. HI reassures ('only an HORT-1') and says he'll call back later. He complains to me afterwards that there is too much duplication since Traffic 'put them out' to the beat but sometimes do them themselves and forget to cancel, with the result that the beat men end up following up, only to find the documents have already been produced.

We continue and check the house of a hospitalized old woman to see whether kids have been in again and pinched sweets. This is a follow-up inquiry, but, as there is no sign, HI aims to come back in the early evening.

HI then overhears a radio call for a panda to go to a domestic. Being in the vicinity, HI radios the controller offering his services, which are accepted. We arrive. The injured party is a young teenage girl who has argued with another girl and then been hit by the girl's father. Though she is upset, her skin is not broken, though her ear is red. HI explains to the mother that it constitutes only a common assault, over which he has no powers, though he could caution. He asks if that would do. She says, 'Yes, so long as he understands you can't go around hitting other people's kids.'

As the alleged assaulter lives only down the road, we troop off down there, after informing Control so he can redirect the panda *en route*. HI slows down, saying it will give the panda more time to arrive; 'better to arrive in strength' because then there is 'less risk of the bloke cutting up rough'. Leaving mother and injured-party daughter at the gate, HI knocks and, after being invited in by a small boy, we enter what is evidently a fairly 'rough' house. The father is in the sitting room, which is cluttered up with old and greasy car parts and tools. Asked for his side, the alleged assaulter claims the other girl knocked over his daughter and he urged his girl to hit back. He did not actually hit her – though he was about to – because his friend warned him of the dangers. This friend will confirm his story, and his wife agrees.

This denial leaves HI nonplussed, though he still proceeds to warn the man of the dangers of hitting others' children. At this point the panda driver arrives. HI also threatens court next time, despite the man's protestations of innocence. These protestations lessen as the man realizes that HI's threats refer to 'next' time, and finally he accepts blame.

Outside HI explains to the mother that she can take out a private summons, and it will not cost anything. Two women say they will testify because the bloke is a persistent bully and loudmouth who gave the girl 'a right pasting' and who hits his own wife and kids as well as other people's children, but he runs when men come. The mother of the injured girl says her husband has done time for fighting and is likely to take the law into his own hand. The panda driver say it isn't worth it 'for the likes of him' and urges the summons solution.

The parties disperse. HI and the panda driver discuss the man and agree he is a nasty piece of work who makes a living buying and selling motors – with an implication of bent dealing somewhere along the line. After the panda driver leaves, HI tells me it would probably be a good thing if the girl's father gave the man a good pasting – as he probably would were she his daughter.

At 5 p.m. we call at a prostitute's house about her stolen radio. After some movement inside, the door is opened by a woman in a dressing-gown, but the woman HI wants to speak to is not in. HI says he does not know the woman who answered the door. We then start to make our way back to the station. At 5.10 we are picked up by a panda and are 'in' by 5.15. HI books off for a meal at 5.30.

With these examples in mind, and the formal elements that preceded them, we turn, in Chapter 5, to the question of interpretation.

Notes

1 At the time of our study there was only one female officer within the resident beat system, a recently appointed RBO. A recent study of community constables in several forces found a similar dearth of female officers. See Brown and Iles (1985, p. 9).
2 A beat which, because of its size, had recently been split into two halves.

CHAPTER FIVE

A Pattern Emerges

FREEDOM

> Freedom is the big thing about RBO work. Pandas are always on
> the go, delivering messages, call after call . . . If I get fed up with
> this desk work, I can get up and go out for a walk . . . Can't in
> cars. (FG)

The first feature that stands out from the accounts of RBO work in
Chapter 4 is the freedom entailed in the job, which is manifest in a
variety of ways. Apart from the formal freedom of choosing hours
of work and lunch times, it is evident that late arrival for duty and
extended meal and tea breaks are routine. This is not to say that
RBOs are routinely late or always extend breaks, but that when
they do it is unexceptional and unremarkable. No plans are made
to hide the fact, or to cover tracks; it is open and apparently
accepted. We never saw much made of it, neither individuals nor
the group as a whole being spoken to.[1] Indeed this freedom is the
source of much open banter between RBOs, with half-joking
accusations and counter-accusations about lateness, as well as
idleness, being common currency: 'Rumour has it you're going out
on your patch' (IJ to DE); 'Don't worry, you won't be out long in
the cold, not with JK' (the DC to me); HI's mention of EF's 'two-
hour meal breaks'.

This freedom over *when* they work largely extends also to *what*
is worked during any shift. Whilst some work comes via radio
control, this is, as we saw, relatively infrequent, with only some 7
per cent of public contacts initiated in this way. As we saw with
HI, RBOs may well offer to assist, if they are in the area, with a call
to unit members. Other work may be relatively fixed: a further
report due by such-and-such a date; unoccupied premises which
need regular checks; a school visit arranged, and so on. But for the
most part the day can be planned to involve mainly patrol, or
visits, or paperwork, or a judicious mixture of the three. The

predominant constraint is less 'busyness' – so many things that simply have to be done by day x – and more the felt need to fend off boredom or the temptation to 'skive'. As GH said, 'You have to make yourself enjoy it.' And CD: 'There's a lot of . . . time that you could say, "I don't particularly want to go out on my area today", and there's opportunity to sit back in the office and not get on with the work you should do.' Producing a day full of variety helps; but it would be equally possible simply to be bored, or to give in to the temptation to, as FG suggested, 'skive'.

VARIETY
The corollary of freedom, unsurprisingly, is variety. This is observable in the range of activities undertaken, and in the differences in these respects between individual RBOs.

Take the question of activities. These might best be divided into three: non-routine, informal and routine. Non-routine activities include all those occasions when the organization uses the officers as 'other than RBOs'. We return to this point shortly. By informal activities we mean those that cannot in some way be linked to the police function, such as window-shopping, collecting clothes from the cleaner's, discussing the price of cycling impedimenta, or purchasing a shower unit. Such informal activities are not confined to individuals secretly filching police time for their own private purposes. The organization itself engages in such activities too, using RBOs to audit social-club accounts and paint the club bar, to use two observed examples.

The routine activities of the RBO stem from the general responsibility for a beat or area. Drawing on the examples in Chapter 4, this means, in terms of discrete functions: foot (and sometimes car) patrol work, community-relations work, gathering 'intelligence' for the collator, following up assigned 'beat crime' and completing the resulting crime files on occasion, dealing with minor complaints and nuisances, delivering messages, submitting reports of crime and matters 'for process', dealing with miscellaneous paperwork concerning 'community' matters (for example, filling in five-a-side-football entry forms) and completing 'visit-book' entries and monthly self-reports (which go forward, via the RBO sergeant, to the Superintendent).

'STYLES'
Variety is also observable in the differences between individual RBOs. Different officers spend different amounts of time on particular activities and particular kinds of contact work. Indeed, the differences are marked with the consequence that it is possible

to talk of distinctive 'styles' of RBO working. To employ the idea of 'styles' is, of course, to recall the conventional Weberian notion of 'ideal types': categories useful for descriptive purposes, indicating a tendency, rather than fixed and absolute categories. It is therefore necessary to make the usual provisos at the outset: in this case, that individual RBOs do not so much embody certain absolute 'styles', but display tendencies towards one or other of four styles, with some straddling more than one style. The four styles to which we return later we call 'public relations' (PR), 'educator', 'spy' and 'patrol'.[2]

An Organizational 'Reserve of Personnel'

The freedom of the RBO as an individual to police his or her patch, in their own way in their own time, has an organizational corollary: the use of RBOs, either individually or as a group, as a source of staffing when particular temporary jobs arise outside the normal routine. In other words, when the organization is faced with excess demands which need somehow to be met, the obvious source of available personnel is those who otherwise would simply be wandering around their patch, drinking tea, visiting a school and so on. Certainly, our examples bear this out. FG complained bitterly of the 'other duties' that kept him from his patch, as he was undertaking one of them, namely, door security. Moreover, since no other unit member was deemed available, it was *another RBO* who was sent for to replace him. On another occasion it was also an RBO who acted as switchboard relief. It was not unusual, also, for some or all of the group to be used at football matches (for some this would be on overtime, of course), as a 'reserve group' on public-order occasions (such as the strike which kept the whole group occupied for several days), as an impromptu vice squad (to raid 'dirty' bookshops or conduct a prostitute patrol), or on one of a number of 'special' occasions (such as the special court-room day which kept some of them from their patches, mentioned in the above GH account, or the racial troubles which kept all the RBOs on town-centre patrols for four months), (cf. Brown and Iles, 1985, pp. 21–2).

The point about the use of the RBOs to offset manpower shortages or to deal with emergencies is not that other groups of officers are never so used, but simply that it is the RBOs who are used *regularly* and as a *first choice* in such situations. Such usage is in direct contradiction to the firm requirement that beat officers shall not be withdrawn from their beats except when absolutely unavoidable. This is a point to which we return.

Relative Absence of Legal Work

Though variety – manifest in the range of activities undertaken and the range of possible styles – is an undeniable feature of RBO work, it is not unlimited. Specifically, and principally, there is a relative absence of legal or offence-related work. Indeed, during the entire observation period, we saw no RBO arrests, for example.[3] Preventive patrol, a dominant RBO activity, is not primarily designed to produce 'on-view' detection of crime in progress, a notion dear to the heart of police fiction writers but soon given up by young constables once experience teaches them that such events are stumbled upon by luck not planning. Crimes reported to the police usually produce a radio call from Control to a mobile patrol, in which case an RBO in the vicinity might offer or be given a supporting role, as we saw with HI and the domestic. This absence begins to account for the recurrent need we observed to 'make yourself take an interest every day' (AB) in order to fend off boredom. More generally, as we shall see, it is this *freedom from* legal work which is funda-mental in explaining the *freedom to* undertake the plethora of activities they do.

A Range of 'Respectable' and 'Known' Public Contacts

The range of activities undertaken enables RBOs to make a variety of public contacts, which may be either 'reactive' (such as the contacts made in consequence of a particular beat crime or minor complaint when police react to a request from the public for assistance) or 'proactive' (in the cases where RBOs seek out contacts on their own initiative – a new 'tea spot', a community centre not visited before and so on).[4] These contacts, as the above accounts bear witness, can apparently be as diverse as the commu-nity being policed: the 'yobs' in the pubs; councillors and commu-nity leaders; 'at-risk' youth hanging around on street corners; youth and community workers; 'rough' families; local head-teachers; shopkeepers and shoppers. In short, the whole spectrum from the 'respectable' to the 'rough', the law-abiding to the criminal, the 'disorganized' to the 'organized', young, old, black, white, male, female, middle class, working class, make up the range of RBO contacts. For particular individuals, the numbers of each type of contact will depend partly on 'area', and partly on chosen 'style'. However, there is a relative absence of non-respect-able or 'toe-rag' contacts – an observation which is linked, as we shall see, to the relative absence of legal work. The continuous traversing of the same beat ensures that many of these contacts will be with known locals on a regular basis.

Generalizing from our observations of contacts recorded in our accounts, there appear to be five reasons for contacts:

(1) to acquire information about particular crimes or of potential relevance to the process of criminal detection (*intelligence*);
(2) to prevent crime amongst especially the potentially delinquent or 'at-risk' populations (*education*);
(3) to build up a credit balance with the public (*public relations*);
(4) to succour the weak and helpless (*welfare*);
(5) to pass the time (*social*).

The acquisiton of information about particular crimes, or more general, potentially relevant criminal intelligence information, is clearly an expected part of the role, with a collator provided to record it all. This may be achieved as part of a conscious proactive strategy (for example, GH's desire to emulate the CID by spending time in the pubs in order to glean information, or by the conscious cultivation of a law-abiding, 'respectable', community Nosey Parker informant). Or information may be gathered reactively, as a chance result of a street encounter (for example, GH being told by the old man of the suspicious night-time digging) or a routine 'tea and a chat', when local comings and goings and 'unusual' activities may form part of the conversation and reveal, incidentally, information about criminal activities.

Contact with social services departments enables the regular informal exchange of information about individuals and families whose conditions of life are seen to be, broadly speaking, criminogenic (or 'at risk'). Social services client populations are generally thought to be 'at risk' because of a common conception of the relationship between poverty and/or other disabling attributes requiring social services intervention and certain types of crime. Thus, contact with such departments can provide both a source of particular information about individuals (for example, HI on their co-operation over addresses) and more general relevant information of a background nature, 'for future reference'.

Contacts with school headteachers and youth workers are usually cultivated less for information about the delinquent or potential delinquent and more for the opportunity to gain access to the 'at-risk' population itself for preventive or educational purposes. School visits are not, therefore, primarily criminal-intelligence gathering missions but 'crime-education' or long-term crime-prevention interventions.[5]

Since the contacts involved – between police, social services departments, schools and youth clubs – may appear to be similarly motivated, it may be useful to explore further what differentiates the 'at-risk' populations provided by the schools and youth clubs from those provided by social services departments, since it is only in the case of the former that access to the population itself, rather than information about it, is sought. Two additional elements are important here: the notions of the *intractability* of the crime problem and the *salvageability* of the 'at-risk' population. Thus, whereas youth, like social services recipients, are by definition 'at risk', in that the genesis of much crime is seen as a consequence of those features of youthful existence – immaturity, boredom, high spirits, or 'bad company' – to which all youth, in varying measure, are potentially susceptible, the crime problem presented by youth is, additionally and paradoxically, both intractable, in its general nature and extent (cf. DE's fatalistic conception of the relationship between being in a gang, an apparently endemic feature of adolescence, and 'going bananas'), yet, given its youthful genesis, potentially open to remedial or 'salvaging' action in particular instances ('if they start thinking for themselves': DE). By 'intractable in its general nature and extent' is meant that the crime problem generated by youth (predominantly minor damage to or theft of property) is such a trivial (in the legal sense of the term) yet endemic feature of this stage of life that traditional detective methods are either inappropriate, that is, not able to justify the resources involved, or ineffective, given that each new generation will have its youthful 'criminal' fling.

Yet, though intractable in general, being tied to a particular stage of life, the crime problem involved – given its presumed origins in immaturity, bad company and so on – is essentially the product of 'youthful' not 'criminal' minds. Were it otherwise, were the genesis of these crimes to be attributed to bad (that is, 'criminal') character, then correction, not education (conceived of as 'persuasion by appeal to moral reasoning' or 'dissuasion through fear of punishing consequences'), would be seen as more appropriate. As it is, given the pre-formative youthful origins of much of this crime, the notion of salvageability, of 'nipping in the bud', is thought relevant. In sum, it is the *combination* of these three elements – a universally 'at-risk' population; the intractability of the crime problem generated by such a population; and the potential for remedial action in particular cases – which determines that the contacts generated, in this case with schools and youth clubs, are in general concerned with long-term crime prevention rather than the simple gathering of useful or potentially useful crime-relevant information. The latter might also be a particular motive on occasions, and some officers may well regard such contacts as primarily to do with public relations – selling a favourable police image. Finally, these crimes though largely trivial or minor, are not simply ignorable on that account, given their visibility and annoyance to the local community.

A third reason for generating contacts with the public flows from the list of specified job functions. Building up a 'credit balance' with the public, a balance which can be later cashed in terms of crime information or more general support – the so-called 'public-relations' or community-relations role of RBOs – is achieved, in part, as a subsidiary function, through maintaining contact with various individuals and the agencies – social services, schools, and so on – already mentioned. Such contact, once again, can be maintained 'reactively' – through regular street contacts with members of the public during routine patrol work – or proactively – through the deliberate cultivation of particular individuals. Deliberately maintaining a presence in populous areas like shopping centres, where the chances of informal contact are high and the consequent pay-off in PR terms (aside from the incidental virtues of simply 'showing the flag') is estimated to be good, represents one way of executing the former strategy. Contacts with individuals connected with groups and associations variously representing the community, for example, tenants' and residents' associations, can be proactive examples of PR work, though they might also be undertaken partly in order to be able to anticipate and if possible defuse potential trouble, and even for the purpose of long-term crime prevention: in these instances, through generating and developing a community consciousness with respect to crime prevention. (Neighbourhood Watch Schemes currently seem to fit this bill.)[6]

Some contacts have no obvious relation, however indirectly, to crime at all, as part of neither an intelligence-gathering, a crime-prevention, nor a public-relations strategy. Examples of these include contacts with the old and infirm whose ability to offer items of exchange – information, or simply 'support' – is very limited. The visits of EF to the old bedridden lady, and of CD to the woman who had recently had a mastectomy, seem to fall into this category. In so far as it is possible to view the reasons for these contacts in more than simple 'welfare' terms, it could be that the evident concern for the welfare of these usually old people is part of a wider concern with 'victims' of crime, of whom the weak and the helpless elderly are archetypal in popular mythology. The old and infirm, then, in that they are, as a category, conceived as generalized symbols of crime victims, become potential objects of solicitude.

A further reason for making contacts with the public is for purely social purposes. These might be simply in order to pass the time (for example, EF talking to the residents of the community home), or in order to find out about something of purely personal relevance, such as the price of cycle accessories or where to go for a bargain item of one kind or another.

So far we have settled for presenting a picture of resident beat-work against the background of the formal elements identified in Chapter 4. We have also begun to sketch in some central structural features revealed in the description. In the next section we begin to develop these topics further and to introduce some new material: from observational data not set out in Chapter 4 and from our interviews with five relevant supervisors, eight RBOs and one DC. As with the unit beat system, we begin with the question of organization and examine how various features combine together to produce the outcomes just delineated.

Organization

The organizational and occupational aspects of resident beat-work that we must consider amount to five: the conditions producing the different 'styles' of work; other types of work; the relevance of supervision; the relations among the RBOs; and the question of the role of management. The last of these we propose, as we did for the unit in Chapter 3, to postpone until we have looked at the legal and democratic aspects of resident beat-work.

DIFFERENT 'STYLES' OF WORK

If the observable differences between individual RBOs were examples of a variety which was itself a corollary of the observed 'freedom' of RBO working, they can be traced, in particular, to the relative freedom from colleague influence or socialization experienced by RBOs. The result of choosing hours of work and how to fill them on distinct and separate patches with their own particular clientele and correspondingly peculiar policing problems is a set of 'unique' work conditions for each and every RBO. This uniqueness provides the basis for individual differences which must be tolerated because they can be justified.[7] Relative freedom from a group 'working norm' is the result.

This means that the individual is free to decide how important a priority to make 'crime arrests'. For some (for example, GH, whose most important work 'is done in the pubs', that is, a place to glean information) it holds a fairly conventional place high in the list of priorities; for others (for example, FG, who virtually can't remember his last arrest) the value of prevention is a genuinely higher priority, and arrest statistics are treated with considerable scepticism. It is this ability to decide how to spend time which is the basis for the emergence of distinctive 'styles' of work, styles which we called, respectively, public relations, educator, spy and patrol.

The *public relations* style involves maximizing contact activities. It involves maintaining regular contacts, seeking to initiate new ones and utilizing excuses for chance encounters. Street encounters and official encounters, whether regular or irregular, with organizational representatives or individual citizens, will be used for general PR purposes, though they may also have other more specific purposes. Contact with 'at-risk' populations, for example, will be utilized as much for PR purposes as for the purpose of long-term crime prevention. It is a style in which a prime function is the marketing of a product: the self as representative of a cordial and benign police *service*. At a personal level, bearers of this style may feel the need to compensate for a bad police image, or to be popular and liked, or to gain personal satisfaction through 'helping'. Of the opening accounts, EF represents probably the clearest example of this style. It may be relevant that he worked once in sales.[8]

The *educator* style will maximize opportunities for contact with 'at-risk' populations such as schools and youth clubs. Opportunities will be sought to develop and extend these. Thus to be concerned with 'at-risk' populations is to be concerned with long-term crime prevention, and contacts with community representatives will be conducted through the prism of crime prevention rather than PR. The causes of crime will be a genuine concern. On a personal level, bearers of this style could well end up in community relations, or leaving the job altogether given the inherent frustrations of a concern for the causes of crime in conjunction with constant dealings with an intractable crime problem. DE is the most obvious example of this style. He was indeed interested in a spell of community relations, and genuinely frustrated with his felt inability to make a real impact on juvenile delinquency.[9] CD, an ex-trainee teacher, had some of the hallmarks of this style in the observed emphasis placed on mediation,[10] as did FG with his genuine concern about crime prevention and lack of interest in 'feeling collars'.[11]

The *spy* style will maximize opportunities for gaining criminal intelligence or information for individual action, or the collator's records. Contacts with the public and with agencies possessing information about 'at-risk' populations will be used to satisfy the spy role. Befriending the public is part of a manipulative strategy to cultivate informants, not simply for PR purposes. Conversations will be focused around crime intelligence, unusual events and so on. The concern for intelligence demonstrates an interest in crime. It thus tends to be associated with an orientation towards beat crime. On a personal level, the RBO role is conceived of as a crime challenge, a training possibility for eventual CID work. GH, whose beat-work, he claimed, was done 'in pubs', falls most clearly into this category.[12]

Lastly, the *patrol* style. This style attempts to maximize foot patrol work interspersed with public contact, and this corresponds most closely with the traditional 'bobby' image. It is predicated upon traditional notions of the deterrent values of the police presence and of the reassurance to the public the sight of walking bobbies fulfils. 'Friend' to the community characterizes this style, though contact with schools and young people tend not to loom large as activities. A traditional friendly image for a middle-aged community is the aim, not any more forceful strategy of community intervention. On a personal level, bearers of this style may well be traditionalists with long service stretching back to the mythical golden age of policing; they may also like walking, fresh air and simply meeting people.

The best example of this style was AB,[13] though BC appeared also to be in this mould.[14] BC was the dutiful community servant, careful to respect its wishes and tolerant of its foibles, rather than an interventionist in the PR or educator style. HI represents another variant of the patrolling style but one of later vintage. His close liaison with the drivers on the unit points to an affinity with modern patrol unit work; as we saw in Chapters 2 and 3, the pattern of discrete incidents and routine inquiries, a willingness to work with others and the response to an emergency call are typical of this more mobile and motorized form of patrol work. His first preference was to become a dog-handler, but recognizing the difficulties of entering such a small department, he applied for the SPG in search of action and glamour. The RBOs, though 'good experience', are still given the 'rub jobs', he thought – as, we might add, are the members of the patrol unit.

Although contacts apparently motivated primarily by welfare considerations were in evidence, as we saw in the case of EF and CD, these contacts were never so dominant with any one individual to enable us to talk of a welfare style. Since all the styles have some kind of connection, however indirect, with crime prevention, it may be the absence of such in the case of welfare which accounts for its limited appearance.[15]

OTHER TYPES OF WORK

There are very few other types of work besides the fourteen RBOs independently working their respective beats. In all, these amount to three: the detective constable, the collator[16] and the sergeant in charge. We deal first with the DC and the collator, before looking at the sergeant when we come, in the next section, to the whole question of supervision.

In fulfilling the liaison and advisory functions, the DC operates primarily as the 'servant' of the system for administering the legal work of RBOs. To the extent that the Superintendent and sergeant determine the policy with respect to RBO working; to the extent that the DC is essentially an 'outsider', subject to the CID command structure, operating within a uniformed system subject to a separate command structure; and to the extent that one of the primary roles is precisely that of 'negotiator', managing the sometimes delicate relationships between the CID 'base' and uniform 'location', a more active leadership role – encouraging a greater crime orientation among RBO officers, for example – is effectively precluded.

The collator's role appears to be largely executed in terms of a series of appropriate administrative routines: maintaining records, issuing bulletins and so on. Given the importance formally attached to the role of 'intelligence' within the whole system, and the formal requirement to promote the use of the system, it is salutary to consider why such an apparently 'passive' role is adopted. Whilst some might wish to opt for an explanation in terms of the selection procedure – which tends to favour mid- or late-career constables with few promotion prospects – and the generally low status surrounding the post, these are simply symptoms of a deeper issue concerning the organizational inattention to generating criteria by which information might be meaningfully sifted. Thus, the collator maintains a classified index of cross-referenced information based on significant legal criteria. This produces a universal system which provides a resource for searches for individual items, and which will tend to be instigated by officers concerned with individual investigations. In addition, the collator issues regular bulletins which are essentially general 'updates' using the same legal criteria which inform the entire system. What is absent is a means for tailoring the supply of information to the requirements of particular organizational roles; no means, in other words, of making selections from incoming data and directing this selected material towards particular groups of officers for whom it might prove significant. The inability to select affirms the general relevance of information to all officers, since all are constables. The consequence is the individual search by individual officers, coupled with a global bulletin over-replete with information and distributed universally – and the reduction of the collator's job to a series of administrative routines.[17]

REDUNDANT SUPERVISION?

The freedom largely to choose hours and styles of work is compounded by the absence of direct supervision. Direct patrol oversight is extremely rare, as the RBO accounts bear testimony. All sorts of people may be bumped into on the patch, but the one person an RBO can be sure *not* to meet is the RBO sergeant. It might appear that supervision was impossible because of the difficulties involved in the direct supervision of fourteen or fifteen officers – a far higher number than any one sergeant on a unit is required to supervise – and the correspondingly higher volume of paperwork generated, and because of the peculiar problems of keeping tabs on a group who, in reality, are fourteen individuals, working their own unique patches in their own chosen time, adopting their own chosen style.

In reality, direct patrol supervision is seen as largely redundant or unnecessary. This may have something to do with the collective experience of the officers, which is generally greater than that of the unit. It certainly was perceived as having something to do with the notion that contacts, like informants, are personal and that the presence of a third party is at best redundant, at worst counter-productive. As the RBO sergeant put it, 'If I went out with them [the RBOs], contacts wouldn't say anything with me around anyway.' But it has most to do with the fact that direct patrol supervision would serve no purpose, in view of the relative absence of activities to supervise. Given that drinking tea on duty is part of the job ('I know all their tea spots . . . They'd be inhuman if they didn't have them. I expect them to' – RBO sergeant), and that maintaining contacts justifies any chat, however lengthy on what-ever premises (except licensed premises in uniform, according to the force standing orders; but, then, RBOs can, and do, undertake plain-clothes work, thus enabling 'pub work' to be openly done), it is hard to envisage what a patrol sergeant might accomplish, short of advice with respect to the quality of interaction. This, as we have seen, is precluded by the personal sanctity attributed to such contacts; but also by the notion that interactive skills or objectives are not 'police' matters for which supervision is appropriate – a point which goes some way to explaining the lack of training given to RBOs. Moreover, as we see in the next section, direct supervision is seen as unnecessary because of the 'exposed' nature of RBO work.

If direct patrol oversight is deemed unnecessary, due to the relative absence of legal work and the failure to produce alternative, supervisable indices of work performance, it is also true that the most common form of indirect supervision – keeping tabs on the quality and quantity of legal process work submitted – is not easily applicable either, the more so since the attached DC, as we have seen, supervises most crime-related paperwork.[18] And traffic offences are as liable to be dealt with informally as otherwise. Thus, unsurprisingly, the form of supervision most in evidence is essentially self-recording, for example, visit-book entries and monthly self-report sheets. Indeed, the latter, which normally include details of visits, activities and crime arrests, are destroyed once the Superintendent has seen them.

Supervision by the sergeant, then, is an instrument largely confined to overseeing the paperwork of all kinds generated, offering advice to individuals, informally or through the appraisal system, dealing with minor disciplinary matters and passing on the 'advice' of the Superintendent, to 'keep up regular school visits' and so on. One result of this supervisory relationship is to throw a greater burden on informal arrangements. This appears to have had two observable effects: (1) a noticeable egalitarianism in the relationship between the sergeant and his officers as persuasion and personality are forced to stand in for the absence of more formal supervisory modes. Thus the relationship is rather like that with an experienced colleague, adviser and, in some cases, friend than with a supervisor in the strong sense. (2) There is a heightening of the importance of the informal reward structure at the disposal of the RBO sergeant – primarily the capacity to reward officers with interesting 'non-routine' details, which is itself partly a function of the largely discretionary, unquantifiable nature of RBO work whereby, as we have seen, removal from the patch is relatively unproblematic. One RBO, for example, was 'rewarded' by being used to 'keep obs.' (observation) on a private house suspected of showing obscene movies, to make test purchases of pornographic material and to assist in the construction of an inventory subsequent to a 'dirty' bookshop raid (which itself employed a number of RBOs among others).

PEER COMPETITION AND CLIQUES

This informal mode of supervision can contribute to competition amongst colleagues, individual intrigues and the formation of small cliques, as individuals and cliques vie for favour and for the chance of an alternative to the routine of beat-work. This is exacerbated by the unique, individual conditions of work in which peers rarely know in detail how colleagues spend their time, though colleagues preferences – for school visits, for general patrol work and so on – will be generally known. Thus, apart from those occasions when the RBOs are used as a group – at football matches, or 'public order' standby (in which case they cease to operate *as* RBOs; as CD says, 'The resident beat officers work as a unit in the Home End [at the local football ground], acting as an almost special patrol group, ready to go where the fights are and sort them out') – there are few opportunities for group cohesiveness or occupational consensus (a working norm) to emerge.

This situation is intensified by the other side of the fact that RBOs work alone on unique patches, namely, the peculiarly 'exposed' nature of the job. This is also a further reason why even indirect supervision is not seen as necessary. For whilst the RBO sergeant admits to having no time for direct patrol oversight and suggests, in any case, that contacts would dry up with a stranger around (certainly not something we experienced) his main argument for not directly supervising patrol work is that it is not necessary because he gets feedback by phone calls asking for RBOs by name: 'They must be making some contact if that is happening.' His other sources of information, he claimed, were letters from the public, arrests and 'the grapevine', the latter source echoed by at least one of the RBOs. The Superintendent too, talked of letters from the public, as well as feedback from his sergeants. The ironic corollary of having a patch to hide in is that, if that is done, the RBO also hides from the community with the result that positive feedback – phone calls and letters – from the community will not be forthcoming.

This 'exposed' nature of RBO work – the areal responsibility which ensures that any visibly recurrent problems occurring on the patch (a large number of complaints, a spate of crimes and so on) are easily located as the responsibility of a particular RBO – and the extensive community contacts possessed by the Superintendent as a consequence of his community-relations responsibilities ensure that community feedback on the nature of the policing of an area is both constant and instantly available. This direct community access to the Superintendent ensured that officers did gain different reputations (deserved or otherwise), a factor which compounded the element of competition in colleague relationships.

Lack of direct knowledge, the unquantifiable nature of beat-work, competition for favours and the divisions instituted by the acquisition of different reputations: all these aspects are conducive to the circulation of rumours about comparative workloads, numbers of contacts, time spent on patch, style of working and community knowledge – matters beyond easy knowledge, quantification, or, in consequence, refutation. But these matters are none the less 'real' (in their consequences) in precluding the formation of a strong element of colleague-group control.

We have seen some of these points illustrated, sporadically, earlier, but here is one RBO (HI) on these questions:

> At the moment our RBOs are not working as a unit, there's too many little groups. You can't compare what KL does in town to what I do ... because it's different. Each patch has got its own individual problems. DE still gets to know his people a lot ... but I don't think he gets on his patch as much as perhaps GH does. [cf. DE's earlier expostulation that GH should get out on his patch more.]
>
> Perhaps DE gets a lot of favouritism in choice of jobs, and which gets him involved in other things away from his patch.[19] I can't say, I wouldn't know, but I shouldn't imagine AB perhaps visits his schools as often as I do. I don't know whether he's got any contact with the social workers in his area, or probation officers on his area.
>
> There's this clique amongst the RBOs of which some people, obviously BC and LM with this A-team/B-team stuff ... The atmosphere at the moment ... isn't right, but I think you've always got to have disagreements. No two people will, you know, no two RBOs will agree on anything.[20]

Legal work

'BEAT CRIME', MINOR COMPLAINTS AND LEGAL DOMAINS AND FORMS

Though we talked earlier of the relative absence of legal work performed by RBOs, symptomatic of which was an absolute absence of witnessed arrests, it is important to an understanding of the relationship between the determinants of resident beat-work to consider the nature of that legal work which *is* undertaken, and why work which could be construed within a legal frame of reference generally is not. Take the case of a relatively simple theft, as we saw in the case of AB and the stolen sports equipment, or any other straightforward crime. Once the crime report is completed, it is forwarded to the CID where the decision is made as to whether it constitutes a 'beat crime'. This term simply refers to those crimes the CID chooses to reassign to the RBOs. The concept was originally generated ostensibly to promote a greater 'crime-consciousness' amongst beat officers otherwise concerned wholly with crime prevention and PR. Analysis of crimes reassigned to beat officers reveals that the criteria for reassignment generally coincides with the conditions, already noted, for crime-prevention measures such as school-liaison work. That is to say, beat crimes by and large are those crimes which are widespread but 'trivial', committed largely by a 'non-criminal' population, which makes them intractable in traditional detection terms, and thought to be more amenable to education than the criminal process. In other words, beat crime work is, so far as it involves young people, the other (reactive) arm of school-liaison work; it involves primarily the same population (local juveniles) and the same problem (petty, 'youthful' property crime). Thus beat crime, by definition, involves legal work only sporadically in the shape of case files, giving evidence and so on, as the RBOs, in their different ways, recognized:

> You are still given the rub jobs, you know, the dog bites, the petty thefts, things like this.   (HI)

> You probably get more mundane jobs than anybody else as well. You can spend twelve hours a week on minor complaints.
> (GH)

> The CID are putting a lot more stuff through to us now, but basically a lot of the things are minor damages, complaints from elderly people.   (FG)

> The crime that I've sorted out, while I've been up here, it's all petty stuff.   (BC)

Minor complaints are simply incipient 'beat crimes': similar activities that have failed the 'crime' test.

Translating the notion of 'beat crime' into that of legal domains and forms means we are talking of either activities existing within the ambiguous border zone between civil and criminal law (nuisances, domestic disputes and neighbour disputes), or those unambiguously criminal activities for which the form of the offence (in terms of the complexity of its definition, the nature of the evidence required and so on) is, for all practical purposes, irrelevant, since these crimes are, as at least two RBOs put it, the 'insolubles'. In both cases, the ambiguous 'domestic' or the 'insoluble' petty crime, their legal relevance to police is very limited.

There is, however, one type of offence which is unambiguously 'criminal', and easily solved, since the only evidence necessary is a set of objective facts which can be easily produced by the observations of the police, and, moreover, lends itself to the routine foot patrol activity of RBOs, namely, stationary traffic and other similar offences (for example, a skip with no lights). Yet interventions in this area are rare or, where interventions are made, are rarely made subject to the legal process. In the above examples, we saw how AB declined to deal with an out-of-date tax disc. This behaviour was observed on at least two other occasions with other RBOs: once when the owner of a car outside a known (that is, local) prostitute's house was warned about his out-of-date disc, and once when such a disc was simply not 'seen', though potential offences in connection with the car were under discussion. The car owner, in this instance, was an (informal) informant. Similarly, the skip parked on the road overnight without lights was dealt with informally.

Then there is the question of public order, which is unambiguously the province of the police, easily 'solved' since the only required evidence is that of the police themselves making subjective assessment on the basis of observed facts, and hence 'simple'. As with traffic offences, informal rather than formal interventions are clearly the norm. The question to which we must now turn is why there is such a reluctance to invoke the legal process even in those (admittedly few) situations – stationary traffic offences and public order – where there is a clear opportunity to do so. In other words, we must now look at motivation: at what influences the use of discretion in those situations which have a direct legal relevance for the police.

PRACTICAL JUDGEMENTS AND THE PRIMACY OF A 'CREDIT BALANCE'

There is a contrast between the response of walkers on the unit to simple, stationary traffic violations and the responses of patrolling RBOs to the same offences. The former, as we saw, were less reluctant to issue tickets in general, and used attitudes to the police as a rough guide to decision-making in the case of the more frequent and trivial offences; 'stroppiness' invited enforcement.[21] The other feature that characterized these unit interactions was the 'random' nature of interactions. For the most part, unit police–public interactions were between strangers.

An examination of non-enforcement by RBOs reveals this last feature to be the critical one. All occasions where car tax disc offences were ignored involved people either known to the RBO or living on the patch. Even the case involving a car outside a known prostitute's house – arguably 'fair game' given the likelihood of the car's owner coming from the 'stroppy' or 'antagonistic' (to police) classes, a fact confirmed when the PNC check revealed the owner to be a known 'ponce' – was dealt with by a warning, once a woman appeared on the doorstep saying it would be seen to. AB's non-enforcement of a similar offence also involved someone whose general behaviour might be generally construed in police thinking as placing him in the 'stroppy' classes; according to AB he was on the dole, cohabiting with a similarly placed woman, doing free-lance repair work and running two untaxed cars. But again, he was 'known' and living on AB's patch.

The 'knownness' of the offenders in these simple traffic offences overrides 'stroppiness' as a factor in the decision whether to enforce. Although AB excused his non-enforcement by saying he could 'do him any time', it is more likely that GH's policy on out-of-date tax discs – 'If person lives there, warn' – is the standard solution (even though GH also claimed it depended on his mood). As JK put it, after warning an Indian builder about not having lights round his skip at night, 'After all, I've got to live with them on my patch.' (The corollary of this can be a hostile attitude to the *stranger* committing offences on *known* 'members' of the patch; remember, for example, GH's vehement threat to bring in a motorist for failing to stop for his crossing lady.)

The underlying reason for this preference for informal dealings in the case of relatively trivial, technical offences has to do with the priority accorded to other aspects of the role.[22] The non-enforcement by JK against the car owner who was also an informant indicates the importance of one other aspect – intelligence gathering – which was also the reason given by GH for not enforcing the gambling licence laws in relation to the café owner. More generally, non-enforcement interventions are opportunities for *contacts*, where building up a 'credit balance' for public-relations or potential intelligence-gathering purposes appears to have a clear precedence over law-enforcement purposes (cf., Banton, 1964, p. 130).

Public order is approached with a similar 'motivational set'. On the couple of occasions when groups of youngsters were talked to about their 'noisy' or otherwise 'unacceptable' behaviour in the evening, the predisposition was always towards the informal mode. Even when on one such occasion the response of a black youth to being warned was laughter (construable as 'stroppiness'), there was never any danger of a formal intervention, merely another warning: 'Don't laugh, otherwise I'll get nasty'; and to me afterwards: 'They are just like I was at that age.' Whilst these two incidents were at best only incipiently, if at all, public-order occasions,[23] the general point about resident beat officers' attitude to public order is reinforced by comparing their responses with those of the SPG to football hooliganism. As we have said, RBOs regularly police football matches and, on such occasions, will often be deployed together, as are SPG units. Yet there is a significant difference between the way the SPG and the RBOs (and divisional officers generally) perceive similar behaviour. These different sets of perceptions result in a differential level of activity, with SPG officers noticeably more 'active' – a level of activity which is not simply attributable to their deployment in the expected 'trouble-spots', since RBO officers in a similar vicinity simply do not 'see' (as offences) those which the SPG (with their different, learned norm) do. This different level of activity leads to SPG complaints that divisional officers 'ignore' offences and, from the divisional side, that SPG officers 'arrest for nothing'.[24]

We have already said that the individual style of RBO working is not conducive to the construction of a general group 'working norm'. However, this ability to construe youthful chanting, shouting, gesticulating, jumping and pushing at football matches as 'exuberance' rather than 'sanctionable offence', when combined with their observed attitude to 'noisy' youngsters on their patches, is suggestive. What it indicates is that the prism through which youthful misbehaviour is viewed (which is fairly general and constitutes something of a standard perception)[25] is that of school liaison, with its operating philosophy of 'preventive persuasion'. In other words, other aspects of the role, in this case education, have a prominence over law enforcement in the public-order sphere where juveniles are concerned – though not necessarily in other spheres, where juveniles have been cast as 'real' criminals (cf. GH's attitude to the juvenile suspects in the Co-op break), nor in other modes of work (for example, RBOs responding in a night van to 'trouble' at a pub clear-out will not exercise the same 'educator' predisposition). Given the simple, subjective nature of public-order offences, this is perhaps the clearest possible example of the general orientation of RBOs towards non-enforcement.

Once again, we checked the character and importance of legal work within resident beat policing through a survey of our observational data on RBOs' duties. This revealed that of 181 public-contact events observed, only 69 (38 per cent) were offence-related, and of these some 22 (32 per cent) were activated by a controller short of a panda driver to send, rather than through routine RBO activities. Since none of these were arrests or traffic citations, only 2 were offence warnings, and 3 the accepting of crime complaints, the vast majority constituted the mundane preliminaries or *ex-post-facto* activities associated with the 'ambiguous' (for example, the domestic), the 'insoluble' (for example, employee theft) or the trivial (for example, HORT-1 inquiries). Indeed, there is strong evidence, witnessed in at least eight instances, of RBOs transforming victims' 'crime' complaints into minor (or 'non-crime') complaints, such as the complaint about bricks being thrown two nights running at the window of a woman's flat. This becomes redefined as a possible 'domestic' once the woman reveals a possible connection between these events and the threats and assault she occasioned a week or so previously from the wife and daughter of the husband with whom she was having an affair; alternatively it is an 'insoluble' ('probably kids'). This absence of important offence-related activity and the massive tail of peripheral activities, together with an observable trend (20/69 or 29 per cent) towards the use of warnings or reduction to the minor complaints category, confirms our observations concerning the relative absence of 'legal' work.

PROCEDURAL FORMS AND PUBLIC RELATIONS

In thinking about the importance of procedural requirements in influencing RBO work, it might appear that the absence of witnessed arrests makes the question of procedural forms of law irrelevant. In a strict sense, this is so. However, if we look closely at the use of offence-warnings we can very occasionally see its function when an RBO has admitted (to us afterwards) an unsureness of their precise powers. Some other 'warnings', though not so admitted, would appear to fall in this category. One way of thinking about the use of warnings, in the context of absent or uncertain powers, is in terms of the manipulation of powers – not, as was the case with the unit, in the interests of arrest and conviction, but in the interests of other aspects of the role, that is, building up a public indebtedness (for *not* taking formal action) or 'credit balance' for later encashment in terms of public relations or criminal intelligence. Seen in this light, offence warnings can represent both 'decriminalization' *and* pro-

Table 5.1 Public Contacts by Resident Beat PCs in the Period of Observation

Number of contacts

Types of person(s)	Elective						Non-elective					
	Adult		Juvenile		Total		Adult		Juvenile		Total	
	Offence-related	Other	Offence-related	Other	Offence-related	Other	Offence-related	Other	Offence-related	Other	Offence-related	Other
(1) Males												
Black	1	0	0	2	1	2	5	3	1	0	6	3
White	4	5	0	2	4	7	12	33	0	0	12	33
(2) Females												
Black	0	0	0	0	0	0	0	2	0	0	0	2
White	7	5	4	1	11	6	12	22	0	2	12	24
(3) Non-individualized groups												
Black	0	0	0	0	0	0	2	2	0	0	2	2
White	1	0	0	0	1	0	5	3	1	1	6	4
(4) Unclassified individuals and groups												
	3	1	0	0	3	1	4	13	0	0	4	13
	0	1	1	4	1	5	1	8	5	2	6	10

Notes

1 'Juveniles' and race are subjective categories based on field observations.

2 Non-individualized groups and unclassified individuals and groups refer to contacts about which information is in some respect incomplete because, for example, the actual contact was not observed directly, or members of the group were not individually counted.

3 Totals for percentage contacts by sex, race and age were calculated as follows: sex (1) and (2); race (1), (2) and (3); age (1), (2), (3) and (4). Thus there were 68 male (14 elective + 54 non-elective); 55 female (17 + 38); 18 black (3 + 15); 120 white (29 + 91); 155 adult (28 + 127); 26 juvenile (14 + 12) contacts. Of all 181 contacts, 69 (21 elective + 48 non-elective) were offence-related, other contacts amounting to 112 (21 + 91).

cedural irregularity (in the interests of a 'higher good', namely, public relations).

The Democratic Relation

RBOs' relations with the public have to be set within the context of a relatively uninfluential legal structure and the consequent organizationally sanctioned 'freedom'. One manifestation of this freedom is the much greater variety of contacts as compared with the unit. This question of variety affects particularly the 'systematic contacts' of resident beat officers, which we come to shortly. But first we need to examine the role of the elective public (those who initiate a contact with police) as opposed to the non-elective one (those contacted by the police) and contrast our findings here, including those concerning the social basis (age, sex, race and class) on which this categorization is superimposed, with our unit beat findings discussed in Part II.

As with the unit beat, we start with a table (Table 5.1) showing a classification of PCs' contacts with individuals (or groups) according to age, race and sex and type of contact (elective, non-elective, or unclassified). 'Spots' are again classified according to the immediate circumstances of the contact.

THE ELECTIVE PUBLIC
Since the elective public is rather more likely to contact the police for an offence-related matter than otherwise, its relative insignificance in RBO work (23 per cent of total contacts; 17 per cent, without Control-initiated ones), and when compared to similar unit contacts (61 per cent of total contacts), is unsurprising. Moreover, since offence-related activity is relatively unimportant and 'call readiness' not a necessity, there is a broader notion of the 'legitimate' complainant with a genuine police-related problem. This is not to say that the 'boundaries of relevance' established by an RBO do not have overriding power over public wishes, as with the unit, nor that the subjective police relevances concerning legal pertinence that we detailed for the unit do not also apply. It is simply that the notion of the legitimate complainant is broader than that adopted by the unit. For RBOs, the basis of consensual relation with complainants need not rest solely on the narrow legal (to police) relevance of the matter, but can encompass a variety of other reasons for contact (education, PR, welfare, social). None the less, it is for the RBO to determine if and when – in accordance with their 'freedom' to sustain contacts for other than strictly

legally pertinent reasons. For example, an anxious allegation of regular assault, from a woman concerned about the regular beating up of a male extended family member by a cousin and his friend, can be defined as a 'domestic' and then ignored ('I don't interfere when it's family ... often makes it worse'); whereas an equally concerned allegation from a woman that a man recently convicted of indecently assaulting her son was frightening both her and her son with 'vindictive and leering' looks – arguably a less serious allegation than regular assault in *strictly legal* terms – can become the subject of sustained legal counselling and general support for PR reasons. That this difference between these RBOs' responses has more to do with chosen style than 'type of family' can be confirmed by the fact that, whereas the former involved a known 'toe-rag' family, the latter involved another 'taboo' category – an emotionally 'difficult' family that the RBO concerned had been warned by the previous RBO to steer clear of.

The centrality of chosen style, and the difference this makes compared with the unit response, holds true even in conflictual situations. Whereas, for the unit, these are the situations most likely to produce an intervention based on the most apparent legal indicators available, in the interests of being seen as impartial, the RBO may approach matters differently. Whilst we *saw* no example of this, RBOs rarely finding themselves (as the absent arrest figure indicates) in highly conflictual situations (as RBOs), a story by GH (mentioned earlier) summarizes the point, and the differences from the unit. It concerned a local fight with which the attendant panda driver was having 'a pig of a time'. GH arrived, and the fighting stopped ('Stop fighting, GH's around'). He then sent the fighters home and had them together the next day over a cup of tea. Subsequently, they became 'the best of mates'.

As for the social basis of the elective public, apart from the black female there is no obvious omission. Juveniles (at 12 per cent of the total) are certainly less in evidence than adults, and blacks (at 9 per cent of the total) than whites, but both make some call for attention. Females, on the other hand, are well represented. Whilst, at 55 per cent of the total, they are only slightly more prominent than males, this is in contrast with their more usual under-representation. But, as with all these figures, their significance become clear only when we contrast them with the 'non-elective' figures, and both with the figures obtained for the unit. It is to the non-elective public, therefore, that we turn next.

THE NON-ELECTIVE PUBLIC

In the first place, it is evident that the vast majority (77 per cent) of contacts are of this kind, that is, police-initiated. Since we also know that the majority (65 per cent) of these are *not* offence-related, this would appear to suggest a consensual basis for most of these exchanges, even if only minimally with regard to those situations deemed 'trivial' and unworthy of police attention. When combined with the exchanges witnessed in connection with the elective public – with their greater likelihood of a consensual basis – we can see that the vast majority of public contacts in the RBOs are non-conflictual. The consensual similarity between elective and non-elective contacts for RBOs is reflected in their similar social bases. Thus, whilst there is an increase in the percentage of male non-electives (from 45 to 59 per cent), thus altering the male–female ratio from 1:1 to 1.5:1, and in the percentage of blacks (from 9 to 14 per cent), the percentage of juvenile non-electives shows a decrease (from 12 to 8 per cent). In short, the change between elective and non-elective contacts is less overall, and more mixed than that observed in the unit. Here the percentage of male non-electives increased (from 52 to 70 per cent), thus altering the male–female ratio from 1:1 to more than 2:1, as did the percentage of black contacts (from 8 to 15 per cent); most spectacularly of all, the number of juvenile contacts leaped from 1 to 23 per cent. Since these social characteristics of sex, race and age all have known offence significance (in statistical terms),[26] and the unit's relations with the public are centred on offence-related activity, this shift is comprehensible – as is its relative absence in the case of the RBOs, given the much lesser significance of offence-related activity for them.

It could well be that the increase in the percentage of non-elective black contacts has to do with the general encouragement given to RBOs to make community (meaning especially ethnic-minority) contact in order to improve public relations. This reading would also explain why Asians, in contrast to the unit, were not noticeably absent but, in some cases, were deliberately sought out and systematically contacted. It would also help explain why the percentage of juvenile non-elective contacts *decreases*; for it is in the elective sphere, not in the non-elective sphere as it is for blacks, that systematic consensual contact is sought, most obviously through an invitation to address a school class.

If the lack of offence-related activity for RBOs begins to explain the largely consensual nature of RBO encounters, it also accounts for the relative absence of 'toe-rag' contacts; again, this is reflected in the similar social bases of elective and non-elective contacts. This is well illustrated with two contrasting examples of offence-related contacts with juveniles. The first concerned a story told by DE, about how he had caught some lads breaking school windows and had, with the parents' consent, forced them to do community work in the school, repay the cost of the windows and subject themselves to a caning. The second concerns the outcome of GH's tracking down the lads who had been seen by an old man 'burying something in the garden'. When he mentioned this to the DC co-ordinating information on one of the lads, who was a persistent young thief, the DC already knew about everything bar the digging, and was already on the verge of 'bringing him in' the next day.

In the first incident the lads are classically the youthful 'pre-criminals' that RBO school-liaison work is designed to catch and correct. Small wonder that DE is 'delighted' that the police, school and parental triad was able to co-operate in producing a creative if unconventional punishment. For what this co-operation demonstrated was that the informal, educative philosophy behind RBO work with juveniles could be made to work, and without simply going soft; both were important to DE in his dual role as educator and police officer.

In the second incident, GH's initial elation ('See what I mean? Few minutes chat here and there may clear up the break') is clearly not going to last; the CID are already on to the suspect and are going to take it over. GH will not see this lad again.

The difference between the two cases is that the second involves someone who has crossed the border from latent to actual 'toe rag'. As such, he can be legitimately and enthusiastically pursued as a 'real criminal' – even if he is only youthful and even by an RBO – but is then 'lost', as is the case with all 'real' soluble crime, to the CID. Whilst GH, a 'spy' according to our typology, might *desire* to spend more time amongst the 'toe rags', out of uniform and in pubs, even he recognized that the opportunities for such work are in reality limited. (Our analysis of the apparent reasons for all RBO contacts with the public, using a generous definition of 'intelligence' which included all contacts where any intelligence potentially relevant to any crime was mentioned, produced only 29 all told, or 16 per cent.) And even when stumbled across, as in the above example, these cannot be seen through to a satisfying conclusion. This CID monopoly on legal work involving known criminals, a product of an organizational decision making the CID responsible for defining 'beat crime' and hence what constitutes 'their own' crime, means that the RBOs have no access to the only

items of exchange of relevance to such groups, that is, legal
favours. And the ability to work regularly in plain clothes afforded
the CID, but only 'on request' to the RBOs, means that inconspi-
cuous contact – a necessary feature for regular contact with
'criminal' populations if the sides are to retain credibility with their
respective peer groups – is denied the RBOs except intermittently.

This finding about 'toe rags' is as applicable to race as to age.
Indeed, given the organizational commitment to good community
relations – of which race relations were constantly the key indicator
and the RBOs the chief 'front-line' means to achieve the desired
relations – this need not surprise. Whether it was true as a result
that, in practice, blacks were treated *more* favourably, as some
seem to think (GH: 'With white lads, you'll clip an ear: not with
black lads'; cf. a similar unit quote, p. 108), is debatable. But, in
any event, we never saw a black ear clipped – nor a white one, for
that matter – by an RBO.

If certain organizational features have enabled the CID to regard
known criminals, the 'professional toe rags' we might say, as 'their
property', it is the set of organizational features we have already
described at length which have enabled the unit to regard the *ad hoc*
criminals, what we might call the 'amateur toe rags', as 'their property'.[27] These features – 'call readiness' and a vehicle – ensure that a
panda or first-response car will usually arrive first at a scene of conflict, except when a nearby RBO offers to assist a call and gets there
first, as was the case with HI and the domestic, or the unavailability
of a vehicle prompts a request for RBO assistance, which is usually
an indicator of a relatively non-conflictual situation. Thus, even in
those offence-related, non-elective conflict situations RBOs do find
themselves in, they get there *after* the unit has arrived. It was significant that GH's story about the fight on his patch had him arriving
after the panda driver (who was having 'a pig of a time'). If the
conflictual incident involves a known criminal, then, the CID will
deal with it; if an 'unknown', the unit. Only if it is possible to transform a conflictual exchange into a consensual one by informal means
will the RBO get a look-in, as happened with GH and his fight.

This consensual basis of resident beat contacts, even non-elective
ones, suggests, in so far as the organization has an interest in maintaining such a consensus, a certain power in the hands of the community. This is nowhere more evident than in those systematic contacts
regularly maintained. It is to the nature of these we now turn.

SYSTEMATIC CONTACTS

Systematic contacts are a regular feature of RBO work, whatever
an individual's preferred style. Certainly the latter will determine,

to some extent, the nature and number of such contacts; but the minimal need to 'know the patch' requires some systematic contacts, apart from explicit instructions requiring schools (and pensioner police officers) to be regularly visited. The five reasons for contact outlined earlier (intelligence, education, public relations, welfare and social), all require, for maximum effect, a degree of regularity in the contacts sustained. Our attempt to analyse all RBO contacts quantitatively, according to the apparent reason for contact, produced the following figures: 19 (10 per cent) 'educational', 29 (16 per cent) 'intelligence' and the rest (108 or 60 per cent) 'public relations', 'welfare' or 'social' – the latter containing incidents, some fairly insubstantial, which it was therefore difficult to allot to any one specific category. A good many of these were 'systematic' in the sense of 'known' or regular 'spots' where tea, chat and information were regularly exchanged.

So, whether the preferred style keeps individual RBOs in regular contact primarily with individuals in the community, schools, youth clubs, social services departments and other official agencies, groups variously 'representing' the community, local 'worthies', publicans, shopkeepers, people in the street, or the elderly at home, such contacts are maintained *regularly*. Regular contact both requires and produces consensual relations – something made easier by the fact that all these contacts are with local 'respectables'. This is true even of contacts maintained for intelligence purposes, given what we have said about the CID monopoly on 'toe-rag' informants. Unsurprisingly, then, a vicar's wife – not a local drug addict – was HI's informant on the local drug scene.

Whilst such recurrent and consensual relations with all respectable sections of a local community may present problems for impartiality and diligence, as we suggested in talking about unit 'spots', they do not present a problem once the organization has redefined the task of RBOs as the production of systematic consensual relations with the public. However, the absences are potentially problematic. The absence of systematic contacts with 'toe rags' for the reasons we have outlined means the RBOs have built up systematic consensual relations with all sections of the community except the regularly 'policed' – who are dealt with by the CID and the unit (and by the SPG at football matches and demonstrations). It is this feature which can account for 'explosive' relations building up between sections of the community and the police, even in areas where community relations are said to be 'good'.[28]

In conclusion, whilst the reasons for contact with the public are many, whether such contact is maintained electively, nonelectively, or through systematic contact, the lack of offence-related activity ensures that consensual relations are apparently everywhere in evidence. Yet closer inspection reveals that such relations, again because of the lack of offence-related activity, are with the respectables and the 'known'. 'Toe rags' remain unknown, and outside the consensual relations, whatever the style adopted. This exclusive conception of consensus can prove problematic.

The Wider Organizational Setting: Management

Thinking about management in connection with resident beat-work means to address the role of the Superintendent, for he is the main conduit for management influence.[29] It would appear, at first sight, that Superintendents, like sergeants, are redundant supervisors. Despite the 'exposed' nature of RBO work, the relative absence of legal work appears to fatally undercut this supervisory advantage. To stop there though is to overlook the correlative freedom enjoyed by the Superintendent to define his understanding of the RBO's task and hence his ability to influence working practices.

Just as the RBO may adopt one of a variety of styles – given the diversity of activities implicit in the term 'community policing' – a Superintendent has a similar freedom of interpretation. This freedom provided the opportunity to exert a definite influence on RBO working. In broad terms this amounted to being in a position to determine, to some extent, how much time was to be given over to interventionist community initiatives and how much to traditional criminal investigation on beats. One result of this could be a marked difference in RBO arrest rates between very similar subdivisions.

For example, the Superintendent of the subdivision studied in depth was in favour of a strongly community-oriented interventionist strategy:

> It all depends on how much accent the individual Superintendent puts on the work of the RBOs . . . whether he's prepared to strike him off for two or three days to organize a football competition, like we did here for forty-five teams of all sectors of the community . . . whether he's prepared to strike one of his sergeants off to work in a youth club, whether he's prepared to strike off resident beat officers to take . . . deprived children to holiday camps. I would, because I think it's part of our role.

His opposite number on a very similar, adjacent subdivision had a different view of such special projects:

> It's nearly as bad as putting them in bloody cars, you know, taking them and doing these little projects. There have been instances on this division where police officers have gone down with a boiler suit on and spades and shovels and barrows . . . and cleared derelict areas and made them into play areas. It was never intended that that should be the role of a police officer, in my opinion.

Whilst the former thought that his orientation was compatible with a traditional orientation to crime ('Don't run away with the idea that if you do community policing, you don't do your natural enforcing role. Nothing can be further from the truth') and was not dissimilar to that of his opposite number ('His attitude is basically the same as mine'), there was no doubt his RBOs noticed a difference in practice. For them, the more traditional attitude of the crime-oriented Superintendent meant a greater freedom for his RBOs to follow up crime on their patches because of his readiness to allow them to indulge in plain-clothes observations for as long as it took to clear up particular crime problems.

The Superintendent certainly confirmed this view of himself:

> Down in the —— area, which is a bit of a rough area, I've got the RBO for the area, and the detective who's attached to the RBO. they've spent about four or five days down there in plain clothes on observations and inquiries. If they've got a problem, I don't care how they resolve that problem. They can dress up as Santa Claus if they want. If they've got a problem on their area, I expect them, if they can, to resolve it, and if they can't resolve it on their own, to call for assistance from anywhere.

Whilst we witnessed occasional plain-clothes working by the RBOs, there was never anything on this scale.

It was this different attitude to plain-clothes work – an apparent willingness to strike RBOs off for 'crime work' as opposed to the 'community-oriented' Superintendent's confessed willingness to strike RBOs off for community projects – which the RBOs we observed saw as the reason for the consistently better arrest figures of their counterparts. The community-oriented Superintendent was not unaware of this difference either; at a time when the 'crime-oriented' RBOs were getting sixty-odd prisoners a month and his own only thirty-seven, he told the RBO sergeant that this could be improved to fifty, a desire clearly motivated by a knowledge of his neighbour's superior statistics. But this exhortation was not accompanied by any reordering of his obvious priorities, or by greater facilities (for plain-clothes working, for example) for his officers to achieve this objective; hence it remained an exhortation. This was no doubt because he felt genuinely closer to senior management on this issue; for example, whilst he mentioned 'a good team of breakers brought in and convicted' as something he found satisfying about his job, this was only the second of three items mentioned, the others being 'nobody injured at football matches' and 'when initiatives taken by the RBOs bring a response from the community'.

His 'crime-oriented' counterpart had a singular response: 'I like to come in on a morning and see a full apprehension sheet.' The latter was aware of his differences from management on this issue ('I've been criticized by the Deputy Chief before for a wrong deployment of my RBOs'). Whilst the determinants of these differences are interesting – the crime-oriented Superintendent was very near retirement and had spent eleven years in the CID, whilst the community-oriented one was younger, ambitious, without significant CID experience, and had been especially drafted in after a serious local racial incident (see Chapter 8) because of his experience of community policing in another difficult area – the essential point, for our present purposes, is the effect such differences can have on the system of RBO working. We return in Part IV to draw out the implications of this.

The managerial processes that have been exemplified in the case of the RBOs display a number of features that may allow us to discuss the broader question of police management. In the first place there is an obvious contrast between the practices of the RBO sections resulting from the preferences of their respective Superintendents – this despite the similarity and proximity of their locations. The power of the Superintendents in each case appears to arise from their responsibility for deploying officers and arranging their duties. But this form of influence can also be identified at the higher level; the community-oriented Superintendent was introduced as a result of deployment at a higher managerial level. Thus at each level we find the significance of deployment as an instrument of management.

In the second place there is evidence of another managerial instrument but one perhaps less readily shown to be significant in terms of influencing practice. At the subdivisional level we have noticed how one of the Superintendents attempts by exhortation to raise the arrest statistics in some degree. On the other hand, this advice appears less pressing, because there is also an awareness on this Superintendent's part that senior management is sympathetic to his general 'community policing' style, and to that extent less anxious about arrest statistics. So the exact weighting of the advice remains somewhat uncertain. The other Superintendent's more straightforward crime orientation produces an atmosphere of encouragement for successful arrests; but there is also an indication that senior management is less encouraging towards the related neglect of 'community-police' projects. Advice, at each level, bears a less than straightforward role, not possessing a guaranteed authority or automatic influence. Nor is there any obvious source of guidance, in terms of policy order, which might represent a means for the resolution of any question of this nature. Rather there appears to be no means of standardizing different emphases on what are equally legitimate goals for the organization: the detection of crime and the building of community relations.

The question of managerial discretion thus must be posed within a set of institutional parameters in which the use of managerial instruments exhibits significant differences. Deployment, a clear bureaucratic prerogative, appears more powerful than supervisory advice; perhaps this is to be expected, yet we should note here the invisibility of any more direct means of guidance such as would be represented by specifications of work duties at each level. The police force certainly possesses such specifications to a plentiful extent, in the shape of the regular orders issued periodically. What we must therefore signal is the significance of the police force's preference for less authoritative means of securing its objectives in the important areas of discretion discussed here, particularly when we also consider the widespread use of authoritative orders dealing with the minutiae of technical and administrative procedures.

Our argument, which we shall expound at length in the chapters on policy (Part IV), is that a coherent answer to this apparent discrepancy can be produced if we bear in mind that the central questions covered here – crime arrests and preventive measures involving the community – impinge directly on the discretion of officers bound generally to uphold the law. In other words, they concern matters on which each officer as a sworn constable has an implicit duty and a significant measure of discretion; in these matters advice is the preferred managerial instrument – not so with the various procedures that constitute a mere means to fulfilling the ends of the police, that is, upholding the police mandate in its various aspects. For these latter ends, an organization of consent through advice, rebuke, exhortation and praise is required. We shall try to substantiate these points in detail when we examine, in

Part IV, 'policy files' and 'policy meetings', which concern precisely the range of topics – from technical procedures to particular crime phenomena – to which such differentiated treatment is given.

Testing Hypotheses

Having conducted an examination of resident beat-work, we are now in a position to complete this interpretive exercise by testing rival hypotheses against these data and these findings.

Hypotheses Stemming from Existing Problematics

If the 'machine' model and the resulting hypothesis have some affinities, as we saw, with the form of unit policing, this is certainly not true of resident beat policing with its emphasis on freedom and the variety of resulting 'styles'. There it was the variety of messages from the centre dutifully received by officers which allowed some validity to the notion of the unit as a machine in action. Here, the almost complete absence of messages, and hence of a contact between the centre and operating edge, produces the reverse effect: a series of autonomous styles. Not that these styles represent an absolute discrepancy between the centre and the operating edge. As we saw, different Superintendent orientations can influence arrest rates. So, it could be said that rank-and-file behaviour *broadly* reflected organizational (the machine's) requirements, as mediated by Superintendents. Where these emphasized community-relations objectives as against traditional crime-detection ones, rank-and-file behaviour produced less arrests, and vice versa. However, it is a very permissive kind of 'machine' that can tolerate such a diversity of styles, which could hardly have been predicted by the model. Moreover, this diversity of styles had nothing to do with a 'blockage in communication', as the hypothesis stemming from the model would have it in explaining discrepant behaviour, for there is no evidence of such a blockage. Indeed, as our analysis has demonstrated, relations between RBOs and their immediate supervising officer are remarkably open, even egalitarian. Furthermore, the channels between a subdivisional Superintendent and the RBOs are kept open, formally in terms of the monthly self-report sessions and occasional meetings, but also more generally in the sense that the Superintendent plays the role, to some extent, of the Inspector on a unit. There are, in short, no structural impediments to the free-flow of communication. Thus we must look elsewhere for an understanding of how such styles emerge.

On the surface, the 'subculture' model's interest in the working norms of officers would appear to be of assistance. However, when we turn to the subculturalist's hypotheses, namely, that we would find two subcultures (those of management and rank and file) which would be in conflict, and that supervision in consequence would routinely fail to have any significant impact, we find that they cannot take us far in explaining the emergence of a variety of styles, *all* apparently acceptable to the organization. Moreover, our comparative look across subdivisions suggested that what differences there were occurred *horizontally*, not vertically – between subdivisions, not between management and rank and file. Thus, as we saw, Superintendents got broadly the behaviour – community-relations activity or crime arrests – they favoured; and even if individual RBOs could, in the way we suggested, deviate to some extent from a Superintendent's preference, we did not observe two opposed subcultures lining up either side of the managerial divide.

Within this context to talk of supervision 'failing' would be nonsense. The 'permissiveness' of the supervisory style matched the 'permissiveness' of the RBO task. What was supervisable was supervised (numbers of visits, arrests and so on); what was not – the vast bulk of RBO activities – was subject only to the broad steer of superintendent preference. Within that broad steer, the diversity of RBO styles was not merely tolerated, but welcomed as the necessary concomitant of the 'peculiarity' of local patches and of individual personalities (with different skills and background experience) faced with an omnibus function

Does the 'environmental' hypothesis, that environment shapes behaviour, fare any better? We have already suggested that this approach, whilst fruitful in general, suffers from being too imprecise and that our approach is concerned to develop more adequately the notion of environment. However, it is worth pausing a moment, for, if anywhere in the police organization, it is in the RBOs with their community-relations remit that we would expect to find strong 'environmental' influences in the shape of the community. Yet, as we saw in our earlier discussion of the relationship between the RBO, the Superintendent and the community, the relationship is complex, and community influence is dependent on the Superintendent's preferences, which themselves do not bear a standard unproblematic relationship with the organization. Thus 'environmental' influences bear a complex, mediated and attenuated relationship to RBO behaviour.

Similar points can be made about the class-functionalist hypo-thesis about class determining police behaviour. Superficially, the finding about the systematic contacts of RBOs with the known and the respectable, and excluding the 'toe rags', supports the class-based thesis of policing. But this would be to imply that the 'respectables' dictate the pattern of policing, a point which ignores the mediate and attenuated way such influence works – which was precisely our point at the outset, that is, the need to *develop* the ways in which class and other social factors are complexly related to the practice of policing. This brings us finally to our own hypothesis.

Hypotheses Stemming from our Reconceptualized Problematic

Legal institutions appear at first sight to be weak as determinants of the working of the RBO system. The bulk of RBO work either is not law enforcement work, or operates in a borderline sub-legal domain consisting of public nuisances and minor complaints. In the case of those beat crimes that do come their way (petty thefts and criminal damage, for example), the legal constraints will vary with the complexity of the offence, the degree of citizen involve-ment and so on; but the time spent on such work is not great, unless there is authoritative advice from the Superintendent to the contrary. The relative lack of involvement with 'legal' work ensures too that RBOs are not routinely subject to the legal constraints related to the use made by citizens and legal authorities of their legal powers. Their infrequent court appearances, together with their infrequent involvement in law enforcement work, makes them less routinely susceptible to the constraints of either judicial advice and admonition or complaints. In the case of the latter, the high visibility of their work, and of themselves as local people, and the fact that much of their legal work involves juveniles with the extra check such involvement usually entails, the likelihood of invoking complaints, in other than a sporadic and arbitrary fashion, is remote.

However, it is *precisely* this absence of legal work, and the consequent weakness of legal institutions as a constraint in a direct sense, that creates the conditions of so many other features of the way the system works. In the first instance, an absence of legal work renders much of RBO work essentially unquantifiable and beyond the conventional processes of police supervisory practices, organized, as they are, to cope with legal process work and encounters centred on legally pertinent matters. It thus creates the fundamental conditions which enable a range of styles to emerge, since there are few legal demands to impose more uniform working styles from 'without', and few supervisory instruments to structure activities from 'within'.

It thus ensures that contacts will be largely with 'respectables' and helps explain the absence of 'toe-rag' contacts. It helps explain why the RBOs are the first to be used when extra manpower is needed; engaged essentially in 'non-legal' activities of an unquantifiable nature, their withdrawal from active duty has the least disruptive impact on a system fundamentally organized around legally pertinent public contacts. And it helps explain why the sergeant, lacking conventional indices of performance except for legal tasks, is largely forced into an egalitarian mode of supervision. Finally, it may well help explain the absence of a cohesive peer-group culture; lacking conventional indices of performance, peers lack an instrument, such as comparative arrest rates, to socialize 'deviants' into uniform work practices and performance. The argument here is that an absence of strong and extensive legal demands does establish certain base-line conditions – unquantifiable activies, problems of supervision – which enable certain other features, for example, distinctive styles, to emerge. In this sense the attenuation of legal influences exercises a *fundamental* determinacy by allowing non-legal factors to come prominently into operation; or, in Althusser and Balibar's (1970) terms, to become dominant. We need to examine these non-legal factors further.

The fundamental feature of contact work with the public is its breadth and, within limits, variety. Most RBOs, dependent in part on 'chosen style', routinely maintain contact with individuals within the community, with representatives of the community and with public officials working in organizations with various responsibilities to the community. Contacts with 'toe rags', as we mentioned earlier, are not routinely maintained. Community contacts are thus largely with 'respectables', often with representatives, and usually consensually based. We have already mentioned that the 'exposed' nature of RBO work enables the Superintendent to have immediate access to the working of a patch – through direct community contact or the crime figures. If he chooses the former performance measure, he is clearly reliant on the community reputation established by the RBO, in which case the community has an influential lever, and, through the cultivation of that reputation, so, indirectly, has the PC concerned. (In so far as this power of RBO officers lies in their ability to cultivate community relations, the inattention to stationary traffic offences, where these involve local people, has a ready explanation.) If the Superintendent chooses the crime figures (which need not necessarily be in conflict with community reputation) he has a performance measure which overrides that community influence. In that the Superintendent is himself responsible for community relations on his subdivision, much depends on how he conceives 'good' community relations, in terms of 'relations' between an RBO and community contacts or in terms of the crime figures. Consequently, the potential community influence on police activity would appear to be high. Indeed, we can go further; given the nature of much RBO work, consisting to a large degree of a series of personal interactions the *quality* of which is known only to the participants, and the effectiveness of which defies easy measurement, the most important general form of assessment becomes 'community reputation' which lies largely in the hands of community contacts.

However, the importance of 'reputation' as a performance measure is dependent on how the Superintendent perceives his community-relations responsibilities. Thus he can choose to highlight the issue of beat crime and judge the success of RBOs in these terms rather than those of community reputation. In this way, it is possible, given the weight of legal duties, for the community influence to be perceived in terms of more traditional police concerns and performance measures. Thus, whilst democratic influences are potentially strong with respect to RBO work, this, in its turn, is conditioned by the 'common-sense' orientation of the Superintendent.

We have noted that colleague influence is characterized by competition rather than emulation. Individuals on 'unique' patches, working discretionary hours in a discretionary fashion, favour the development of individual styles, not a collectively approved working norm. We have also noted that the sergeant's supervisory role is less important, due to the 'exposed' nature of RBO work, than that of the Superintendent with his general preferences. It is his orientation to the community, as we have just seen, his decision to take note of community 'opinion' or to utilize more traditional performance measures, which is ultimately decisive. However, to complicate matters further, such an orientation has to take account of the 'peculiarity' of the area with its particular policing demands. The idea of the uniqueness of particular areas and hence of the justification for personal ways of handling them is strong in police thinking both historically and currently (cf. Critchley, 1978; Alderson, 1979). The idea of 'local' policing depends upon it.[30] This notion recognizes and justifies a range of styles, and hence a certain amount of RBO 'discretion'. Thus, though democratic influence is conditioned by organizational requirements, through the Superintendent's orientation, where these are not entirely consonant the 'local' needs can be invoked by the RBO as a counter. To put the matter concretely, RBOs with a good community reputation might successfully invoke this where a Superintendent favours a more crime-oriented approach on the grounds of peculiar local demands. In so far as both crime investigation and community relations are desirable police objectives, the one 'common sense' can be played off against the other, given the discretion inherent in the role.

Let us, finally, summarize the foregoing in relation to our starting-points: the legal, work and democratic structures and, crucially, the relation between these. The initial absence of pressing legal demands is the condition of the emergence of a degree of freedom in relation to RBO work. Beyond that, however, there is the question of the precise relationship between the work and the democratic structures. The relative absence of legal demands is accompanied by a complementary absence of anything such as an agreed doctrine of rational effectiveness. 'Common sense' necessarily fills the vacuum. Given this, and the absence of a colleague-group occupational culture, the question essentially is how does the work structure relate to the democratic one? However, a prior question involves the relationship between the four identified styles and the organization. We have established that the Superintendent – the organization's field representative – has a degree of freedom, basically in terms of how much weight to attach to community initiatives as opposed to traditional crime ones; so we need to ask about the relationship between the four styles and the two 'options' available to Superintendents. If we examine the former more closely, it is possible to equate the two: the 'educator' and the 'PR' style are manifestations of the newer community-oriented common sense; the 'spy' and 'patrol' style represent the more traditional one of routinized crime prevention (patrol) and detection (spy). The former is a much more recent arrival and has much to do with 'managing consent' and establishing 'legitimacy'; the latter is a more traditional attempt to deal simply in terms of system 'inputs' and 'outputs'. We therefore suggest the terms the 'new' and the 'old' bureaucracy respectively.

Without as yet finalizing the matter, we can say that the community will be 'offered' one of two possibilities: a type of policing drawn from the old bureaucracy, or one drawn from the new. The question of which version of 'common sense' will be offered will partly depend on how much 'freedom' the superintendent is given to determine priorities, which itself will partly depend on the boundaries – the formal allocation of responsibilities to the various departments (crime, traffic and so on) – established by the organization. Where these boundaries are set, and the conditions of any changes in this regard, is ultimately a historical question.

In the case of the RBOs under discussion, the most important historical moment was a highly traumatic racial incident for which the police were totally under-prepared (see Chapter 8). This provided the stimulus to restate the centrality of RBO work – the operational arm of community policing – to the overall objectives of the police force: restaff unallocated beats, clear out the 'dead wood', bring in new, enthusiastic and ambitious faces and provide more 'back-up' resources of various kinds. Within this context, revamping the RBOs at the level of the organization was about instituting the new bureaucracy: to reorganize consent and re-establish legitimacy. Whilst this organizational initiative could not entirely eliminate the discretion and hence the traditional 'common sense' of the Superintendent – given the failure to develop coherent rationally effective criteria with which to evaluate RBO work – the fact that the incumbent Superintendent of the subdivision on which the troubles occurred was quickly moved sideways was an obvious message of intent. The revamped RBOs were the vanguard of the new bureaucracy. Consequently, the local commander can go only so far in encouraging traditional crime work, since the 'new' community-contact work remains primary. Whilst, within this, the commander might emphasize a particular form of contact work (for example, in schools), community acceptability represents in each case a crucial validation. Thus the democratic structure ironically becomes more influential the more it demonstrates, in some form or another, its lack of satisfaction with, or consent to, aspects of the 'old' policing.

It nevertheless has to be asked why traditional styles ('spy' and 'beat') remain dominant. Although it is difficult to place some officers with any precision, for the reasons mentioned earlier, the best estimate delivers four spies, six beat patrollers, one PR and three educators – a clear majority favouring the old bureaucracy over the new. A simple answer indicates the lack of developed criteria for evaluating the effectiveness of the new, a point we have already made. However, this only pushes the question back a stage: why no developed criteria? The answer is as simple as its implications seem difficult to grasp; given the unspecific police mandate simply to 'uphold the law', the new bureaucracy can *never* replace the old but can only exist uneasily alongside it. Indeed, the old bureaucracy, given the mandate, necessarily remains constant; the 'new' is more volatile, liable to become important at particular times and less so at others. In the light of this, it takes a great deal of commitment to side completely with new; safer, perhaps, to stay with the old, but with an open and positive attitude to the new in line with management thinking. That, probably, best explains this finding of the pull of traditionalism even with a 'revamped' group of RBOs.

That the two bureaucracies are indissolubly linked has been recently highlighted by Scarman. Whilst the Brixton 'riots' prompted Scarman to emphasize the importance of community consultation and positive community policing, he was clear this did not mean a turning away from traditional notions of law enforcement; the SPG and the RBOs were, according to Scarman (1982, pp. 139–46), equally necessary. Indeed, the very same situation (that is, the riots) which produced a renewed emphasis on the 'new' paradoxically demonstrated the need for the 'old', even though that situation was itself a product of the old, namely, the swamping 'arrest-oriented' policy of law enforcement.

There is, finally, no once-and-for-all explanation of the relationship between the organization and democratic structures. Nor given the discretion inherent in the concept, is there a fixed relationship between the management and subdivisional Superintendents, or between the latter and their RBOs. If this feels, ultimately, indeterminate, we are still a very long way indeed from the indeterminacy of the subculturalists since it is, at least, a *structured* indeterminacy, one whose conditions and limits can be spelled out.

Notes

1 However, it was mentioned at one RBO meeting that, if they were making complaints (to the Superintendent about how some controllers were using them), they needed to cover their tracks – which meant not allowing controllers to come back and remark on the extended meal breaks being taken. I saw one example of a young RBO spoken to by the sergeant for lateness, but that was probably because he had (inadvertently) kept me waiting!

2 For a summary of the existing literature on typologies of styles, see Reiner (1985b, pp. 103–6). These all appear to be based on observations of unit rather than resident beat officers. On the area constable as 'spy', see Mawby (1979, p. 75).

3 Unlike the unit, where we witnessed six. This difference between the two forms of beat policing echoes Smith (1983, p. 79), who found 25

per cent of home beat officers in London to have been involved in an arrest in the previous seven days, compared with 42 per cent of 'relief' or unit constables. On the low proportion of 'crime work' undertaken generally by RBOs, see Brown and Iles (1985, p. 23).

4 The terms 'reactive' and 'proactive' are terms easily misunderstood in the police debate, because both have positive *and* negative connotations. 'Reactive' is used to refer to the (positive) act of responding to a public request for assistance, and to the (negative) act of a too hasty and insensitive response (sometimes called 'fire-brigade' policing). 'Proactive' connotes both the (positive) act of initiating public contacts characteristic of good RBOing, and the (negative) act of stopping and searching large numbers – as part of a 'swamping' operation, as happened in Brixton just prior to the riots of 1981.

5 This is not to deny that school visits raise important issues about the role of police in education, but to insist that such issues hinge fundamentally on the terms upon which police enter schools as *educators*, not, for the most part, on the potential visits have for intelligence gathering.

6 For information on Neighbourhood Watch, see the various working papers emanating from the research project funded by the Libertarian Research and Education Trust, 9 Poland Street, London, W1.

7 Whilst the uniqueness of an area might be used to justify the adoption of a particular style, we found no positive relationship between kind of area policed and chosen style.

8 'Selling' policework may be seen as a manipulative strategy, and for some indeed it may be; but it is not necessarily. Certainly EF talked of RBOing being 'the closest that I've been to what I class as true policework . . . mixing with people, being with people, and being one of the people'. Nothing we have said about this style contradicts this self-conception.

9 In reality the situation, as always, was more complex. The force recognized his abilities in this direction, and he was indeed 'wanted' by the sergeant. DE was less sure because of being uncertain of the motives of those offering him the job. Part of him wanted promotion, another part wanted a spell in the divisional stolen-vehicles squad. Variety if anything was the keynote. Being an 'educator' in terms of observed style, then, does not preclude other motives or interests. (DE did get his spell in the stolen-vehicles squad.)

10 Once again, the general concern, whilst an RBO, with patient preventive work did not preclude alternative ambitions. In the case of CD, a specialist squad – vice or drugs – was the goal.

11 FG, more predictably, expressed a preference for community-liaison work, though 'I'd have to . . . spend some time with them to see if I'd enjoy working there', and a positive dislike of the CID: 'I've never liked the CID. It never interested me.'

12 Although GH enjoyed his present job, he considered it a dead end. In line with his chosen style, he thought the 'plain-clothes' squad was where he would like to end up. (His last known posting was to the SPG.)

13 AB 'wouldn't mind an attachment to the CID for, say, six months', especially if he could be 'doing the firearms inquiries'. But he was 'very happy . . . being an RBO', because 'being a large man . . . I want plenty of exercise'.

14 This was perhaps partly a consequence of the beat he was on, which he found 'too quiet' with too few opportunities to get 'his fingers into something'.

15 For an alternative view of police welfare work, one which sees police as 'the secret social service', see Punch (1979b).

16 Now collators, but during the research period there was one collator, plus a PC (nearing retirement age) in charge of arrangements concerning football who also 'helped out' the collator.

17 A major examination of the collator's role was in progress during our study, which resulted, among other things, in the recommendation to have two collators.

18 This is not to suggest that the RBO sergeant has little or no paperwork to oversee. On the contrary, this can be broad in character, involving reports on activities with local associations and agencies as well as more routine matters, and can be quite voluminous, given the continuous 'case-work' character of much RBO work compared with the more incident-based work of the units. If there is no specially assigned RBO sergeant or inspector, as Brown and Iles (1985, p. 11) point out, the extent of supervision is more variable and dependent on unit supervisors.

19 However, DE did get turned down by the sergeant when he requested to help with the scheduling of the material seized in a 'dirty' bookshop raid. The sergeant said this would be done by IJ and EF since they had been involved with the raid, hence it was 'only fair'.

20 It was noticeable that those RBOs who were probably furthest from the central nexus around the sergeant (which allegedly constituted the 'A' team) talked most about the 'A' and 'B' teams.

21 For a similar finding on 'stroppiness', see Piliavin and Briar (1964) on the importance of 'demeanor'.

22 This was something not confined to stationary traffic offences but also observed on other occasions: selling over the legally allowed number of disco tickets (DE), a missing gambling licence in the case of a café owner with pinball machines (GH), having shop sunblinds too low (BC). In all these cases the offences were mentioned, by either the RBO or the offender, so were clearly known about.

23 Youthful 'misbehaviour' was clearly a concern to some local residents. I witnessed at least three occasions when people complained to an RBO in the street about such misbehaviour.

24 For a full account of the working of the SPG, from which these remarks are drawn, see Jefferson and Grimshaw (1981).

25 Even one of those whose general style was 'spy', not 'educator', was observed to warn juvenile offenders riding bikes on the pavement.

26 We stress the statistical dimension since it is *recorded* crime that police respond to. We cannot here deal with the complex question of the

relationship between 'real' and 'recorded' crime rates, for which, see the exemplary discussions in Box (1981, pp. 56–93, 157–207).

27 On the question of the liability of 'any category of citizens ... to become police property', see Lee (1981, p. 53). He suggests power-lessness as the key shared characteristic.

28 It can also perhaps render comprehensible police claims about being taken by surprise by riots, and the frequency of explanations blaming 'outside agitators'.

29 At the time of the research, all superintendents were men.

30 This is a notion successfully advanced throughout the history of modern policing, most recently in the Royal Commission that preceded the Police Act 1964; see Royal Commission (1962).

Conclusions to
Parts II and III

The results of our observational study on beat-work have now been presented. Before commencing a study of policy within the police organization, it is appropriate to summarize our findings as they relate to the principal hypotheses established at the end of Chapter 1.

The 'machine' model suggested the importance of communication as the key to organizational relations. Controls would succeed to the extent that communication was maintained with the operational sector of the organization. Reviewing our evidence from the unit and the RBOs it would appear that communication was not a problem for supervisors in either case; rather the issue was the appropriateness of communication. In the unit the supervisors were able to adopt a human-relations approach in order to motivate the group; in the RBOs contact with the supervisors was open and regular, but the nature of the task was defined as discretionary, though management evidently took an interest in the kind of activity undertaken. If, on the other hand, management in the unit appeared somewhat remote, this distance again was produced by the perceived nature of the task, bearing in particular on legal duties or on the contingencies of incident response. On key questions of control, the 'machine' model is thus inadequate to embrace the type and relevance of communication. It is this question that a structural approach can perhaps more plausibly address.

The relation between legal and work structures (to use our terms) was the subject of a competing series of hypotheses from the subculturalist perspective, which emphasized the existence of police 'subcultures', their opposition along the dividing line of rank and the routine failure of supervision. These three points can be dealt with in turn.

(1) It was hypothesized that the structure of law would determine how and to what extent work values would prevail. In neither resident nor unit beat-work did we discover large quantities of legal work. In the former case this absence manifests itself through the optional nature of the work pattern in which individual management priorities and constables' preferences generate *tendencies*, sometimes reinforcing, sometimes contrary, towards the adoption of work styles more or less capable of fitting local circumstances. The legal structure reveals its discretionary, limited aspect here, its possibility of 'non-appearance'.

In the case of the unit the organization of work is compulsorily geared to high productivity and generates a significant number of offence-related contacts but produces tasks of low actual relevance. Thus the legal structure asserts itself as an important context, both negatively (in diminishing the importance of routine tasks) and positively (in providing a constant focus of attention). The permissiveness of the legal structure was revealed at the moment of offence-related contact when typifications of relevance came into play, in the cases of the unit and RBOs equally. In neither case did precisely articulated legal structures enter the task, and the attitude of supervisors reflected this state of affairs.

(2) The incidence of value differences and opposition within the organization was hypothesized to be a function of contrasting tasks, whether in the shape of differences in work situations or of distinctions in legal remits. The frequency of conflict was limited in both the chosen case studies. For resident beat officers its most obvious manifestation grew from the absence of a collegiate standard, instead of which a series of rumours laid the basis for cliques and individual envy. With no sense of a common task or standard approach, officers were left to construct a partial and dubious 'league table' centred on the judgement of a primary figure such as the RBO sergeant. The indefinite nature of the task precluded a clear sense of unity. In the case of the unit, emphasis was placed on solidarity and on a group standard, since various factors, especially the common work situation, combined to isolate the group and integrate unit members. A hierarchy of competence could be constructed on the basis of the perceived differences between jobs, while an equitable distribution of jobs among members consolidated group unity. An administrative value system was embodied in the formal elements of the task which officers sought to transcend by their operational activity. Hence the issue lay in the task rather than in value conflicts themselves. Opposition can thus be related to definitions of the work task.

(3) Supervision was felt to be likely to succeed when tasks were

not defined as matters of obligation or directive. The evidence of the case studies confirmed the significance of task definition as a determinant of supervisory effectiveness. The resident beat system was felt to require a delicate cultivation of local contacts in which direct supervision was felt to be redundant or intrusive. Hence the principles of the task determined the scope and nature of supervision. In the unit, supervision was 'automated' to a certain extent by systems of radio control and paper report but was supported by a 'human-relations' style of leadership, in which known personal qualities received attention from supervisors. Where tasks such as law enforcement were felt by officers to require a pragmatic approach, the attitude of supervisors complemented rather than contradicted this perspective.

Finally we chose to combine together the 'environment' and 'class-functionalist' hypotheses in order to suggest the importance of a complex relation between policing and various social categories. In addition we argued that the resulting democratic structure would be constrained in its effects by legal and work-related influences. In the unit the democratic influence appeared 'weak' and disparate, as a result of the fleeting and contingent nature of the contacts. The composition of the 'democratic' public revealed some gaps and disproportions which require a complex 'environmentalist' analysis to disentangle. The same can be said of the RBO system with its orientation towards local 'respectables'. Most importantly for the RBOs, we found that the resulting 'community reputation' was influential in legitimating styles of work. From the point of view of testing our hypothesis, the difference between unit and RBOs in the significance accorded to 'the community' testifies to the important intervening variable – task definition, which in the case of the RBOs determines the weight placed upon feedback from the 'public'. No such definition was to be found in the unit.

We are therefore left to conclude that the structure of law manifests itself indirectly in beat-work – as a reflex in the unit, as a resource in resident beat-work measured against the search for consent. The alloted task in hand, equally, defines the possibilities of opposition and of supervisory 'failure'. The capacity for democratic influence over policing thus remains a function of legal and organizational structures.

The hypotheses broadly have thus proved to be sustainable in dealing with two kinds of beat-work without foreshadowing the concrete connections that a theoretical case study can supply. It would seem possible to consider applying the hypotheses to the study of other sections, other forces and so on, and to develop them in ways that contribute to a more comprehensive theory of policework. We hope to have shown the relevance of a theoretical critique of existing positions to the development of general theory, using an investigation of contrasting forms to distil general structures. Having presented an observational study of police operations, we shall now pose the problem of policy within police organizations. Once again, the utility of considering policy as a structural feature of policing, with a specific definition and relevance, will be at the forefront of our investigations.

PART IV

The Policy System

Introduction to Part IV

Having looked at both unit and resident beat-work, and tested the various hypotheses, we come now to 'policy'. While we have been arguing for a new way of interpreting policework, we were doing so in relation to ground already traversed by others. Hence we proceeded, via a critique, to our empirical examination. But in moving on to policy we come to that about which, as we argued in Chapter 1, nothing is concretely known. If our hypotheses have validity they must be able to stand up here too; but before that we have first to define our object. What follows in the next two chapters, then, will offer, in line with our general orientation, a concrete definition of policy, in addition to adopting the structural form familiar from previous chapters. But since offering such a definition introduces a novel element, the structure of what follows will not be so immediately familiar and will probably benefit from some signposting.

We start Chapter 6 with the competing hypotheses, stemming from the competing 'models' of policework, which posit as their respective starting-points an unspecified (assumptive) definition of policy (all models bar 'ours') against a specific (empirical) definition (ours); though the contents of our definition at this stage remain to be filled in.

The next section commences the task of defining policy by outlining the formal elements ('machine'-model style) in a way which highlights the role of the structures of law, work and democracy. This is followed by a definition of policy – one intended to enable a concrete, empirical examination. The definition of policy is followed by a consideration of some other managerial instruments – advice, command, supervision and so on – in order to begin the process of clarifying what 'policy' is, by demonstrating what it is not. We extend our focus to include the process of policy consideration. This new focus enables policy matters to be defined in sites where such 'consideration' takes place.

This is followed in Chapter 7 by a concrete exemplification of one of the key institutions where policy is considered: meetings. Such a look reveals the distinction between operational and administrative issues, the former characterized by a common-sense discourse and the latter by a rational-scientific one. Before completing our examination of key institutional sites, we offer, at this stage, three examples to illustrate this fundamental distinction: one administrative, one operational and one 'mixed' issue. We end the chapter with a summary.

Chapter 8 focuses on the other key institution for the consideration of policy – the policy files – and on what such an examination can reveal about the relationship between the structures of law, work and democracy. An outline of the methodology in dealing with the files is followed by an exemplification of different types of files: operational, 'mixed' and non-operational (administrative). The significance of the revelation that files are oriented towards the non-operational is gradually shown as succeeding sections consider first how *frequently* external bodies appear in the files considered and then, when we look at two case studies involving operational policy matters, how *influential* such bodies, and the democratic structure generally, can be, relative to the work and legal structures. These case studies, in revealing the determining centrality of the legal structure and the discretion it vests in the constable in operational matters, 'explain' the symbiotic relationship between operational matters and common sense, the inherent difficulty of formulating other than permissive policy in this sphere, and the consequent dominance of the work structure as well as the dominance (just noted) of non-operational matters in the policy files. A comparison of the hypotheses, which follows, shows how none of the other hypotheses with their (unexamined) unitary notion of policy can begin to explain any of these findings. We end by mentioning the theoretical and conceptual bases of the analysis, by way of a pointer to the central theoretical theme of Chapter 9.

CHAPTER SIX

What Do We Mean by Policy?

Alternative Hypotheses

The *machine* model is based on the mechanistic notion that law, policy and practice should simply coincide and that failure to do so results from some 'blockage' in the machine preventing the message getting through. Policy is regarded unproblematically as that set of lawful instructions, guidelines, or principles which informs practice (cf. Etzioni, 1964, p. 30). We could say, generally, that this approach sees policy as 'super-relevant' to the question of practice. In terms of an hypothesis, apparent discrepancies between policy and practice are to be explained as a failure of understanding or communication.

The *subculture* model broadly reverses the above assumptions, though policy is still viewed as a set of instructions, guidelines, or principles which subordinates should follow. However, the conditions of policework and the strength of the rank-and-file subculture combine routinely to undermine or disregard policy. Consequently, policy is effectively the public-relations arm of policework, but a 'dead letter' in practice: 'policy as irrelevance', we might say. In terms of an hypothesis, apparent discrepancies between policy and practice are to be explained as the consequence of a subversive rank-and-file subculture constantly at odds with a managerial 'bureaucracy' which it regards as, at best, 'out of touch' with the realities of street policing and, at worst, as cynically disregarding of its interests and safety in a (mistaken) concern to pander to 'the public' and politicians.

The *environmental* model stresses the importance of environment in shaping police behaviour, but works with too gross a conception of the environment: with conceptions of 'law', 'work' and 'democracy' which require the kind of development we have been attempting. Though our model, as we said earlier, has clear affinities with this approach, and though its role is developmental in relation to it, there is no doubt that here, too, the conception of policy adopted echoes that of the first two models: a set of instructions, guidelines, or principles which ought to be followed. The question of discrepancies between policy and practice seems less relevant to this model than tracing the role of environment in shaping both policy and practice. Thus it is difficult to formulate an hypothesis comparable to the previous two; but an appropriate hypothesis stemming from this model might be the general proposition that the environment shapes policy.

The *class-functional* model stresses, broadly, the function of class in determining laws and their enforcement. Once again, we are less interested in denying the broad role of class (though we do deny a simple functionalism) than in *developing* the ways in which class (*and* sex *and* age *and* race) is complexly related to law and to law enforcement. But the model's simplistic interest in law and in law enforcement has precluded other than a simple, unexamined notion of policy; implicitly, like the others, this model regards policy as a set of instructions, guidelines, or principles informing practice. In so far as discrepancies between policy and practice are a concern of this approach, the explanation would doubtless have to be couched in terms of the determinacy of 'class'; laws are enforced so as to favour the ruling class. More generally, an appropriate hypothesis stemming from this approach might be the proposition that class determines policy. 'Policy' is thus either a bland 'cover' for discrimination or a secret encouragement of it.

Our model suggests, in general terms, the hypothesis that apparent discrepancies between policy and practice are best explained by a specific examination of how the three structures – law, work and the democratic – relate to the particular policy in question, explaining the role of the legal structure in organizing the relations between the structures. Specifically, we expect, in line with our earlier hypotheses concerning the practices of unit and resident beat-work, the different discourses or value systems – occupational 'common sense' and the administrative discourse of 'rational-scientific' management – to be repeated at the level of policy and to be task-related. We further expect, in line with this, that policies involving operational and related tasks will be characterized by the values of occupational common sense, and those involving administrative tasks will be characterized by rational-scientific management values. Finally, we would similarly expect the 'success' of policy in influencing practice to be task-related. Thus, the impact of those policies bearing on operational and related tasks where occupational common sense is to the fore will be less decisively calculable and more unpredictable in effect than those policies bearing on administrative tasks where rational-scientific management values can come to the fore.

With these alternative hypotheses in mind, we turn, as in previous chapters on the practices of unit and resident beat-work, to an outline of the formal position with respect to policy.

Formal Elements

Since policy-making refers to one of the activities of the Chief Constable, this fact requires that we start with an outline of the legal obligations and responsibilities of this office. The statute primarily concerned is the 1964 Police Act, though the 1976 Police Act, which made some amendments in the area of complaints, is also relevant. The 1984 Police and Criminal Evidence Act (PACE) enacted after this research was undertaken introduced changes in the area of public consultation and complaints investigation which in the nature of the present research we cannot touch upon; only the situation as it existed in 1978–80 is relevant. The 1964 Act, whose provisions cover both England and Wales, makes a Chief Constable responsible for the 'direction and control' of his force. Certain powers are given him to fulfil this responsibility, i.e. powers to appoint, promote and discipline all his officers up to and including the rank of Chief Superintendent – officers for whom he is held to be liable in tort in the case of a civil action brought against any one of them. A Chief Constable is obliged to supply the Home Secretary and the Police Authority with an annual report, and occasional ones on request;[1] though, in the case of such a request from his Police Authority, he can ask that the requirement be referred to the Home Secretary if he thinks that to grant the request would not be in the public interest, or if he thinks such a report is not necessary for the Police Authority's exercise of its duties. In such cases, the request is of no effect unless confirmed by the Home Secretary. The terms of the Act also oblige a Chief Constable to investigate complaints against his officers and to submit all complaints revealing the commission of criminal offences to the Director of Public Prosecutions.

The 1976 Police Act, which introduced an independent element in the complaints procedure in the form of the Police Complaints Board (PCB), required that complaints not submitted to the DPP be submitted to the board for review (in admitted cases which have been heard and decided by the Chief Constable) or decision (in other cases). Investigations, however, were still conducted by senior police officers responsible to the Chief Constable. (The 1984 Police and Criminal Evidence Act strengthened this independent influence in ways we cannot explore here.)

The 1964 Act obliges each Police Authority to maintain an 'adequate and efficient force', and to keep itself informed of the manner in which complaints are dealt with. Besides the power to call for reports, subject to the Home Secretary's confirmation in the event of a disputed request, Police Authorities are empowered to appoint, discipline and retire, in the interests of efficiency, senior ranks (the Chief, his Deputy and the Assistant Chief Constables), though appointments and retirements are subject to the approval of the Home Secretary, who is also the appellate authority in the case of discipline offences. (Under the 1984 Act the Police Authorities are also responsible for organizing consultative arrangements in their localities.)

The Home Secretary's duty, under the terms of the 1964 Act, is to use his powers so as 'to promote the efficiency of the police'. These powers include being able to call for reports from Chief Constables and to adjudicate on referred requests for reports by Police Authorities, to enforce amalgamations, to institute independent inquiries, to call on Police Authorities to use their powers to retire Chief Constables 'in the interests of efficiency', and to ratify appointments or retirements proposed by Police Authorities.

Whilst the precise demarcation of responsibilities between these three authorities – Chief Constables, Police Authorities and the Home Secretary – principally responsible for the police in England and Wales may be subject to dispute,[2] the conventional meaning, reinforced by relevant case-law provisions (which we consider below), is that a Chief Constable's responsibility for 'direction and control' distinctively embraces police practices (including policy) relevant to *operational* matters; that a Police Authority's for maintaining an 'adequate and efficient' force distinctively covers the question of resources – the sufficiency of the establishment, equipment and building – all matters with financial and administrative implications; and that the Home Secretary's for 'promoting efficiency' encompasses a similar field to that of Police Authorities, though on a national basis, and in an enlarged sense, since the Home Secretary has certain extra powers as we have outlined. In short, Police Authorities and the Home Secretary must be concerned with ensuring that local communities are adequately and efficiently provided for in the way of police; Chief Constables with directing and controlling the instrument of police so provided.

The statutory position which gives each Chief Constable the

responsibility for the direction and control of his force presents no problem for the relationship between officers in a force. Subordinates must obey the lawful instructions of a superordinate authority, i.e. the Chief or his delegates. However, the matter is complicated by the position at common law, which it is therefore necessary to consider; moreover, the common-law position covers the substantive duties of the office of Chief Constable: duties which are assumed but not substantively detailed in the Police Acts. Case law relevant to the question of the relationship between constables – principally established in the judgements in the *Fisher* v. *Oldham* and the two Blackburn cases[3] – endorses the common-law notion of constables as agents exercising an independent authority by virtue of the office. This idea that constables possess an independent duty to the law importantly mediates the relations between constables within a force. Specifically, the requirement to obey lawful instructions is necessarily tempered by this independent responsibility to law – a responsibility which can be legitimately employed to support alternative courses of action, as the *Joy* case re-emphasized (*The Times*, 6 July, 1974).

Independent responsibility to the law, for upholding the law, in a situation where total law enforcement, for various reasons – inadequate knowledge of offences, lack of resources and so on – is simply not possible does not constitute a substantive mandate for Chief Constables; but the Blackburn judgements clarify the position. Broadly these establish that a chief officer must seek the enforcement of the law where offences are apprehended and that failure to do so will justify the intervention of the courts; but that the courts will not interfere in the disposition of the force, though they may indicate matters for consideration by a Chief of Police, since the Chief Constable has an independent discretion in these matters and is answerable only to the law. In other words, so long as efforts are made across the range of laws, in line with the general mandate to uphold the law, particular emphases or priorities remain within the independent discretion of the Chief Constable to determine. Certainly, the Chief Constable's view of Home Office circulars confirms this:

> If the Home Secretary is going to be called to the House of Commons for something that a chief officer of police has done, then that chief officer of police will be a darn fool not to take into account what the Home Office policy is in respect of certain things, and that's really what that one comes down to, that particular circular [a reference to a Home Office circular concerning access to police records] ... Now there are other

circulars which come down, which probably are ... solely of
guidance and which you could ignore, with impunity, if you
wanted to ... Now he can't tell us what to do in an operational
field, he can't tell us that we *shall* arrest prostitutes, or we
shan't arrest prostitutes, that's a decision we have to take.

Whilst an empirical examination of the system at work is
necessary before the precise nature of the structural interrelation-
ships can be unravelled, we can, in line with our hypothesis, begin
to point to distinctive aspects of these arrangements and their
likely broad relationship to our key structures. Take, first, the
responsibility of the Chief Constable to accept the supervision of
key bodies which express their duties in terms of 'adequate and
efficient' policing: the Police Authority and the Home Secretary.
It is perhaps this dimension of the Chief Constable's obligations
which fits most closely into the discourse of what we call 'rational-
scientific' management, the discipline of exact procedure and
regularized information which aims to produce effective and
calculable results in organizations of a bureaucratic tendency. The
impulse to produce 'adequate and efficient' policing can be traced
historically to the bureaucratization of the New Police in which the
Home Secretary figured significantly. Our present interest
however is to see how this particular discourse with its specific
lines of institutional accountability penetrates the decision-making
of the Chief Constable and exerts specific influence on the process
of policy consideration within the force.

On the other hand, there are those responsibilities of the Chief
Constable deriving from the positioning of the police within the
structure of legal duties, powers and discretionary acts. Here the
lines of accountability flow outward to the legal system, comprising a mixture of statute and case law as well as a web of institutions
and offices that constitute legal authority for the police. Our
hypothesis is that this legal institutional connection will employ
different discursive terms and thus point up a contrast with the
discourse of 'rational-scientific' management. While the latter
aspires to a purely rational and universal authority based on
objective inquiry and a calculation of effects, the discourse of law
enshrines a more supple and particular gradation of authority:
things which *must* be done, things which *may* be done, compelling
and permissive powers, duty and discretion intimately intermin-
gled. This difference has substantial implications for our understanding of what constitutes 'policy' in police practice, since it
raises the possibility of different approaches to policy consideration, and different outcomes, depending on the definition of

issues as 'administrative' or 'operational'. If we expect the former to draw on a discourse of 'rational-scientific' management, we expect policy consideration in the domain of legal obligations to draw on a quite different idea, of common-sense decision-making, backed by a notion of discretion which is a legacy of the principle of constabulary independence.

More shadowy in the formal institutional arrangements, there exists none the less a traditional and customary assumption which implies an obligation on the police to be seen to respond to community opinion. This obligation is given statutory recognition in the new Police and Criminal Evidence Act 1984. The belief in 'policing by consent', in harnessing public goodwill, remains as much an habitual feature of the police scene today as it did in the era of the first commissioners of the Metropolitan Police, with their celebrated advice to police officers, recommending a modest and patient exercise of power. The democratic dimension to policing, with its characteristic language of 'community relations', 'public contact', 'liaison' and 'consultation', enjoys a long-standing place in the lexicon of police accountability, especially in relation to beat-work, which forms the preferred mode of 'community policing' in its modern as well as its traditional guises. Here our objective is to inquire how and to what degree the democratic dimension is incorporated in the process of policy consideration. Such an examination will contribute to an understanding of the degree to which the democratic aspirations of beat-work are reflected in the central decision-making processes of the force. Does policy, in relation to either 'administrative' or 'operational' issues, emerge from 'consultation', 'liaison' and so on? Whilst we cannot answer the question here, we can suggest that the impact of the democratic structure on policy will partly depend on its ability to mesh with the discourse of 'rational-scientific' management or occupational 'common sense'. At first sight the fact that neither the discourse of rational-scientific management nor that of *occupational* common sense has a natural 'home' in the lay public would suggest that democratic influences, under normal circumstances, will not be great.

Policy: a Specific Definition

As we suggested in setting out the hypotheses stemming from other approaches, a conventional conception of policy assumes that for each force practice there is a definite set of principles which form an authoritative guide to action. Thus for community relations, or racial attacks, for example, we should expect in each case a series of statements outlining certain questions and containing some definite answers. Yet, in general, we found that the various institutional sites (conferences, meetings and 'policy' files) where policy was discussed did not routinely involve the making, or revision, of such statements; rather, 'policy' was an umbrella term for discussions and statements which only in limited and specific cases approached a degree of definiteness and authoritativeness that we could reconcile with the conventional conception.

Given this starting point – the absence of an adequate definition – we define policy as *an authoritative statement signifying a settled practice on any matter relevant to the duties of the Chief Constable*. 'Authoritative' refers to the source of policy (the Chief and his senior officers), whilst 'statement' distinguishes description from practice. By 'signifying a settled practice', however, we intended that policy point towards a practice, a practice moreover which is more than simply immediate or temporary. The final part of the definition is included in recognition of the statutory position giving the Chief Constable his responsibility for policy that we have just outlined.

This definition enables us to differentiate policy from other instruments available to the Chief Constable and his senior officers. These other instruments include advice, command, supervision, discipline, deployment and training – in short, *all* the other means at the disposal of a Chief Constable which enable him to fulfil his statutory duties. Policy is one *specific* instrument at the Chief Constable's disposal, and our definition attempts to clarify its specificity.

An example of what would constitute policy, if the above still seems a little abstract, would be a statement made by the Chief Constable or one of his senior officers that 'Resident beat officers [the 'operational' arm of community policing] will not be taken off their beats except in exceptional circumstances.' This 'authoritative statement' clearly 'signifies a settled practice' since it has direct implications for the deployment practices of the Superintendents (that they must not use RBOs as a reserve of manpower), implications which are clearly intended to be more than temporary.

Other Managerial Instruments of Control

Advice, Command, Supervision, Discipline, Deployment, Training

The meaning of the above terms is unproblematic since their meanings in this context do not differ from their conventional

meanings. But by defining them in relation to our definition of
policy, and then offering illustrations, we hope to clarify further
the specificity of policy as a managerial instrument of control.

We take *advice* to mean authoritative statements, which either
do not unequivocally signify a particular practice (for example, an
exhortation to 'do your best' or 'improve relations with the public')
or, when they do, signify one which is not settled or general.

Like policy, *command* (or 'instruction') refers to an 'authoritative statement'; but, unlike policy, such statements signify
immediate or temporary and not necessarily settled practice.
Obvious examples are direct commands by senior officers at
demonstrations, where, as the Deputy Chief Constable (DCC)
put it:

> You couldn't possibly police a National Front meeting with
> every individual officer acting at his own discretion ... The
> sergeant says, 'Lads [sic], you stand there and don't move, link
> arms and stay there', and that's it, and they unquestionably take
> the order, and that's our strength.

Supervision refers to all the attempts, indirect and direct, from
the keeping of paper records to direct observation and inspection,
to ensure that advice, commands, orders, policy and so on are
complied with. In this force, the preferred relationship is clearly
'caring' and one based on trust, as the DCC attests:

> Q. How effective do you think the pocket-book is as a means
> of supervision?
>
> DCC: Well ... it's got a role to play because obviously you've
> got to record things in your pocket-book because that's
> the way in which you give evidence, and you've got to
> use other notebooks for traffic and that sort of thing ...
> They ought to be supervised, all books, all charge sheets
> and everything ought to be subject to regular inspection
> by Superintendents ... but I see supervision as a much
> more caring sort of a role ... not a 'trying to catch people
> out' role and that sort of thing, but somebody who has
> got extra experience ... who is looking after somebody
> for the good of that individual and the good of the
> service and everybody's good.

Discipline is what needs to be invoked when the 'trust' breaks
down, as a 'last resort', according to the Chief Constable:

> Now discipline, I believe, should be very much like the law of
> the moving motor car. It ought to be the last thing that you

impose, you ought to be able to encourage people and . . . to try and train them . . . to persuade them, that the way to do things is this, but if in the final analysis they aren't going to do it, then somehow you've got to impose some discipline on them.

Deployment refers to the placing of particular officers in particular posts or positions, either temporarily, as in policing a football match, or more permanently, such as the transfer of officers to the CID or promotions. It is clearly an adjunct to discipline, since one form of punishment is to remove an offending officer from a particular post, most seriously in demotion. It is also an adjunct to supervision, since promotion is about ensuring the right officers are in the appropriate positions. As such, it is a very important mechanism of influence, as the Chief Constable admits.

I remember an old Chief Constable once telling me, and I'm sure he was right . . . when you become a Chief Constable . . . you'll find that murders and rapes and arsons will keep you out of bed at night, but, he said, what will keep you awake at night is promotions and discipline, and I think he's probably right . . . With discipline you are affecting not only a man's [sic] career and livelihood, but his wife and family as well very often . . . And promotions, you are setting the future of your force. If you don't do that well, you put the wrong people into positions of authority, then the efficiency of the force obviously gets kicked, and you're the final arbiter in that kind of thing.

The key to ensuring that advice and commands will be unnecessary, is the internalization of good standards. *Training* is seen as the means for this purpose, not least because of the high level of discretion given individual officers, a result of the independence of the office of constable, as the Chief Constable recognizes:

You can only lay down guidelines [about discretion] and hope that people will use their discretion wisely. You can to some extent train people for it . . . You can give them case studies and all that sort of business, and argue them out in the classroom, but in the final analysis we've got to accept that the decision whether he [sic] should arrest or not will be taken by an individual constable out in the street, and the only way you can . . . can control his behaviour, is by . . . good training.

Let us now return to the distinctive and specific instrument of policy and its consideration.

The Process of Policy Consideration

Widening the scope of the phrase 'the policy-making process' to talk instead of *the process of policy consideration* allows us to conceptualize not simply the *inauguration* of new policy (the *making* of policy in the strict sense and a restricted event, empirically speaking) but *all* the occasions when a policy matter is brought to the attention of significant groups inside and outside the force for the purposes of reminder, clarification, review, or information. Being able to conceptualize all these occasions enables us to make sense of all the policy-relevant data we examined – and not simply of a tiny proportion of it concerned with the inauguration of policy. More specifically, it enables us to identify occasions when policy is reviewed and then changed, as against other occasions when existing policy, or lack of it, is simply considered and left substantially unchanged. This distinction could not have been established without the expanded notion of 'policy consideration'.

It is important, in order fully to appreciate what follows, to be absolutely clear about what we mean by *policy, policy-making* and *the process of policy consideration*. So, at the risk of repetition, a summary may be useful at this point. When we talk of policy being an authoritative statement signifying a settled practice, we intend that for a statement to qualify as policy it must satisfy all the criteria in the definition; where any criterion is absent we are not talking about policy. The definition of policy, therefore, does not include statements made by senior officers which are invisible beyond the immediate circle to which they are directed (such as supervisory advice), nor statements which do not signify a practice (such as an announcement of the need for better relations with the public *tout court*), nor, finally, statements which signify practices which are not meant to be settled or continuous (such as a direct command). When we talk of policy-*making* we refer to the inauguration of new policy, which is but one moment in the wider process of policy *consideration* – a process which can draw upon a whole gamut of resources and result in reminders and information about, or review and clarification of, existing policy, as well as the making of policy.

In order to analyse our data about policy, it will prove helpful to break down the process of policy consideration into a number of significant elements. These elements will enable us to pose analytically a series of important questions about the policy matter at issue, for example: how does it come to the attention of those who consider it, how is it considered and how is it concluded? They will also enable us to answer, for example: who brings it to attention, considers it and concludes it? And what brings it to attention, what is it considered to be and in what form is it concluded? We suggest that these questions can be combined to provide a format for guiding discussion of the various forms of policy consideration we shall later deal with.

The elements which will enable us to answer such questions amount to seven. The first element, which enables us to address the question of *what brings the matter to attention initially*, and hence within the process of policy consideration, we shall call the SOURCE. The second element, which enables us to answer the questions of *how the matter comes to the attention of those who consider it, and of who brings it to attention*, concerns the immediate means by which the matter is made known to those involved in the process of policy consideration. We call this the element of REPORTING. A particularly critical element is that of INITIAL DEFINITION, our third element, since it is this that enables us to clarify later what type of outcome (in policy terms) has occurred as a result of policy consideration. This element enables us to answer the question of *what the issue is considered to be*. The element of DISCUSSION, our fourth element, allows us to answer the question of *who considers the matter* since it covers the contributions of all discussants in the process of policy consideration. INQUIRY, our fifth element, considers the distinctive contribution of inquiry to the knowledge available to discussants and enables us to answer the question of *how the matter is considered*. The sixth element, DECISION-MAKING, is obviously crucial to the whole enterprise, since upon it depends the final definition of the issue under consideration and hence the practice of policework – or combination of such practices – brought forward as relevant to that issue. For our purposes in particular, this element is critical because it enables us to characterize finally the type of policy consideration undertaken in any particular process of consideration, whether it be an inaugural injunction or reminder, or for clarification, review, or information – in short, whether it be an example of policy-making, or one of consolidating existing policy in some way. This sixth element clearly enables us to answer the three related questions of *who concludes it*, *in what form* and *how*. Our final element, IMPLEMENTATION, whose form is prescribed by the decision, *similarly relates to the same three questions*.

Our definition of policy consideration requires us to make it slightly more concrete before examining 'the system working' in Chapters 7 and 8. We need particularly an outline of the institutional arrangements for the consideration of policy existing within the force, though we should remember that these arrangements are themselves within the Chief's discretion to determine and thus, strictly speaking, constitute aspects of the 'system working'. However, we wish merely to outline what these were during our research period, saving an analytical description of them 'in action' for the next two chapters. The principal institutional arrangements for the consideration of policy are: conferences or meetings (the terms are interchangeable); intra-force correspondence; orders; and files. Meetings are conducted at force, divisional, subdivisional and departmental level. The principal force meetings are the fortnightly Management Team meetings, the regular Chief Superintendents' and Subdivisional Superintendents' conferences and the monthly Joint Advisory Committee. At divisional level, the primary meetings are the fortnightly Chief Superintendent's senior officers' meeting and the regular divisional conferences open to all divisional officers. At subdivisional level there are the subdivisional Superintendent's senior officers' meeting and occasional subdivisional conferences open to all subdivisional officers. In addition, RBOs occasionally meet with the Superintendent to discuss problems.

Orders can be issued by Force HQ and by the divisions. Force standing orders are the standing instructions of the force, governing its organization, basic policies and systems, and 'are intended to be a series of guidelines, to advise and help officers better to perform their duties' (extract from Part 1 Police Order). Information concerned with the day-to-day running of the force is circulated in the form of police orders in three parts: Part 1 Orders, which are issued as necessary, are orders intended to become part of regular practice but ones which do not necessitate an item in force standing orders; Part II, which are issued weekly, contain personnel details – postings, transfers, resignations and so on; Part III, also issued weekly, refer to sporting and social events. Force operational orders, which deal with arrangements for major events involving two or more divisions, are issued as necessary. Headquarters circulars are used to control the flow of administrative information and instructions emanating from headquarters and are intended only for Superintendents and above. Occasional other force publications include, for example, contingency plans for major incidents. Divisional orders are issued by divisional Chief Superintendents about essentially local matters; divisional instructions are used to implement force orders when appropriate, and also for small, operational, divisional matters. At the level of the subdivision, memos, not orders, are required.

The system of intra-force correspondence – the issuing and

receipt of miscellaneous memoranda, reports and so on – is an institution for the consideration of policy, as are the files wherein such correspondence, along with matters discussed in meetings or elsewhere and correspondence with outsiders, is routinely deposited. These institutional arrangements, in different ways and different degrees for different matters, as we shall see, constitute the component forms of the force policy process: the process by which policy-relevant matters are signalled, discussed, decided and implemented.

Having spelled out the formal position and its relationship to our key structures, defined policy and the process of policy consideration, and outlined the component institutional arrangements wherein such a process takes place, we are now in a position to examine the system in action. But, as should now be clear, before getting to a consideration of particular policies, we must first describe and analyse the routine of the key institutional arrangements, namely, the meetings or conferences, and the policy files.

Notes

1 Police Authorities are bodies which, in the case of county forces such as the one presently studied, are composed of two-thirds elected councillors and one-third magistrates.

2 For contrasting readings of the 1964 Police Act's implications for Chief Constables, compare Jefferson and Grimshaw (1984b) with Marshall (1965) or Lustgarten (1986).

3 *Fisher* v. *Oldham* (1930) 2 KB 364; *R.* v. *Metropolitan Police Commissioner*, ex parte Blackburn [1968] 2 QB 118; [1968] 1 All E. R. 763; *R.* v. *Metropolitan Police Commissioner*, ex parte Blackburn (No. 3), [1973] 1 QB 241; [1973] 1 All E. R. 324; and endorsed more recently in *R.* v. *Chief Constable of the Devon and Cornwall Constabulary*, ex parte Central Electricity Generating Board [1981] 3 All E. R. 835. For a full discussion of the cases, their relation to the historical practice and their implications for the current position, see Jefferson and Grimshaw (1984b, pp. 14–58).

CHAPTER SEVEN

The System at Work I: Meetings

The Process of Policy Consideration: Analysing the Meetings

In what follows the intention is to offer analytical portraits of the conferences and meetings based on our field observations. In doing so we shall utilize the constitutive elements – source, reporter and so on – we earlier outlined, highlight the type of policy – 'administrative' or 'operational' – routinely under consideration and summarize the kind of forum each is with respect to our three key structures: legal, work and democratic. We end the section with a summary –Table 7.1, quantifying the features of interest to us – and discuss it in relation to our observations.

The classification of agenda items in the following discussion is given full quantitative expression in the summary table. Items were assigned to the following classes: (1) operational, legal, deployment (grouped under the heading 'operational, etc.'); (2) establishment, equipment, supply, finance and conditions (grouped under the heading 'establishment, etc.'); (3) procedure, inspection, organization and systems (grouped under the heading 'procedure, etc.'); (4) recruitment, promotion and training (grouped under the heading 'recruitment, etc.'); (5) extra-police and unclassified (grouped under the heading 'other'). Jointly, (2), (3) and (4) comprise 'administrative' items. As we shall see, these main headings can be related to the principal discourses of policy consideration.

The Chief Constable's Management Team

Management Team meets fortnightly. It is chaired by the Chief Constable (CC) and attended by the Deputy Chief Constable

(DCC), all Assistant Chief Constables (ACCs) and the force accountant. Minutes are taken by a Superintendent member of the CC's headquarters administrative staff. Attendance is expected, and only unavoidable absences will produce a less than complete attendance. If the CC is unavailable, however, the meeting will be rearranged.

Matters discussed include any matters related to the force, but tend to be oriented towards administrative rather than operational matters (75 per cent versus 10 per cent). Novel operational matters, such as an item about the new operational briefing scheme and one concerning 'police/public-relations ride-along programme' (an item about whether to allow the public to 'ride along', US style, with beat officers as part of a public-relations exercise), arise, as can more routine matters ('burglary squads', 'investigation of minor crime'). The implications of new legislation are also aired. But the staple items typically concern establishment, equipment, finance, conditions, procedures, inspection, organization, systems, recruitment, senior promotions and training, though the regular presence of 'extra-police' items – about traffic wardens, special constables, school crossing patrols, police surgeons and the like – should not be overlooked (16 per cent). The regular occurrence of 'financial' items compared with operational/legal ones doubtless explains the regular presence of the accountant and the routine absence of the Chief Prosecuting Solicitor.

The source of items can be field experiments (for example, 'operational briefing'), a Management Dept. project (for example, 'organization of traffic warden service'), a monitoring exercise (for example, 'review of authorized establishment'), reports from headquarters departments of problems encountered (for example, 'personnel carriers – hire'), requests for policy decisions (for example, 'time off for sport'), or statistical returns (for example, 'pipe band – balance sheets'). Problems with force routines which appear to indicate a need for review or fresh initiative (for example, the question of divisional identification in public-order situations) can also become the subject of a report. These 'internal' sources of agenda items are supplemented, very occasionally, by external ones. In the five meetings attended we found seven such sources: the inner-city partnership, the funding agency in the case of a new area police project; the County Council in an item concerning the system of reading County Council papers for police-relevant matters; the Police Scientific Development Branch in the case of protective helmets and other equipment; a United States police force in an item inviting an officer exchange programme; HM Inspector of Constabulary on the subject of his proposed visit; the co-ordinating committee of the local victim support scheme on the question of the condition of police liaison with such schemes; and the 'announcement' of a cut in petrol and diesel supplies. Overwhelmingly, sources, whether internal or external, are organizational and occupational rather than 'legal' or 'democratic'. The only obviously legal source of any item in the five meetings attended was the new legislation on wearing seat-belts, which in the event excluded police officers and so the item hinged on whether there should none the less be a force requirement to do so. As for a democratic source, this enters only indirectly through the mediation of finance or through the CC's concern not to have a critical finger pointed at the force, a reason he cites for having a formal (rather than an *ad hoc*) arrangement for hiring personnel carriers, after putting the contract out for tender, in one meeting attended.

Items are introduced by the CC, the DCC, or the appropriate ACC – perhaps partly dependent on the stage in the cycle an item is at, for once the CC has initially introduced an item it then tends to get farmed out to the relevant ACC. Financial items may be introduced by the accountant – 'management control budget', for example – or by non-team members responsible for particular inquiries – for example, a Chief Inspector in connection with the organization of the traffic warden service.

Inquiry and written report usually precede the introduction of an item (in 78 per cent of items). This means that rational-scientific management techniques of one sort or another are much in evidence; it also means, as we saw, that items are routinely deferred for the completion of the awaited report (63 per cent). But if the rational-scientific report provides the staple basis of discussion, the question of practical implications ensures there is a 'common-sense' input to the discussion: for example, on one occasion the DCC's half-joking reference to using an 'old stager' to 'sell' the new operational briefing scheme.

Apart from team members, discussants tend to include all parties likely to be affected before the final decision. Thus the reactions of the Chief Superintendents and Superintendents will usually be sought before a decision on those questions with operational implications, ensuring a further common-sense input. For example, decision on the question of divisional identification in public-order situations – a matter on which the CC is far from persuaded anyway – is left until the reaction of Superintendents at their conference is assessed. Matters concerning conditions and equipment may be deferred until the views of the staff associations have been sought. An item on protective clothing, for example, was deferred in order that the Operations Department could comment on the Police Scientific Development Branch report, and so that discussions with the Police Federation could take place.

Inquiries are usually made by the relevant ACCs using the facilities for which each is responsible. The Management Department (MD) is fairly prominent in this process. In one meeting, for example, items reliant on its inquiry included 'the organization of the traffic warden service', 'the use of teleprinter message switching system', 'radio communications – speech privacy', 'divisional identification – public order situations' and 'operational briefing'. Rational-scientific forms of inquiry may well be supplemented by an examination of the existing practices of other forces, especially in the case of some doubt about force policy. In one example, the unease about the practical implication of the new 'time-off for sport policy' prompts an inquiry into the Metropolitan Police Districts' practice, since, as the 'Home Office force', its policies and practices are taken as an acceptable standard.

Decisions are made by the CC even though he will listen to team-member views or, in some instances, the views of his operational commanders and the staff associations. But unless he is persuaded by a well-reasoned case he will override even a majority viewpoint. The 'use of force transport – sport and social functions' and 'time off for sport' items on one occasion both demonstrate this aspect of CC decision-making. His prime consideration that policies be such that no one can 'point a finger', neither the public nor the statutory authorities, means, effectively, policies which are lawful, rational, efficient, cost-effective and fair. This consideration prioritizes scientific rationality. However, his willingness to get operational opinion where appropriate, which demonstrates a concern that policies also be acceptable within the force, ensures practical common sense is not overlooked either. Decisions taken in Management Team are implemented in various ways: a police order or circular, a personal instruction, a field trial prior to force-wide implementation, or a decision to consult with the divisional or subdivisional commanders. Thus not all decisions give rise to policy in the strict sense. Though many items are weighted towards the administrative, the 'democratic' structure retains a mediate influence through the desire of the CC to produce defensible policy. In general, however, we have to look to the other structures to explain how policy is considered here.

The Chief Superintendents' Conference

The Chief Superintendents' Conference represents the highest institutional forum of policy consideration below the Chief Constable's Management Team. The sources of the items mainly lie in ongoing reviews of force practice, some prompted by relations with external colleagues and salient representative bodies. The reporting of the items rests mainly with the CC, his DCC and ACCs rather than with the Chief Superintendents. Sources of items reflect the pattern of reporters' activities; complaints and discipline, community relations, technical schemes and the expert management of force housekeeping are important to Management Team members, as we have seen.

The definition of policy issues is given by the powerful reporters of Management Team who in discussion seek, by persuasion if necessary, to secure the consent of the Chief Superintendents. For example, a Chief Superintendent raised doubts about the principles of agreed 'manning' levels, in that discretion was removed from the 'man on the patch'. The CC replied: 'I absolutely agree. But Superintendents must be able to justify overtime when it is vital . . . Chief Superintendents should go round and see how *well* they are exercising their judgement.'

The broad categorization of items is related to the pattern of sources to an extent. For example, a Police Federation suggestion for an organization review is put forward for opinions to be gleaned on its merits because Chief Superintendents represent the CC in talking to Federation representatives. Again, the consent of the CC to a new national system relating to identification of people in custody entailed discussion of its implications for the force's procedures in that area. The CC and his DCC transmit items of concern to supervisors in the individual cases of complaint and discipline they deal with. CC: 'Nobody in the police station saw an injury to a prisoner, yet ten minutes after leaving there was blood coming from his head. I reduced an Inspector to sergeant. I'll leave you to reflect on that.'

The detailed consideration of items reflects assumptions about the shape of particular practices and their scope for direction: that altered working arrangements require discussion with the Federation representatives and some common-sense assessment of the likely reaction of officers in actual working practice; that highly technical systems require technical consideration; that individual disciplinary cases signal failings in supervision. It is possible also to link the items where a pattern of problem-solving presents itself, for example, where the experience of disciplinary investigations and ethnic friction with police induces the DCC to seek to initiate schemes of training in the appropriate operations.

The role of inquirer falls to Chief Superintendents and other discussants as the matter falls within their remit, with provision for the establishment of bodies such as working parties. Inquiry is undertaken in 30 per cent of items. Where global statistical returns are used, straightforward figures indicate cause for concern, or allay such concern. A Chief Superintendent had been asked to report on the relative evidence of damage to places of worship visited by racial groups:

> CS: It's fifty/fifty [between black and white] in the poor area we looked at. It seems there's no difference between black and white in terms of damage ... The poor area is the point.
>
> DCC: Overall figures in the force show a 'black' or 'brown' preponderance.

Decisions reside with the CC or his DCC, though given the type of policy consideration they are not necessarily conclusive. Where, as here, it is the practice of the CC to assign operational control over deployment and work arrangements to Chief Superintendents within their particular domain, the Chief Superintendents may, for example, be asked for a collective opinion on the structure of deployments between departments. This, in representing a standard opinion on the general pattern of deployment, appears to have considerable weight in determining the CC's policy in that area. Thus, after discussion, DCC: 'So I will put it to the Chief Constable, about appointments [to the CID] because it's in authorized establishment. You all agree?' (Agreement is signified). Similarly Chief Superintendents are given the power to dispose of their pool of overtime and to negotiate locally agreed 'manning' levels where necessary.

The broad categorization of issues does not alter much at the decision-making stage. Where individual matters are felt to hinge on supervision then the decision amounts generally to a motivational appeal, exhorting, praising, linking the proper practice with some consensual value such as public expectation, the mediated way the democratic structure enters. Some may appear off-the-cuff as a result of a discussion. The type of policy consideration is aimed at explaining and discussing existing policy, including initiatives and experiments, whether decided or evolving. The implementation of the decision rests with the appropriate agent – an inquiry by assigned agents into a detailed or technical question, or the Chief Superintendents taking notice of the orders, advice and information of superior officers.

The conference as a process of policy consideration illustrates the effective control exercised by the CC and his DCC in that the conference contains the most senior officers outside Management Team. If there were a great many distinctive items and definitions coming from Chief Superintendents to influence force policy we would expect them to be here, yet they are in fact relatively absent; only in policy matters closely bearing on their already policy-defined responsibilities do the Chief Superintendents have weight. The substantive topics of the conference give some relative prominence to operational questions (45 per cent of items), confirming the scope of operational decision-making which is accorded to Chief Superintendents, in particular the divisional commanders. Once again, the important influences are internal, with the 'external' democratic structure relatively absent.

The Subdivisional Superintendents' Conference

The subdivisional Superintendents' conference is a regular, periodic meeting between the Chief Constable (who chairs the meeting), some members of his Management Team and the subdivisional Superintendents, though some department heads and divisional Chief Superintendents also attend. The range of items covered is wide, commensurate with the broad brief of subdivisional commanders, and fairly balanced as between 'operational' (39 per cent) and 'administrative' (45 per cent) items – the remainder (16 per cent) being 'other' items. Absent, however, at least from the two meetings we witnessed, were any items dealing with establishment, recruitment, promotion, or training.

Though the agenda is open for all participants to contribute items, it tends to be dominated by items introduced by the CC and his Management Team members, who between them introduce some 80 per cent of the items – despite the CC's earnest desire that the meetings be occasions when issues 'from below' be given an airing. This tendency towards a 'top-down' introduction reflects the routine sources of agenda items: complaints from departments; discipline cases (for example, pocket-book entries); new initiatives undergoing field trial (for example, 'senior officers – paging equipment'); management projects (for example, 'operational briefing') and headquarters monitoring of administrative and financial matters (for example, 'budgetary control and overtime'). Other sources include changes in legislation (for example, the wearing of seat-belts), and external agencies: bodies with whom the police liaise regularly (for example, the Education Welfare Service); bodies with complaints to make about police action; and representative bodies like the County Council with an obvious interest, financial and otherwise, in police decisions. Thus 'organizational', 'legal' and 'democratic' bodies are all possible sources of agenda items.

The disparate nature of the origins of items ensures that both 'common sense' and 'rational-scientific' discourses are utilized. Initiatives undergoing field trial, for example, are discussed in common-sense terms, as in the discussion of the item dealing with a proposed scheme for the identification of officers at public-order situations. Thus discussion ranges widely and fairly indiscriminately over the comparative advantages and disadvantages of divisional letters versus coloured stickers, of permanent badges versus plastic 'stick-ons', over the problems of identifying particular groups like the SPG which might be picked out leading to 'unnecessary complaints' and over whether divisional identification helps officers feel part of the division or reintroduces an outdated parochialism. The discussion is eventually wound up by the CC, who says there appears to be a case for some form of identification at public-order situations, and remits the item to the item's introducer, the Management Department Chief Superintendent, for a fully costed report with firm recommendations. The reorganization of the vehicle fleet, on the other hand is, presented in the technical-rational terms of relative cost-effectiveness (discussed more fully in Chapter 8). Items are discussed by conference, though the role of the chair, relevant ACCs and departmental heads is prominent. On the other hand, items involving outside agencies necessarily introduce, if only mediately, certain outside bodies as discussants, as was the case with an item discussing the undertaking that had been given to the local Passenger Transport Executive that subdivisional Superintendents would attend its meetings when the presence of a police officer would be beneficial – for example, when discussing assaults on bus crews.

Reports produced by Management Team members or department heads sometimes precede items, as when the CC reported the grievances that had come out of a meeting with the representatives of the non-manual civilian staff. Or discussion occasionally produces a request for a fuller report, as happened, for example, after a discussion about delays in servicing police cars: delays caused partly by an understrength (because poorly paid) mechanics section. The CC ended the discussion with a request for a comprehensive report of the mechanics' wage rates together with the necessary evidence supporting an increase in the scale. The ongoing nature of many report-based items ensures that 60 per cent of the items are 'matters arising', and some 17 per cent are deferred for further inquiry or discussion with other bodies not represented at conference (for example, the police staff association in the case of an item on whether police officers should be made to wear seat-belts, as an example to the public, even though the new legislation exempted them). Items which refer to matters where policy already exists may lead to the CC, after discussion, re-instructing Superintendents concerning the relevant standing orders or policy. For example, a discussion about some problems arising in connection with the submission of exhibits to the forensic science laboratory was concluded with the CC reminding the Superintendents to ensure the procedure was complied with. Alternatively, as was the case with the overtime item, the CC may simply advise them (of the financial situation in this case) and leave the matter of particular decisions on how to achieve the saving on overtime to their discretion. Instructions will generally be accom-panied by exhortation and an outline of the necessity for the action proposed. A good example of this was the CC's patient explanation of the purpose of pocket-books as both a record of original entries *and* a diary. Views will be sought to establish the consensus on particular matters, but final decisions will not be taken simply on the basis of consensus. The CC was thus willing to override the apparent (common-sense) consensus that drivers were losing confidence in a particular vehicle, because the (rational-scientific) evidence did not appear to support the consensus. He noted the general complaint, but overrode it.

The implementation of whatever decisions result from the conference takes either the form, just mentioned, of a direct instruction to do something or to supervise others, or that of 'advice'. Either form is usually accompanied by a motivational 'hard sell'.

Whilst the conference is certainly used to reinforce existing policies, it also seems to serve the function of acquainting the central policy apparatus with the views of Superintendents. By giving Superintendents the opportunity to report back on and discuss field experiments, by using it as a forum to explain and discuss innovations that have been or are to be established, Management Team can hope to be informed as to possible difficulties. At the same time, the team may see the occasion as important in acquainting Superintendents with the difficulties of management and the discourse of rational-scientific management. The problem is how to prevent the meeting turning into a prescriptive monologue: a danger the CC clearly recognized in his own words, spoken to one of us after one such meeting: 'I hope it wasn't just a harangue.' Either way, the 'democratic structure' remains relatively uninfluential.

The Joint Advisory Committee

The JAC is comprised of representatives from Management Team (MT), the Superintendents' Association, the Federation Joint Branch Board, a co-opted member of the force books and forms subcommittee, the force accountant and the CC when available. It is chaired by the DCC or, in his absence, an ACC, and it meets approximately once a month.

Matters dealt with by the JAC comprise, almost exclusively, 'administrative' items of one kind or another, with only some 7 per cent comprising 'operational' or 'other' items. More specifically, items are most often related to conditions and facilities. Thus items relating to catering and equipment, allowances, refreshment arrangements and so on form the staple of the agenda, comprising some 60 per cent of the total. More surprising, perhaps, is the routine presence of items relating to forms, which collectively comprise some 25 per cent of the items. However, since form filling represents an important, and growing, part of a police officer's duties, it can be seen as a 'condition of service'. Moreover, there is the further advantage of operational feedback that discussion in such a forum necessarily gives.

Agenda items tend to originate from the committee's own subcommittees (for example, the catering subcommittee; the uniform and equipment subcommittee), and from certain force subcommittees, particularly the books and forms subcommittee. Subcommittee membership, like the JAC itself, reflects the composition of the force – federated ranks, Superintendents, management, relevant technical specialisms and financial advisers. More indirectly, items have their origins in operational experiences having a bearing on conditions (for example, mobile canteens at major incidents). Given the operational source of many items, and the need to consider the practical implications of items whose source lies within the subcommittees mentioned, the dominant form of the discourse is 'common sense'. Questions of *who* should be issued with protective clothing (should all be issued with reinforced helmets or just new recruits and others when one of the existing two helmets became due for replacement?), *how much* should be issued (was one set of thermal underwear sufficient for motor cyclists?), *how long* uniforms should be retained (once officers were appointed to the CID) and at *what level* of demand staffed canteens should be replaced by food-and-drink-vending machines and a self-service microwave oven – these and other questions are not easily amenable to 'rational-scientific' debate, except cost-accounting. Indeed, financial considerations loom large and can be decisive (hence the important presence of the force accountant). The discussion about the appropriate thermal underwear allowance for motor cyclists, for example, was resolved by the announcement that the Home Office had no objection to a single one-off payment, provided the police committee agreed. On the other hand, issuing protective helmets to all officers was clearly foundering on a financial rock when we left it; there was no money in the budget for such a contingency, according to the accountant; moreover, there was the problem of what to do with the large stock of existing helmets, according to another committee member.

Most items are introduced through the chair or other MT members of the relevant subcommittees. The co-opted books and forms subcommittee member, who is also the head of the Management Department, also figures prominently as a 'reporter'. Items are discussed by the committee – often in relation to prior recommendations by appropriate subcommittees, or the views of appropriate senior officers; for example, matters affecting the CID (such as the format of the CID time book) will have first been discussed with the ACC (Crime). Where representatives wish for more consultation with members, or a MT member thinks it should be discussed at MT, or the CC is absent but wishes to speak to an item, these items are deferred (44 per cent overall). Where further inquiries or reports are necessary, these are conducted by the relevant representatives of the subcommittees or the appropriate ACCs. In a majority of instances (60 per cent) items will be discussed in relation to some previous inquiry or report.

Since the committee's status is advisory, the object of decision is to reach an agreement between the bodies represented which can form the basis of a 'joint' or agreed recommendation to the CC – who ultimately decides on the basis of agreed recommendations advanced by the committee, though, in certain instances, another member of MT with the relevant responsibility – ACC (Crime) in the case of 'scenes of crime register' – might do so. The decision-making process takes the form of an attempt to balance out preferred conditions against demands imposed by various duties and/or finance, as well as, sometimes, force requirements for forms of standardization. This attempt to optimize as between the preferred and the feasible is necessarily a negotiative process. As such, its discourse is essentially composed of competing common senses.

The type of policy consideration conducted by the JAC as an institution of policy is clearly advisory, and then only in relation to the restricted range of topics with which it deals. It has, therefore, a limited role in relation to policy, though it may perform an important function for the constituencies it represents over conditions of service. Even here, it has no powers to implement any of its agreed recommendations. For example, the apparently simple question of when ties need not be worn, an item with no financial implications, had still to be deferred for the views of MT. Routinely absent from consideration are matters relating to 'the law' or 'the public'. Influences are purely organizational and occupational, and the primary purpose is the achievement of a consensus in the matters which come before it.

The Divisional Chief Superintendent's Senior Officers' Meeting

The Divisional Chief Superintendent's fortnightly meeting of senior officers includes all the divisional senior officers above the rank of Inspector. The sources of items can be divided into those concerned with administration of law, those within the force and the division and those outside representative bodies relating to the police in some way. Reporting is usually performed by the Chief Superintendent where matters of force policy are directly introduced, by his deputies where there are failures to comply with existing policy and by the other Superintendents or their deputies where matters arise in connection with the working of force or divisional policy.

The definition of the issue varies. For example, in legal matters linked to the administration of law, the definition tends to reflect the role of the police as independent legal agents; the role of prosecuting solicitors in offering advice – the starting-point in defining an item – might be accordingly distinguished in discussion from that of the police in prosecution decisions. The source may have an impact on the development of the definition; a point on the subject by the CC and accordingly endorsed by the Chief Superintendent had a good deal of weight.

> CS: The Chief Constable is saying that if [a case is] doubtful, then take advice [on prosecution] ... We have to work on the DPP principle – a fifty/fifty chance of success. The Chief Prosecuting Solicitor works on it. We're not giving up the right to mark up prosecutions.

By comparison, discussion on a suggestion from the local prosecuting solicitors that their advice be obtained when prosecution files are prepared was closed by remarks from two Superintendents which stressed the simply *advisory* function of such consultation, a point on which all present seemed to concur. The framework of legal powers and prerogatives is similarly applied to a request from a representative body. Here licensees of public houses concerned about trouble-makers had their request for action referred to the prosecuting solicitors, which pointed out the legal limitations on the police's freedom of action.

A major part of the items are concerned with the deployment of personnel (discussed more fully in Chapter 8) – the filling of vacancies on transfer in respect of divisional and departmental posts; leave arrangements; and so on. These are discussed in terms of common-sense requirements, for example, the experience needed to undertake a post. An undercurrent in such discussions may be the bidding of the subdivisions for personnel resources. A Chief Superintendent consciously concerned to co-ordinate the work of subdivisions will take a strong interest in divisional operations and schemes which require such co-ordination. Football-match operational planning, a night-van scheme to cope with disorder, a shoplifting squad, community-relations training, a community-relations post: such schemes needing divisional co-ordination are defined in order to decide how to deal with any resource needs and to specify the work arrangements. Divisional community relations, defined as exchange of views, will introduce representative bodies as topics of discussion.

Inquiry takes various forms (though it is not prominent, being used in only 17 per cent of items). Thus the Detective Superintendent regularly reports the current detection rate, and a low figure may provoke discussion, but substantial variations mean the significance of a current figure is accordingly limited for the discussants. Significant inquiries with HQ are undertaken by the Chief Superintendent. The temporary co-option to the conference of a specialist is feasible, for example, the PC responsible for football arrangements.

Alongside legal, operational and deployment questions (48 per cent of items) there also rank 'administrative' issues of procedure, use of resources and so on, which are recognizable within any organization that accepts the obligations of scientific management (45 per cent of items). Hence buildings, accommodation and equipment are discussed in terms of practical work requirements. Monitoring of particular failings is done by the divisional deputies who, with a view to improvement, cite individual cases and make general inquiries into actual practice. The input of public agencies may be at this level.

> Supt: I've spoken to the local authority about their means of contacting us. They've taken short cuts – speaking to an

Inspector on the phone; the Inspector makes a report and we didn't know. [There was] even a case of an Inspector replying direct to the local authority [on behalf of] a Superintendent . . . This shouldn't be done.

Decisions rest finally with the Chief Superintendent though they are determined by his assigned role and his approach. Demands for immediate concrete arrangements tend to produce firm conclusions, but ongoing operational matters not concretely defined will be inconclusively discussed. The Chief Superintendent seeks to guard force policy, though reservations expressed in discussion about new policy may induce him to seek confirmation or reassurance from HQ. When introduction cards for RBOs were to be issued, the Chief Superintendent referred to the problem of impersonating officers, should these fall into the wrong hands, but he said that the matter had been looked into by the Management Department and accepted by the CC.

Chief Superintendent (CS)	Reservations?
Detective Chief Inspector (DCI)(1):	Yes
DCI (2):	Grave reservations.
DCI (1):	It's *most* useful for CID. But we stop them doing it.
CS:	Further inquiries are needed.

He may maintain his view on a concrete issue bearing on a specifically divisional policy against subdivisional doubts, but he may be loath to institute a policy of his own where normally separate subdivisional and unconnected practices are shown to diverge. The type of policy consideration is directed at ensuring compliance with force policy, and at concluding, where feasible, decisions on divisional policy. Implementation rests with the subdivisional Superintendents, for the most part, given the scope of their command in relation to the divisional resources as a whole. The form of implementation depends on the substantive demands of supervision, work arrangements and so on implied by the decision. The divisional Superintendents' meeting of senior officers therefore follows other conferences in focusing on a set of policy questions relevant to working practices and in maintaining the autonomy of the police in relation to the law and the public. It differs from them in the possible range of concrete operational and personnel arrangements that lie uniquely within the divisional Chief Superintendent's ambit and become the subject of policy discussion since they require the co-operation of subdivisional Superintendents. Once again, external democratic influences do not loom large.

The Divisional Conference

Divisional conferences are regular, periodic events open to all members of the division. The one attended was chaired by the divisional Chief Superintendent. Various HQ personnel were present – the DCC, an ACC, a Chief Superintendent from the MD, a DCI from the Special Branch and a training school Inspector – as were officers who could be spared from divisional work, those with flexible enough working arrangements (RBOs/CID) to suit themselves and others attending on overtime.

The official agenda was largely comprised of matters emanating from divisional HQ (8/10), with the remaining two from Force HQ: one a Special Branch reminder on the procedures for incidents involving aliens, and the other a training officer on police check-points. However, the presence of HQ staff inviting impromptu questions from the floor produced an 'unofficial' agenda of some thirteen items, more numerous in fact than the official one. This unofficial agenda ensured an opportunity for items to be raised from the floor, but also, equally importantly it appeared, for MT representatives to raise matters they wished to by way of reply. The DCC, for example, in response to a query from the floor about the slowness of a complaint investigation, promised to look it up, and then used it, quite openly, as a springboard to say what he wanted to about complaints and discipline generally, namely, 'Our discipline problems are not external [that is, the result of external complaints] but self-inflicted. The remedy is in your hands. I won't help those not fit to be policemen [sic].'

One consequence of this flexible agenda was that items covered a wide spectrum. Questions from the floor covered staffing, equipment, conditions, training, complaints, procedures and the cost of policing the local football club; those from the podium, supervision, standing orders, form completion, police vehicle accidents, crime, public liaison, training and the new police facilities at the local club. Whilst there is clearly considerable overlap here, the concern expressed about items tends to reflect its origin; thus the rank and file are concerned about inadequate resources, unsatisfactory procedures, unfavourable conditions and so on; management concerns centre on poor supervision, failure to follow standing orders, slow completion of forms, the rise in blameworthy accidents, the importance of public liaison and the detection rate.

Items from the floor were usually cast in the form of questions, often with a critical undercurrent, and sometimes quite overtly: 'Are we going to get an increase in establishment?' 'Are we all going to get issued with reinforced helmets? At [a particular event] the — police were much better off. They all had the same mac, boxes, shinpads. We looked a right shower.' Answers to these tended to stress operational benefits and justifications pertinent to the items in question. For example, after the Chief Superintendent had invited the DCC to add his comments to the item on 'criminal record forms and single centre reporting', an item which hinged on an unacceptably slow turnaround of the forms in question, the DCC said that he appreciated the paperwork build-up, 'but criminal record forms are vital operational forms. The accuracy of form filling helps the later apprehension of villains which you're all interested in – and so am I.' Operational common sense is, then, a key discursive touchstone, but often buttressed by statistical support as in the 'public-liaison' item. The DCC had been outlining various force community-relations projects, stressing that they are *not* soft options for oddball men [sic] but involve doing things *on top of* normal policework'. But he knew well enough that the only really convincing argument, one that meshes with operational common sense, is one that demonstrates its effectiveness in reducing crime:

> Statistics can be used to say anything, I know, but I just give you these statistics. In 19— crime in the force went down by 10 per cent. In the same year crime in the project subdivision went down by 28 per cent. The detection rate is higher [in the project location] than in the rest of the subdivision; the level of information fed in has gone up; the number of complaints has gone down; the incidence of vandalism and hooliganism has dropped.

A further example of operational common sense at the helm was evident in the Special Branch DCI's reply to a question about the problem of knowing who were aliens: 'Good guide is "funny names". Send all "funny names" on to the Immigration and Nationality Department.'

The source of items tended to echo the composition of the conference, with division and Force HQ, as well as the rank and file through intervention from the floor, represented. Items originating from Force HQ were introduced either directly by representatives present for that purpose – the DCI for the Special

Branch item, the training school Inspector, the Chief Superintendent from MD to encourage them to use the force suggestion
scheme and to remind them that the old 'stop-form' system was
being reintroduced – or indirectly, as in the case of the DCC and
ACC using 'question time' to introduce matters of concern to
HQ. Of the five items originating from the division, and actually
dealt with, four were introduced by either the Chief Superintendent or one of his Superintendents, with only one such item –
public liaison – being introduced by a much lower ranking officer,
namely a police sergeant. However, he was in fact the highest
ranking divisional public-liaison officer. The source of all items
was organizational or occupational; the public entered only
indirectly, as in the public liaison item, for example, and law not at
all.

Discussion of items theoretically involved all officers present;
but given the pressure of time (30 per cent of agenda items were
not dealt with), and the clear desire to ensure that representatives
from HQ had their say (a deference which may have had something to do with the fact that the HQ ACPO ranks were senior to
the chair), the chair and other managment representatives tended
to appropriate more of the 'talk time' available, not least because
the thirteen items from the floor were answered by the platform,
mostly by the DCC, until he left part-way through the meeting (a
departure which coincided with the arrival of an ACC). Since
items were not concerned with reaching a decision, the breadth of
discussion allowed was purely at the chair's discretion. Initiation
of inquiry resulted from discussion when questions were not
answered through lack of appropriate information. For example,
the ACC and the Chief Superintendent (MD) promised to find out
when a question from the floor about paying out wages at police
stations [to civilians] was met with incomprehension. On the other
hand, inquiry preceded the introduction of some items, typically
into statistical trends relevant to the item, for example, the trend in
'blameworthy' police vehicle accidents:

Divisional Deputy: [There have been] twenty-three accidents
[over a recent period]: one per week. [This
is] far too many.

DCC: In 19— panda drivers wrote off 25 per cent
of our panda fleet ... Blameworthy acci-
dents [have gone] up; 38 per cent of all
accidents [were] blameworthy in 19—.

Decisions were not reached in the conference. This was partly
because policy with respect to many of the items introduced had

already been set in other institutions. More importantly, perhaps, this was because the function of the conference is not that of policy-making. Rather it is an opportunity, for management, to explain and clarify policy, inform about new institutions, issue reminders about existing standing orders, persuade and cajole, exhort and motivate, re-emphasize and reiterate, proffer praise or harangue, and gauge rank-and-file feelings. For the rank and file, it is an opportunity to air grievances, seek justifications and explanations, express a view, let off steam and generally confront management on any issue. Since decisions are not taken here, the question of implementation does not arise. It is, in sum, a forum for a mutual 'taking into account' of the views of the other; more cynically, it is an exercise in public relations, with both force and divisional senior management offering themselves as willing 'Aunt Sallys' in exchange for the opportunity to 'hard-sell' force policy. Given this feature, the common-sense basis of discussion is hardly surprising. Only internal influences are prominent – though the democratic structure in the form of 'public acceptance' may be invoked, as we have seen elsewhere, to defend or justify force policy.

The Subdivisional Superintendent's Senior Officers' Meeting

The subdivisional Superintendent's officers' meeting is called and chaired by the Superintendent or his deputy and includes all those of Inspector rank, and the RBO sergeant. It is therefore the subdivisional equivalent of the divisional senior officers' meetings. Our characterization is based on observation of a single meeting chaired by the Superintendent's deputy, but nevertheless this contained a number of features of interest. Items originated either from the authoritative centres of policy consideration, with divisional injunctions and items from the subdivisional superintendents' conference reported by the chair, or from the subdivisional experience of members who reported problems. The definition of some issues was therefore given by the nature of the decisions taken at a higher level of policy consideration for information or implementation, though practically minded comments might be registered in reaction. Commonsensical experience of legal work or personnel management might be introduced in reaction to relevant matters. For example, on learning that there was to be no overtime working to cover a forthcoming major election, one inspector was surprised, warning that if there was trouble, 'they' would ask 'why weren't there people?' Recent subdivisional problems produced other items: uniform officers of inspector rank referred to empirical deficiencies of equipment, supply and facilities, some attributable to subdivisional failings – not recording petrol consumption or checking oil, for example. The CID produced items critical of the legal and administrative competence of uniformed officers. Relations with the public did not appear as markedly. The discussion reflected the demands of operational common sense, including legal work, and the responsibility of inspectors for the care of the physical resources assigned to them for practical use, a responsibility which is to an extent formally divided among them. By way of inquiry subdivisional matters might be investigated by inspectors and their sergeants in the course of their normal duties. The decisions of the meeting are made by the chair but only in certain areas. Some deficiencies could be answered by new arrangements; orders, etc. were endorsed by the subdivisional head, for example, the checking of pocket-books by supervisors. But such injunctions do well to prevail over criticisms based on experience of legal work or operational common sense where for the cases in which it is relevant the formulation is not copper-bottomed and brass bound. For example, the "instant" cautioning for crime of elderly people of an age which may not appear to qualify them for the relevant provisions of force orders attracted criticism and debate; but the problems of evidence linked with the readiness of complainants, such as retailers, to accept financial satisfaction produced a factor of ambiguity that ruled out a clear policy. Instead the circumstances would always have to be considered by the officers in the actual case. This is a significant indication of an inability of a process of policy consideration pitched at the lowest level of the force hierarchy and therefore closest to the problems of the 'ground' to generate potent policy on legal and operational practice. Again, an operational priority can be readily invoked to overcome a temporary problem of resource deficiency (for example, depriving RBOs of radios in order to meet other needs), but this is a common-sense redeployment of resources rather than an alteration of operational practice.

Policy consideration is concerned to relay decisions from above, and to cope with empirically perceived problems within the remit of the subdivisional senior officers. Implementation takes the form of injunctions to obey procedures, to supervise, and temporary deployments of officers and other arrangements. The subdivisional senior officers' meeting, despite its closeness to the 'ground', appears to reproduce in a lower register the formats of policy consideration discovered in more elevated regions of the organization.

Table 7.1. *Summary Table of Meetings and Conferences Attended*

	Force								Division				Sub-division		Overall	
	Management Team		Chief Superintendents		Superintendents		JAC		Senior Officers		Conference		Senior Officers			
	No.	%	No.	%	No.	%	No.	%	No.	%	No.	%	No.	%	No.	%
No. of meetings	5		3		2		2		9		1		1		23	
Matters arising	111	64	23	34	25	54	18	47	67	34	0	0	3	12	247	43
New business	63	36	44	66	21	46	20	52	131	66	23	100	23	88	325	56
Deferrals	109	63	15	22	11	24	17	44	29	15	5	22	0	0	186	32
Reports	135	78	20	30	19	41	23	60	33	17	4	17	3	12	237	41
'Operational, etc.' items	17	10	30	45	18	39	1	3	95	48	5	22	9	35	175	31
'Establishment, etc.' items	81	47	14	21	8	17	24	63	42	21	4	17	7	27	180	31
'Procedure, etc.' items	33	19	13	19	13	28	11	29	46	23	9	39	8	31	133	23
'Recruitment, etc.' items	16	9	3	4	0	0	0	0	2	1	2	9	1	4	24	4
'Other' items	27	16	7	10	7	15	2	5	13	7	3	13	1	4	60	10
Total agenda items	174	100	67	100	46	100	38	100	198	100	23	100	26	100	572	100

Notes

1 'Operational, etc.' includes operational, legal and deployment.
2 'Establishment, etc.' includes establishment, equipment, supply, finance and conditions.
3 'Procedure, etc.' includes procedure, inspection, organization and systems.
4 'Recruitment, etc.' includes recruitment, promotion and training.
5 'Other' includes extra-police and unclassified.
6 'Administrative' includes all items in 2, 3 and 4.

Let us now consider a comparison of these meetings, using a quantitative summary table, Table 7.1.

Discussion of the Summary – Table 7.1

The relationship between qualitative and quantitative data is not always as one would wish. In this case, the variable number of meetings or conferences of each kind attended makes even comparisons within the table less than certain. It is easier to be confident about statements made in relations to some meetings – like the divisional senior officers' meetings, Management Team and the Chief Superintendents' conferences, which were attended on a number of occasions and for which we received official minutes to supplement our observations – than others like the divisional conference and the subdivisional senior officers' meeting, where it was possible to attend only once and for which we relied solely on field notes. (The frequency of meetings was very variable – from fortnightly to biannually. Within the designated research period of eight months all the less frequent meetings and conferences it was possible to attend were attended.)[1] Nevertheless, the trends observable in the table broadly serve to reinforce our qualitative observations, even if sometimes these are not always as distinct as one would wish, and they occasionally 'surprise'.

One important, broad distinction is that between those meetings or conferences oriented towards 'rational-scientific' management and those more focused upon 'common-sense' management. Features of the former include an agenda with a high proportion of 'matters arising' and 'deferred' items as well as 'reports' – the first two features related to the latter in so far as they are obviously a consequence of the need for inquiry and report (the mechanism, par excellence, of 'rational-scientific' management) – which results in the routine reappearance of items as reports gradually become available. Such an agenda is also characterized by a high proportion of items of an administrative nature (most obviously, the establishment, equipment, supply, finance and conditions and the procedure, inspection, organization and systems categories), with its scientific discourse, and a low proportion of items of an 'operational' nature (the operational, legal and deployment category), with its common-sense-based discourse. Management Team and the Joint Advisory Committee clearly exemplify this rational-scientific focus, with almost half or more of all agenda items comprising 'matters arising' and 'deferrals', reports being used in 60 per cent or more of them, 'operational' items constituting 10 per cent or less and 'administrative' ones at least three-quarters.

In the case of MT, such a focus is doubtless a consequence of an attempt to push operational decisions 'down the chain' to Chief Superintendents. As the CC put it, talking about the control of overtime expenditure:

> We have been trying very hard over the last twelve months or so to *push* some of this responsibility down the chain, and overtime is a very good example . . . I am *committed* to Chief Superintendents being told, these are your resources . . . now you use 'em . . . It's all part of a philosophy which says *they run their division*.

It is also in line with the CC's perception of his responsibilities, as is evident from the following comment on how he spends his time:

> The one [department] I see *most* of, I suppose, is finance and administration, that kind of area . . . 'cos that's where the money's spent . . . I think my, the main, thrust of your monitoring ought to be on the deployment of the resources, as between one demand and another, I think that's done more in the admin. and financial side, than it is in the operation departments . . . operating departments.

In the case of the JAC, this finding is probably a consequence of its close relationship to MT – which it 'advises' about rank-and-file 'feelings' on new forms, equipment and so on, and, again, of a policy decision to confine discussion to such issues.

In contrast are those meetings or conferences characterized by 'common-sense' management. Here the features just outlined are systematically inverted. There is a lower proportion of 'matters arising' and 'deferrals', with, in consequence, less of a need for 'reports'; a much higher proportion of items of an 'operational' kind, and a lower proportion, relatively, of items of an administrative kind – though administrative items are clearly salient in all meetings and conferences, never dropping below 44 per cent of the agenda. The best representatives of this trend are the Chief Superintendents' conference and the divisional senior officers' meeting (run by a Chief Superintendent); 'matters arising' constitute only about a third of the business, only one in about every six items is deferred; 'reports' are less used (in up to one item in three); 'operational' items constitute almost half the business and administrative ones most of the rest. Here, if anywhere, is the site of operational policy consideration. This is not only in line with the CC's policy, as we have just seen, but it also reflects the reality of the situation. For without the support of departmental and divisional commanders, the success of operational policy – given its common-sense basis – cannot be guaranteed. Even with such support, 'persuasion' is the only possible route to the operational goal, as the CC recognizes in talking about how to enforce an operational policy to get officers to use pocket-books as a diary:

> I'm afraid it's . . . it's got to be enforced in the same kind of way as any other policy. I have to sell it to the Chief Superintendents . . . Now, if the Chief Superintendents are unhappy with that as a system, then I would hope that they will tell me so. If they're not unhappy with it, they think it's a good system, then they should persuade the Superintendents that it's a good system, and so on all the way down the line.

However, here we encounter a somewhat surprising finding. In line with the above, it might reasonably be expected that 'operational' common-sense management looms ever larger the more we descend from the 'heights' of MT to the comparative 'lowlands' of the divisional conference, the Superintendents' conference and the subdivisional senior officers' meeting. Here the picture is variable, but not fully in line with our major trend. Our attendance at these meetings was low; in fact, we attended, as we mentioned earlier, only one divisional conference and one senior officers' meeting. We have no reason to suppose these were atypical, but we should be a little cautious nevertheless. The most interesting point is that whilst the proportions of 'matters arising' (0–12 per cent), 'deferrals' (0–22 per cent) and 'reports' (12–17 per cent) are low for the divisional conference and the subdivisional senior officers' meeting, so too is the proportion of 'operational' items (22–35 per cent). By contrast, the proportion of administrative items is high (62–5 per cent). It would appear that in these two forums administrative matters predominate but without the associated features such as 'deferrals' and 'reports'. This perhaps reinforces the impression that these are occasions for 'selling' administrative decisions to operational senior officers and the rank and file themselves, albeit stressing their operational, common-sense features in doing so, *after* inquiries have been instituted, reports discussed and decisions made higher up the chain. The comparative absence of operational items might be explained by the fact that, at this level, the discussion of operational matters is a routine daily occurrence. What is more significant here is the absence of operational policy consideration precisely at the level of the organization where it would be most relevant; this points to a structural issue about the nature of operational discretion.

The Superintendents' conference fits neither the 'rational-scientific' nor the 'common-sense' pattern, nor even this more mixed one just described. What it does display is a pattern fixing it squarely between MT and the Chief Superintendents' conference. It is neither as 'scientific' as MT nor as 'commonsensical' as the Chief Superintendents' conference. If MT represents the pre-eminent site of 'rational-scientific' management and the Chief Superintendents' conference and the divisional senior officers' meeting the locus of 'commonsensical' operational policy consideration, it can be argued that the Superintendents' conference represents an intermediate form.

Considering the meetings/conferences as a whole, certain trends emerge. Interest in 'operational' items is very variable, varying from 3 per cent to 48 per cent, but overall amounts to only 31 per cent of total items. Moreover, operational items were generously interpreted, deliberately, where there was some room for doubt. Clearly, then, in relation to all other matters under consideration, operational matters are not predominant. By contrast, 'administrative' matters, though they also vary (44–92 per cent) as a proportion of total items, constitute more than half (58 per cent) of all items discussed, though recruitment, promotion and training items hardly surface as issues anywhere (range 0–9 per cent; overall 4 per cent). This is also true of the 'other' category (range 4–16 per cent; overall 10 per cent). This dominance of administrative items reinforces our feeling that the consideration of operational policy, with its common-sense discourse, is seen as less suitable, generally, for the instrument of policy consideration.

The variations in 'matters arising' (0–64 per cent), 'deferrals' (0–63 per cent) and 'reports' (12–78 per cent) are altogether greater, but the overall mean results show that meetings are almost, though not quite, split between 'matters arising' (43 per cent) and 'new business' (56 per cent); one in three items is deferred (32 per cent); and reports get asked for in almost half the cases (41 per cent). The overall strength of administrative discourse and procedure is perhaps reflected in these figures.

We end by reiterating our starting-point: that these findings should be read in connection with the qualitative pictures already discussed; and that they should not be 'over-read', given the variation in numbers of meetings it was possible to attend and the difficulties of *post hoc* classification. Despite these caveats, the data are consistent with our major feeling about the relative importance of the distinction between types of policy issues, operational and administrative, and the concomitant distinction between their appropriate discourses: 'common sense' and 'rational-scientific'.[2]

Though not visible in this table, we should end with a reminder that these discourses are primarily internal in origin. The comparative absence of the democratic structure within this set of institutional arrangements for the consideration of policy is noteworthy. We return later to its significance.

Types of Policy Issue and Types of Discourse

The Process of Policy Consideration

In order to secure the points about the distinction between the two types of policy issue and their respective discourses, and the comparative absence of the democratic influence, and before moving on to examine the other key institution for the consideration of policy – the files – we intend to present three examples of 'policy consideration'. These issues surfaced at one or other of the meetings and conferences we have just dealt with and often reappeared in others. The first item – 'replacement traffic cars' – is an administrative policy issue and demonstrates the 'rational-scientific' discourse at work; the second – 'deployment and divisional policy' – exemplifies a clear operational policy issue and shows the 'common-sense' discourse in action; and the third – 'controlling petrol consumption' – is an example of a 'mixed' issue which consequently illustrates both discourses uncomfortably attempting to occupy the same 'space'. All demonstrate the exclusion of the democratic structure.

An Example of an Administrative Policy Issue and 'Rational-Scientific' Discourse: 'Replacement Traffic Cars'

This item is a good example of a policy matter which is resolvable completely within the terms of a scientific management discourse. Given that, it takes up little time, an uncontested decision is quickly taken, and discussion of it is confined to Management Team. The Chief Superintendents are later told of the decision taken, but the Superintendents learn of it only indirectly; certainly it does not become an item at one of the Superintendents' conferences.

The item surfaces on the agenda of a MT meeting. The relevant ACC delivers the gist of the report that is being prepared. Car A is going to be cheaper than Car B and hence will be recommended, though Car A's figures are based solely on motorway driving. The CC defers the item until next time when the figures are available.

The full report is available at the next MT meeting. The

relevant ACC summarizes the report. Car A clearly comes off best, but there is not enough money for them. Car B is definitely 'not on', whereas Car C is slightly underpowered. Since Car D would appear to be ideal, the suggestion is to go for this car. 'Traffic' has suggested either all Ds, or three As and the rest Ds. This latter proposal would leave a budgetary shortfall, which would be made up by taking (out of the budget) two other vehicles.

After this introduction, the CC asks the treasurer's opinion. He feels that since the As are 'out' for reasons of cost and because they have not been tested (that is, fully) he favours the first suggestion.

The CC then asks another ACC. He favours Ds; he has seen petrol-consumption figures of As used in another county but doesn't believe them. The CC thinks it would be difficult in this force area to sell the idea of switching to another make – a reference to the presence in the area of a major car manufacturer and the first hint of another notion (namely, public acceptability) creeping into the otherwise completely 'scientific' debate. He adds that As are out of service longer. However, he is prepared to go for three As and twenty-five Ds, but wonders about the proposal to take the vehicles out of the budget since he has already told the Police Committee he needs them. The relevant ACC comes to the rescue. He says, order the vehicles now, but pay out of next year's budget since they won't be here before April next year anyway. The CC agrees.

The decision having been made, the CC ruminates more generally about replacement principles, attempting to make the whole business a pure matter of scientific administration. He says the force will get twenty-eight cars, that is, a complete traffic fleet; what is needed is a staggered programme, replacing some every year. The relevant ACC says he has Traffic Department thinking that way. The treasurer adds the 'financial' seal of approval; the idea of evaluating a few at a time is good; a cost-effective argument for the new cars can then be presented.

The CC concludes that he has found the traffic report very helpful and that if the meeting had had that on a much earlier occasion the matter could have been settled then.

Despite the options presented by the need to balance money available against value for money, given that the clear front-runner could not be afforded, the discussion never veers from the questions of finance and testing. Rather, as in a Consumers Association *Which* report summary, there are always features about the best performer – too costly; repairs take longer (as was the case with Car A) – which ensure others are also considered. But subjective common-sense amendments have no place here, though the CC's mention of 'public acceptability' added another reason to the cost argument for sticking largely with Car D. *Alone*, however, that qualification might never have withstood a serious scientific-financial onslaught. In these areas police managers become, like any other managers, interested in cost-effectiveness, optimization and all the other terms of 'rational-scientific' administration.

An Example of an Operational Issue and Occupational 'Common-Sense' Discourse: 'Deployment and Divisional Policy'

The centrality of deployment to the concerns of divisional policy consideration was confirmed by our earlier look at the divisional senior officers' meeting. How the senior officers go about the task of discussing the issues of deployment can be illustrated by considering the case of a divisional foot patrol experiment.

The Chief Superintendent (CS) introduces the topic of town-centre operations at night, noting that it is 'a bit controversial'. He has talked it over with one of the divisional Superintendents and then used three pairs of officers, with a supervisor, on a foot patrol, after incidents outside a night-club. He and a deputy personally joined the patrol. He thinks the experiment has brought a great deal of benefit and has advantages over motor patrol; he proposes to organize a permanent divisional patrol on nights. The two subdivisional Superintendents most directly concerned then speak in support of the plan in principle, but point to shortages of personnel. There is a current of support also for the previous system of a *subdivisional* night van worked by officers on overtime. But the CS favours a foot patrol on a divisional basis without overtime assistance. One Superintendent agrees that he has told his Inspectors that those in the van must get out and walk in pairs. It depends on the calibre of the sergeants, he explains. Arrests made by the van patrol over the last month justify it, particularly by comparison with the arrest rate of the SPG, who never walk.

One of the CS's deputies then raises the possibility of using resident beat officers for this purpose, as in all other parts of the force. The CS however refers to the DCC's remarks about their proper use. It would be for only one night of the week, comes the reply; the example of the use of RBOs at football matches is also cited. The CS reiterate his wish for a system drawing on all three subdivisions.

A compromise proposal for a routine *divisional* van, yet one operated by officers on overtime, emerges from the CS. Additional queries concern the possible shortage of volunteers for overtime and the problem of initially picking up officers dispersed on three areas. A further complication is the possible unwillingness of personnel from the outer subdivision to volunteer, and it is proposed they be excluded. But the CS insists, seeing the practical viewpoint of doubters but not wanting to segmentalize the division, proposing a compromise plan which will involve a tripartite contribution but one excluding sergeants, though not PCs, from the outer subdivision. The possibility is mentioned that one pair will be walking if there are four pairs in all, plus a sergeant.

One Superintendent suggests that an alternative could be found if each resident beat were given two officers instead of one. But the CS doubts that officers could be found for such a proposal and points to the consequent reduction in night cover. Another Superintendent agrees, preferring more flexibility in deploying extra strength. The CS refers to the CC's view that RBOs are not needed in town centres but says there would be no objection to selective doubling of resident beat coverage.

Some general points can be made before we discuss the development of this particular item of policy consideration. In the first place, the court of appeal implicitly, for all participants, is occupational common sense and experience, the touchstone against which the proposal for a divisional foot patrol is measured in the course of debate. There is minimal reference, for example, to detailed quantitative information or analysis or to scientific principles of occupational practice; the characteristic focus of scientific management on the results of objective inquiry is relatively absent. Rather the debate is largely governed by the reference to personal observations, 'what everyone does', 'the practical viewpoint', as the CS put it. As this form of evidence is accumulated it steadily shapes a series of qualifications and queries around the proposal which the CS initially introduced with some confidence and decisiveness. There is also a more specific background assumption which is endorsed by common sense and experience: the pre-eminence of the status quo.

Thus the practicality of the proposal is implicitly judged against the value of what is already being done, the latter being taken for granted. A further and connected feature is the displacement of the topic as a series of conditions which are shown to be problematical for the scheme's success are introduced. Regardless of the merits of the plan, which may indeed be accepted, the preconditions for its operation are unfavourable, these being once again rooted in the status quo. All this takes on a particular significance when we also bear in mind the rather tangential way in which the pronouncements of the CC and his Deputy can be treated when raised in connection with a particular operation. They are clearly not the first or the most authoritative source of policy consideration in such operational matters.

The CS's original proposal rests on various arguments: the centrality of divisional organization; the importance of foot patrol; his personal observation of a successful experiment; the need to reduce overtime, which has been endorsed by the CC, and to keep RBOs on their beats, likewise a force requirement. Deployed against the proposal were a number of points and queries. First, while footpatrol was fully accepted as a principle, the arrest rate of the van patrol was a point in its favour, especially by comparison with the SPG, who, we were told, never walk; depending on 'the calibre of the sergeant' (a vague but common-sensical qualification) van patrols could be *combined* with foot patrols, as past instruction had made clear. In addition there was a fundamental problem of personnel shortage: where were the officers to be found? One answer in line with common practice was to offer RBOs, at least for one night (an offer the CS was bound, as we saw, to refuse). There were also question-marks to be raised against divisional organization: the problem of volunteers recruited on a division-wide basis; the logistics of transport. These arguments steer the discussion towards the acceptance of a compromise based on the status quo – a *van* patrol operated by officers on *overtime* with a *lesser* involvement from one subdivision than from the others. It was envisaged that only *one* pair of officers would be on foot, an ironic conclusion in the circumstances. We see here how the practical arguments based on experience and the status quo operate against an innovation, even one personally advocated by the CS. What is distinctive here does not lie in the concession of power by the commander to his subordinates but in the accepted force of common-sense discourse which we see marshalled against a proposal which starts out with some not inconsiderable advantages in its favour. The authority which invests the CS must make its way against the argued experience of junior officers in a matter of operational significance. The CS may seek to defend the requirements placed upon him from above – for example, on RBOs – but he cannot decisively enforce them against requirements emerging from below. He had also to concede the force-imposed limitation on overtime in order to secure his basic objective. External considerations are not an issue at all.

An Example of a 'Mixed' Issue and Competing Discourses: 'Controlling Petrol Consumption'

The following narrative concerns a policy which straddles the two areas of concern to police management: upholding the law and managerial efficiency. The former entails the discourse of occupational common sense, the latter that of rational-scientific management. Thus, in discussions of issues which straddle both areas, we would expect these dissonant discourses to appear, uncomfortably, side by side. This tension provides the basis for a degree of humour as a principled scientific managerialism comes up against a pragmatic, constantly shifting and ultimately subjective common sense, and for a degree of irresolution. We hope to illustrate both these aspects in the following; moreover, we end by pointing to the structural roots of this tension and (inevitable) irresolution.

The story begins in the early summer with an announcement, in the form of a loose 'warning' by the DCC, that, due to the oil shortage, the force is to suffer a 20 per cent reduction in petrol supplies and 10 per cent in diesel. The ACC responsible for such matters spells out the details and implications. Stocks are 'OK' at the moment but fuel is going to become more expensive or more difficult to obtain. Meanwhile he has asked the Transport Manager to supply details on a divisional basis of the average consumption over the last three months. However, it is for MT to decide by how much to cut consumption. Discussion follows. The CC suggests that an alternative to cutting consumption would be to reduce vehicles to six pandas per subdivision. The ACC thinks this would simply mean the six doing the work of those removed from duty. The CC then thinks that a reduction in the amount of petrol available in the pumps would be necessary; the ACC disagrees, arguing the need to keep the pumps topped up if 'all does break down' (that is, petrol supplies completely dried up). The CC feels a cut is necessary given that telling Chief Superintendents to cut down on overtime has had no effect; but the ACC's disagreement takes him back to 'trust': the need to rely on the Chief Superintendents 'to play the game'. Effectively the ACC's point has been conceded, and he takes full advantage of that by mentioning that the monitoring of mileage can be done from HQ, suggesting a cut of one-third, but that Traffic should be excluded. The CC wonders about subdivisional first-response cars, suggesting that economies cannot be expected from them. The ACC reiterates his point about excluding Traffic, citing, its 'emergency' role as his reason. Another ACC and the DCC do not agree, on the grounds that Traffic goes to 'minor stuff'. Yet another ACC wonders what would happen to the men immobilized by such a cut. Static accident-prevention squads, is the CC's answer. The DCC, following up his objection to excluding Traffic from the envisaged cut-back, argues the case for keeping pandas on the road because they are 'part of community policing'. So now Traffic, first-response and pandas all have their advocates as the mobiles most necessary to maintain on the road. A final compromise intervention by an ACC – suggesting that pandas could be cut 'on nights' – is followed by a decision by the CC; the ACC responsible is to draft an order in line with his original suggestion that divisions should be instructed to cut their petrol consumption by a third. However, first-response cars, Traffic cars and Summons and Warrants Department vehicles will not be affected. Divisions will be supplied with details of their petrol consumption so that they can monitor the situation. A final note is added by the ACC in charge of Management Department; some constables will ask for bikes; an alternative to cars is clearly needed; the department is looking into the question.

The objective 'science' of monitoring constantly comes up against a more subjective 'common-sense' logic. In some of these encounters (monitoring versus restricting pandas to six per subdivision; monitoring versus restricting the amount of petrol in the pumps), the 'common-sense' arguments are undermined because they are seen to be operationally dangerous. But in other cases science has to concede; there must be 'exceptions', for operational emergencies, to an across-the-board cut. The question of which mobiles best fill this 'emergency' role is, given the level of disagreement, clearly a subjective, common-sense assessment.

Later the same month bad news about petrol consumption is being discussed at a divisional senior officers' meeting. Despite efforts and exhortations the situation remains beyond easy control. One particularly concerned Superintendent claims to have been doing everything in his power, giving instructions, going on parades to deliver the message in person, talking to controllers, singling out particularly heavy 'driver-consumers' – but to no avail. The Deputy blames the controllers; the CS says, taking up the CC's rejected argument about withdrawing pandas, that cars will be withdrawn unless there is an improvement. His solution is postponement; wait for the latest monthly figures. The Superintendent of one subdivision is more sanguine; they are losing cars anyway due to a garage go-slow.

The question is returned to, in the following month, at a divisional senior officers' meeting. Petrol consumption, the CS has learnt at a Chief Superintendents' conference, has not decreased at all; on some divisions it has even increased. A policy of waiting for the next set of figures is not possible, since by then the petrol might run out. He ends expressing surprise; he thought the division was using less. One of the Superintendents, who previously has done 'all he can', claims to have been doing a lot of research and making practical interventions such as stopping cars on nights and going on parades. But the figures revealed by his research are unreliable, varying from 17 to 76 miles per gallon as a result of officers failing to record. The CS thinks they will have to monitor the issuing of petrol. The Superintendent believes this will be difficult to control; because the station sergeant and station are too busy, individuals help themselves. 'It is monitored at Traffic HQ,' replies the CS. The Superintendent reiterates that his (very unreliable) figures indicate a saving of the order of only 5 per cent. Leave until the end of the month and then check the pump figures, is the CS's suggestion, recording divisional and non-divisional usage separately. One Superintendent thinks that would be impossible, to which the CS replies they will need to contact Traffic HQ to see which pumps they (the non-divisional users) are using and what they are doing to cut consumption.

Here, clearly, the attempt at monitoring, despite 'research', exhortation and personal interventions, had made no impact on operational exigencies, which remain firmly at the helm.

In early autumn another divisional senior officers' meeting is the scene of a further report-back on petrol consumption. The CS reports continuing difficulties but he will await the latest monthly figures before bringing up the matter for discussion again.

During the same month the question is given a further airing at a Chief Superintendents' conference. The relevant ACC announces that the County Council has said that there is no more oil available than last year (which was a poor one due to a tanker drivers' strike), with the result that there is no point in ordering any more since it will not be forthcoming. In reply to a question from the floor about the new clubhouse needing oil supplies, the CC takes a hard line; they may have to stop using the clubhouse; there will be no sympathy from the County Council; the police service is the only service not cut; there are plenty willing to accuse the police of waste. The relevant ACC adds that so far there has been no overall saving in petrol consumption but, as with oil, it must be cut. He then reveals, as explicitly as anywhere, the knife-edge this narrative is concerned to demonstrate. He says he is working as an administrator, but the job is to balance the 'operationally desirable' with an administrator's view. In practical terms, he intends to leave the figures out so that all can compare 'their' performance with that of other Chief Superintendents – a sort of persuasion-by-inducing-guilt if 'out of line'; he adds that the allocation given is calculated on the average consumption of the last three months which, though arbitrary, gives a base-line for the cut.

The CC reinforces the message by mentioning a discipline charge he has dealt with involving the illegitimate use of the car. He stresses also the need to ask 'why' when the reason for doing something is not obvious. The DCC echoes this by talking of the importance of 'front-line' supervision and of the controller – something Chief Inspectors do not recognize. The CC murmurs approval. Here, then, the most sophisticated – if arbitrary – scientific approach to the problem of cuts (average consumption over the previous three months as a base-line) is explicitly balanced against the operationally desirable, to a background of exhortation.

At this point, the saga ends, or rather, here we leave it, rumbling (fitfully) on. At one level, the question of petrol consumption looks to be a purely administrative matter. However, the purely administrative reaction (cut back by one-third in relation to some predefined base-line, such as the last three months' consumption or last year's figures) can never be absolutely imposed because the legal issue of *operational* efficiency is also involved. Consequently absolute (administrative) directions are necessarily precluded because the highly unpredictable 'direction of the law' is paramount. The predictability necessary for competent administration and scientific management is entirely lacking; the 'emergency' and the 'exceptional' have to be allowed for. What constitutes an 'emergency' or the 'exceptional', who is best fitted to deal with them (pandas, sub-division first-response cars, Traffic) and so on can all be discussed, but ultimately, given the overriding commitment to upholding the law, only subjectively, in common-sense terms.

The result, as we have seen, is constant tension, some humour, as the battle between common sense and scientific management produces some bizarre images, and endless prevarication, postponement and irresolution. As the ACC said, he talked as an administrator, but that was different from the 'operationally desirable'. In so far as the public enters, through the question of 'waste', its influence is constantly mediated by (and ultimately subordinated to) the occupational common sense of the 'operationally desirable'.

Summary

Thus far we have suggested various competing hypotheses about the policy–practice relation corresponding to the various models of policework. Our own hypothesis centred on the expectation of discovering two kinds of policy issue – administrative and operational – each with a characteristic discourse, namely, 'rational-scientific' and occupational common sense, and each with different expectations of success in terms of influencing practice on the ground. The following examination of the formal structure suggested the way these competing discourses were related to it, 'rational-scientific' management deriving directly from the statutory requirements of 'adequacy and efficiency', occupational 'common sense' indirectly from the constitutional discretion vested in the constable. This constitutional examination also revealed the highly shadowy presence of 'the public'. A specific definition of policy was followed by illustrated examples of managerial instruments other than policy in order to concretize the definition. A definition of the process of policy consideration followed, which enabled moments of 'policy-*making*' to be distinguished from moments of 'policy *consideration*'. We then looked at one of the key institutions for the consideration of policy: meetings. This revealed the expected distinctions between 'administrative' and 'operational' issues, a revelation which was further enhanced by a detailed look at the policy consideration of three concrete examples, demonstrating respectively 'administrative', 'operational' and 'mixed' issues. Both sets of data also demonstrated the comparative strength of internal influences as against any external 'legal' and 'democratic' ones.

It remains to complete our consideration of the key institutional arrangements for the consideration of policy by examining the policy files to see if the hypothesized expectations still hold, and then to review the whole in relation to our hypotheses. Those are the tasks of Chapter 8.

Notes

1 The one subdivisional conference that came up during the research period was, unfortunately, cancelled.
2 On 'rational-scientific' management, see the classical view in Taylor (1911); for a more distanced perspective, see Etzioni (1964) and, more recently, Brown (1979). On 'common-sense', see Gramsci, (1971, pp. 323–33, 348, 419–25).

CHAPTER EIGHT

The System at Work II: Policy Files

Introduction

This chapter will complete our examination of the policy system, by examining the repositories of policy consideration: policy files. Specifically, it will start with an outline of our methodology in approaching the files, exemplify our key findings and then move on to consider the implications of these for understanding the relationship between our key structures – law, work and democracy. This latter task will involve a look at the numerical appearance of external bodies in the files in order to demonstrate something of the comparative strength of the various structures; then a consideration of two operational issues, one of particular relevance to unit beat-work – unit car speeds – and one of particular relevance to resident beat-work – racial attacks. Both demonstrate the centrality of the legal structure in determining the relationship between the structures: in the former instance, its ability to override organizational and occupational concerns of efficiency or welfare; in the latter, its ability to override the democratic structure where there is a clear and pressing example of public concern. Finally, by way of an overall summary to Part IV, we review the policy system as a whole in relation to our starting hypotheses.

The Process of Policy Consideration: Analysing Policy Files

Methodology

The study of policy files was conducted in the light of the information gathered from observation in particular sections of the organization, including the unit and resident beat systems. The aim was to illuminate the relation between practice and policy and to do so in relation to these specific sections. At first sight the task seemed formidable in that a listing of all classifications and subclassifications from the main index produced a total of 759, very largely comprising file titles (the remainder, estimated at about 10 per cent, being solely headings). In order to construct a sample of relevant items, we therefore selected those titles that seemed of interest, generating a smaller list of 342 (or 50 per cent) file names. These files reflected our interest in the specific sections we had observed but, in addition, were oriented towards operational matters – matters which brought police into contact with the public. From the second list we indicated certain files apparently of particular interest and relevance, giving a total of 62 names. Of these, we managed to see 28 (or 45 per cent). A further 33 on related topics were given us from the larger list of 342 and 8 from outside the 342, though cognate in certain respects.[1]

Our procedures in examining the files had to take account of the highly variable way in which the files were compiled. Some, for example, proved to be extensive and detailed, containing a long historical narrative of changing force policy and policy consideration, some were extremely brief and some were empty. In addition the files were composed of every type of force record that was relevant to the topic, thus containing items of correspondence, records of conferences and meetings, documents, orders, circulars and memoranda. Within the files there was variation in the length of consideration. Some items were shortly dealt with while others were long-standing. These features created significant difficulties for any attempt to find standard methods of analysis and description, both for the files and for their contents.

Classifying the Files: Some Examples

Given this difficulty of analysis, we divided files into one of three broad categories: 'operational', 'non-operational' and 'mixed'. The former included all those files which contained items exclusively dealing with operational, legal, or deployment matters. 'Non-operational' files, on the other hand, included all those files which contained all manner of items *except* those dealing with operational, legal or deployment matters. In other words, such files contained items which fell within our 'administrative' (establishment, equipment, supply, finance, conditions, procedures, inspection, organization, systems, recruitment, promotion and training) or 'other' (extra-police and unclassified) categories.

'Mixed' files contained both 'operational' and 'non-operational' items. Though no files are typical, for reasons we have outlined, the following are examples of each of the three categories.

'OPERATIONAL': RACE AND COMMUNITY RELATIONS – INCIDENTS ARISING FROM RACISM

This file, which covers a period in the late 1970s, during which one racist became a *cause célèbre* amongst National Front supporters after his imprisonment for racist remarks, consists of four incidents arising from racism and the police responses to each: first, the burglary and damage to a local community-relations office and the police follow-up inquiry which showed that police attention had been lacking on the night; second, the racist daubing of a local club wall, and the unsuccessful follow-up inquiries and night-time observations; third, a claim by a trade union that attacks on some of its members, Community Relations Council workers, were increasing and were not being treated with sufficient urgency by police, and the police denial of a lack of urgency; fourth, a complaint by a local Asian workers' association about racist attacks on an Asian restaurant and a threatening letter to another, and the subsequent police response: inquiries, arrests, continued observations. Since incidents, and the follow-up activities these generated, are unambiguously operational, there was no difficulty in classifying this file as 'operational'.

'MIXED': ARRESTS – STOP AND SEARCH

The file, which covers a period in the 1960s and 1970s, consists of Home Office requests in response to parliamentary questions and complaints to police forces for details about their current powers, procedures, practices and relevant statistics, including convictions, in relation to 'stop and search', and the force responses. It also embraces Home Office circulars about desirable procedures and practices. The force responses comprised internal inquiries to check the existing position, supplying requested details, ensuring procedures and practices conformed to Home Office requirements and, where necessary, amending force orders. Whilst the early part of the file centres on the possibility of introducing a national power to stop and search for stolen goods, the rest focuses, in the aftermath of the Misuse of Drugs Act 1971, on stop and search for drugs. The file is concerned with force stop-and-search practices, an 'operational' matter, but it is also about ensuring the adequacy of procedures in this area, hence its characterization as 'mixed'.

'NON-OPERATIONAL': ORDERS – POLICY ON POLICE
DIVISIONAL ORDERS
Here we find concern expressed to the CC by an ACC about the
method of informing HQ about changes of policy or practice,
emanating from divisions in particular. Any divisional orders had
to be consistent with force standing orders. At Management Team
a new system of collating information about standing orders was
agreed, and the existing restriction on divisional orders was
reaffirmed. At the Chief Superintendents' conference the ACC
drew attention to that restriction and stressed the need to send a
copy of a divisional instruction to the CC. Since the issue here is
the administrative system of communication and control, the file
was classified as 'non-operational'.

In the event, the majority of files (29) were 'mixed', followed by 20
'non-operational' and 13 'operational' files. Given our interest in
police–public encounters and consequent bias in selection towards
the operational, this finding may suggest a clear preponderance of
other than operational items in the generality of files. Even if this
prediction were not to be fulfilled, there was no escaping the sheer
amount of 'non-operational' items within the files. Only 13 of 62
were unambiguously operational. Since the most contentious
policing matters arise in the operational field, we initially found
this surprising. However, since it echoes our finding about the
meetings, where less than one-third of the items were operational,
it ought not to. Once again, the unpredictable exigencies of the
operational appear to escape the grasp of policy consideration.

The Relevance of External Bodies

Here we wished to begin to estimate the possible relevance of
outside bodies, by adopting a simple quantitative index: the
frequency of appearance in the files displayed by particular outside
bodies. This referred to the presence of correspondence or reports
originating from or addressed to individual bodies; only *one*
appearance per file was counted. Their frequency of appearance
was compared according to the classification of operational relevance given to particular files. However, we were mainly concerned with the total number of appearances. Individual bodies
were assigned an individual category or grouped in a broader
classification; since our aim was to look at the relevance of bodies
with some degree of formal distance, we excluded other individual
police forces on the grounds that these provided 'normal' contacts
with 'peers'.

Table 8.1 *The Frequency of Appearance of External Bodies in the Sample of Policy Files*

| External bodies | Frequency of appearance | | | |
	Operational files (N = 13)	Mixed files (N = 29)	Non-operational files (N = 20)	All (N = 62)
Home Office (including Inspectorate)	6	18	9	33
Local council officers	4	12	2	18
Association of Chief Police Officers (ACPO), etc.	1	12	3	16
Police Federation	1	9	3	13
Parliamentarians	3	6	2	11
Police Authority/Watch Committee	1	9	0	10
Complainants	2	7	0	9
Commission for Racial Equality (CRE), etc.	2	4	2	8
Local councillors	1	4	3	8
Media	1	5	2	8
Select committee/ government minister	1	5	2	8
Local non-statutory associations	2	2	3	7
'Special-interest' associations	3	3	1	7
Director of Public Prosecutions (DPP)	2	2	1	5
Judiciary (including magistrates)	1	3	1	5
Local councils	1	2	2	5
Non-local council officers	0	4	1	5
Other government bodies/officers	0	4	1	5
Business	1	2	1	4
Political groups	1	2	1	4
Educational	2	0	1	3
Local authority associations	0	2	1	3
Clerk to the justices	2	0	0	2
Non-local councils	0	0	2	2
Probation and Aftercare Service	0	1	1	2
Religious	0	1	1	2

Table 8.1 (*cont.*)

Superintendents' Association	0	2	0	2
Police Complaints Board	1	0	0	1
Other groups and individuals	1	4	0	5

Notes
1 ACPO, etc. includes the Chief Constables' Association and the Central Conference of Chief Constables.
2 CRE, etc. includes the Community Relations Council and community-relations officers.
3 'Special-interest' associations include pensioners, students, trade and professional groups.

The distribution of appearances according to the type of policy file is shown in Table 8.1. We should note first the frequency and distribution of appearances of the Home Office, or its representative the Inspectorate. For each type of file these protagonists recur most frequently. But for other statutory bodies the picture is less impressive, with the Police Authority much less in evidence (a total of 10 appearances against the Home Office's 33). The DPP and the Police Complaints Board were less well represented (5 and 1 respectively).

A frequent input is to be observed from a group of local government figures, headed by local council officers (total 18) accompanied by local councillors (8) and councils (5). Another dimension of *national* institutional involvement is signified by the appearance of parliamentarians (11) and those in a more specific parliamentary category – House of Commons select committees and government ministers (together making 8). The community-relations arm of the government is also significantly represented (total 8), while the remaining government bodies and officers number in all 5. None of these has a direct responsibility for policing; it is therefore thought-provoking to consider why the Police Authority and other statutory bodies (apart from the Home Office) do not appear more frequently. Other legal figures have a less substantial presence, the judiciary and the clerk to the justices appearing on 5 and 2 occasions, respectively. Non-local councils (2) and officers (5), not unexpectedly, feature with a lesser frequency than their local counterparts.

A strong representation is evident in the case of occupational staff associations, with ACPO, etc. (16) just outnumbering the Police Federation (13). Both were significantly represented in the 'mixed' file category. This strong representation of ACPO, etc. was endorsed by the Chief Constable's view of ACPO's relevance and importance: 'My line, . . . generally speaking, is that if ACPO has a policy, I'm a good soldier and I'll follow it, unless there is a very pressing reason why we shouldn't.' The few appearances made by the Superintendents' Association (2) tend to point up the contrasting position of ACPO.

In the broader category of public opinion, it is not surprising that complainants lead the field (9), followed by the media (8), with various associations in the rear, including specific categories of association representing 'special interests' (7) and local non-statutory associations (7). Further classifications of public contributions yielded no more than 4 appearances in each case. However, these help to confirm the sense of a somewhat disparate public 'audience' for police decision-making.

Table 8.1 on its own does not tell us very much about the specific weight of the outside bodies in determining police thinking, as it is concerned simply with the *frequency* with which they appeared in our sample of files; moreover its findings largely relate to the sections we cover in this text (not the CID, for example). However, it helps us to compare the degree to which certain types of institution recur in the processes of policy consideration, across several topics. The pre-eminent presence of the Home Office can be attributed to its manifold responsibility for 'efficient' policing and its wide remit as a recipient of reports, though there is also no doubt that the influence from the centre has grown, perhaps especially in the operational field:

> CC: The Home Office over the last ten years . . . has become more and more active, in operational police matters. I can remember the day when the idea that you were going to talk about football hooliganism, let us say, to Home Office officials, well you know, it was just never thought of, you never dreamt of talking to them about operational matters.

But other statutory bodies fare less well, notably the Police Authority, which has in principle a comparatively large role in questions of 'efficiency' and a lesser one in the matter of reports; were the latter responsibility, in particular, to be fulfilled adequately one might reasonably expect to find a greater general frequency than appears to be the case. As we have noted, other local contacts seem by comparison to be almost as frequent, with local government a comparatively significant presence. A consistent level of appearance can also be attributed to the principal police associations, testifying to the occupational interests represented within policy consideration. The wider public is more disparately represented.

Summing up, it would seem that the broad scope of Home Office involvement is consistent with expectations derivable from a study of the statutory system of accountability. This scope is arguably attenuated in the case of the Police Authority, while some democratic forces – councillors, MPs and so on – and occupational interests – ACPO, etc. – play by comparison a role of some significance.

This hierarchy of relevant 'audiences' was echoed in the Chief Constable's own assessment of the bodies or constituencies he had to take into account, though not quite in the order they appear in our table:

> CC: In the final analysis . . . he has to satisfy his own conscience . . . The most important audience is his community . . . the area that he is policing and the people who live in it . . . Secondly, there is the Home Office as an audience because you have got also to satisfy the Home Secretary. I'm accountable to him . . . Another audience I have – I think this is another important one – is my own force, and members of my own force, and the way in which I fight their battles for them or am seen to be fighting their battles for them . . . My Police Authority, obviously I've to satisfy them. I have to take into account what they think and what they don't think and through them the County Council. Then there is ACPO as an audience as well; I want to be liked by my peers.

These remarks tend to highlight the perceived importance of a range of democratic and work-related audiences, buttressed by statutory obligations in some cases but not in others. The findings of Table 8.1 noted above provide a quantitative gloss on the actual lines of response and consultation, on which the Chief Constable has given his more personal perspective.

It remains to be seen, despite the Chief Constable's perceptions, how *influential* democratic and work structures can be in relation to the legal one. Our next two examples – one from unit and one from resident beat-work – address this issue in particular, in so far as they represent *operational* problems in which the legal structure is clearly invoked. The relative infrequency of operational files applied to our chosen sections as to others, thus requiring us to choose as illustrations the most developed examples of a very restricted category.

Policy Files and the Unit: the Example of Beat Car Speeds

A process of policy consideration in relation to beat car speeds was begun in a force that was to become a component of the present force. This happened in the year prior to the amalgamations that produced the present force. Standing orders said that car patrol officers would not check and report speeding motorists, drive at excessive speed, or chase stolen cars. A unit sergeant reported to his senior officers on his experience of frustration in dealing with speeding motorists. In his opinion there was a need for flexibility in policy in relation to unit beat car drivers, who should be allowed to deal with excessively fast drivers who flouted the law in their view, provided the police drivers were well qualified and the speedometer was checked. An Inspector, and the Superintendent who had cautioned drivers dealt with by the sergeant, agreed with the sergeant's opinion, the Inspector claiming that chases of cars involved in crime should also be permissible. The Chief Superintendent of the division, on balance, disagreed; it would be sufficient for a panda driver who encountered a speeding motorist to take the car's number and to trace the driver later. The ACC (Operations) concurred.

The ACPO Traffic Committee became involved in the same question from a different perspective, when a Police Federation letter was received referring to dangers experienced by panda drivers assigned by controllers to tasks requiring excessive speed. The reply declared that it was difficult to frame an order to prevent danger, but in general unit beat cars were not used for dangerous purposes

Attention returned to the topic as the present force was formed. A Part 1 Order was issued reminding officers of the dangers of high-speed pursuit in unit beat vehicles. Instead Traffic units were to be called to assist. Normally unit beat cars were to observe statutory speed limits except when it was necessary, in an emergency, to detect offences, or to perform a particular duty. Speed limits up to 10 mph over the statutory limit were to apply. At a Chief Superintendents' conference, almost two years later, the CC said that he could not lay down firm guidelines, but supervisors should ensure orders were observed. The following year a Superintendent asked for the order to be made permanent as a standing order; the report was passed through the Management Department and the Traffic Department to the ACC(O), who endorsed the request. The order was drafted by the Traffic Department. The draft drew attention to conditions of safe driving and contained the advice that unit beat cars should exceed the speed limit only in cases of emergency or serious crime. The Chief Superintendent of the department wrote that there was no need for formal limits. The ACC(O), however, decided not to authorize the proposed draft.

The issue was an implicit theme in the inquiries that preceded the internal reorganization of the force. Research by the Management Department, reported to a district regional planning officers' conference, showed that emergency calls were being assigned to unit beat cars rather than to Traffic patrol cars, which were not being properly used for high-speed chases. The new system introduced first-response vehicles, under subdivisional control, in order to ensure the proper use of resources. At a Superintendents' conference it was said that the reorganization meant that the panda driver was not now required to drive at high speed. Shortages of higher-powered vehicles were a problem; an Inspector asked whether a qualified first-response car driver in a vehicle normally used for panda work might report speeding motorists; the Traffic Department officer consulted was against such a proposal.

The ACC(O) then authorized a new order on the subject. The order reminded officers that the unit beat car was not intended to deal with speeding motorists or for use at high speed. Speed limits should be observed at all times except in extreme emergency. While it was not desirable to lay down hard-and-fast rules, under normal circumstances it should not be necessary to exceed limits by more than 10 mph. Primary responsibility for speeding offences rested with Traffic; first-response cars might be used as necessary. Where panda vehicles were used as first-response cars it was necessary to observe the same limitations that applied in normal panda work.

If we take the continuing question of panda vehicle speeds as one process of policy consideration we note certain themes. The sources of policy consideration lie in the activities of the lower ranks and the reviews of policy stimulated thereby. Officers working close to the ground report on matters of concern to them; supervisory reporting is also generated, independently. The definitions of the basic issue contain a number of elements. Implicit in the version of the problem at source and in the framing of the orders is the idea of the individual police officer's duty to law. The sergeant who started the issue said that he had been overtaken on two occasions by speeding motorists who when stopped and verbally cautioned said they did not think they could be reported by a panda driver. He had reported two speeding motorists, only to be advised about existing policy by his Superintendent, who cautioned the motorists in question. The problem faced by the sergeant was posed by the deployment of resources within the force which assigned the duty of dealing with speeding offences to specialist officers with the right kind of vehicle. The sergeant was expressing, against the implications of that efficient deployment, the duty of the police officer to enforce a law within his discretion. The orders which followed from the persistent nature of the problem recognized implicitly that it is not possible to restrain officers from pursuing a legal duty which they as individuals may be capable of fulfilling. The problem of holding down the speed of unit beat car drivers was thus to be solved only by framing a set of possibilities in which judgement had to be the final arbiter, supported by supervision. This definition persisted through successive organizational circumstances, as the example of the order finally noted has shown.

The assignment in practice of emergency calls to panda drivers followed a similar logic. The police officer nearest to the problem would be given the job of dealing with it. The ultimate policy answer was to compromise with the logic of these assumptions and to deploy first-response cars at the disposition of subdivisional controllers. The national intervention of the Police Federation, curiously, went against the logic of the operational assumptions of its membership; it blamed central control policy for accidents arising from job assignments to pandas. The denial of risk by ACPO, the senior ranks' counterpart of the Federation, seemed to block a general occupational concern on the matter. The efficient deployment of resources is therefore a theme also supported by the demands of welfare; moderate speed is safe. These two themes are at odds with the legal factor of constabulary duty.

The policy decisions about unit beat car speeds are made in the light of inquiries by departmental specialists. The field of discussants is enlarged to include officers of various ranks, from lower ranks through supervisory ranks to the ACC(O) and the CC, who make decisions. The general continuity of those decisions is marked, as is shown by the ACC(O)'s decision not to accept the even less categorical draft order prepared by a departmental specialist. The type of policy consideration involves the review and reinforcement of policy through orders and appeals, the implementation of which resides importantly with supervisors. The example of policy on unit beat car speeds shows that, where legal duty is a factor to be taken into account, policy formulations on grounds of efficiency or welfare cannot prevail unequivocally in the final policy. The public appears only through the reported voices of recalcitrant motorists.

Policy Files and Resident Beat-work: the Example of Racial Attacks

Police policy for the last twenty years has been heavily influenced by 'the community' – by which is meant, for all practical purposes, ethnic minorities.[2] This has resulted in the development of a set of community policing policies, usually involving provision for consultation with community representatives, in most forces whose areas encompass concentrations of ethnic minorities. At the same time – as the recent riots in Handsworth, Brixton and Tottenham unhappily make all too plain – this form of policing has apparently failed to assuage ethnic-minority grievances concerning policing, even if in particular areas at particular times relations between police and community have not always been hostile.[3] We hope to demonstrate that the resolution of this apparent paradox is to be found in an understanding of how it is possible for a high level of concern about community relations – which in the force studied pre-eminently involved the resident beat system (the 'cornerstone of force policy' according to the DCC) – to coexist with a policy vacuum on particular matters of concern to the ethnic-minority communities.

We start with a narrative account, which for the sake of brevity has been reduced to essentials. We then consider it in relation to our notion of the process of policy consideration in order to illustrate our central point.

Community Policing: an Exemplary Narrative

A series of criminal attacks on black youths and rumours of further violence were followed by a confrontation of black and white youths in the street after the pubs had shut. In the course of dispersing the groups, fighting took place and some police officers were injured. The incident was taken seriously enough for the DCC to attend in person. He then informed community leaders, in particular the local Community Relations Council (CRC) and the Home Office. The following day the local press carried reports of Ku Klux Klan attacks; and a hooded youth was arrested. In the aftermath a local Anti-Racist Committee was formed which organized a march (which the CRC declined to support) and prepared a dossier of evidence of racial harassment and police indifference which it presented to the police. At the same time as the dossier was received by the police, a man appeared in court charged with criminal damage, an arrest which led to the clear-up of the original series of attacks on black youths. A public meeting organized by a county-based ethnic association was attended by the CC, his Deputy and the local divisional commander. The local Police Liaison Committee met, and two police constables attended to answer questions put to them.

The Anti-Racist Committee dossier, which referred to examples of attacks on both blacks and Asians, alleged various instances of neglect of duty by police (for example, the escape of a white arrestee) and one case of police assault. The police on the basis of inquiries formed several conclusions about these matters: the assaults had been detected, or a private remedy had been advised; the Director of Public Prosecutions and the Police Complaints Board had been sent details of the police assault; the escape of the arrestee had indeed been due to police error. An unofficial tribunal was established to consider the Anti-Racist Committee allegations contained in the dossier. The DCC told the CRC of the police conclusions about these matters, mentioning that assaults are normal matters in any community. The Anti-Racist Committee march, which was nationally attended, took place and was protected from attacks by whites, though one of the organizers – a local student – was arrested in a scuffle. The Anti-Racist Committee mobilized support amongst community organizations, councillors and the CRC on the basis of the original incidents. A nationally attended meeting followed which passed off without incident. On the anniversary weekend of the original black–white youth confrontation a pre-emptive police operation was successfully mounted; and the local divisional commander was informed by the organizer of the local youth club attended by many of the black youths involved in the original confrontation that local 'agitators' had failed.

During the course of these events the local Member of Parliament became involved. As a consequence the MP addressed a party conference on fascist sympathizers in the police and on complaints about police action. The Home Secretary asked the MP for the evidence upon which the allegations were based. On receiving this, he sent it to the CC with a note saying that no action was required. The MP's evidence consisted of four components: first, the unofficial tribunal report, which concluded that there had been no attempt to disperse the white youths prior to the confrontation, that blacks clashed with the police after racialist taunts, that the 1970s had witnessed a history of complaints by blacks concerning police behaviour and that the Anti-Racist Committee dossier evidence was a case to answer; second, the miscellaneous media reports of racial attacks by the National Front circulated to MPs by the defence campaign established to support the student organizer arrested on the Anti-Racist Committee march; third, the indication of support for an inquiry into police–black relations proffered by a local CRC representative; and fourth, the reference in *Spearhead*, the National Front paper, to National Front supporters in the police.

On receipt of this evidence and despite the Home Office letter suggesting that no action was necessary, the DCC advised the CC to explain the situation to the MP. He added that the allegations were without substance, inquiries had been undertaken with respect to all relevant matters, the tribunal had had no impact; and he suggested a meeting with the MP. The Home Secretary replied to the MP's allegations, saying that there was no evidence of police fascism and outlining the relevant law and police regulations. The MP remained unsatisfied and wanted to know what measures were being taken.

The CC invited the MP to meet him, his Deputy, the head of community relations and the local divisional and subdivisional commanders. In preparation for the visit, the local divisional commander ordered reports to be prepared by his subdivisional commanders of racial attacks in their subdivisions during the previous months. (Prior to this, the DCC had already expressed an interest in details of such attacks.) A divisional report was compiled, based on details supplied by the subdivisional commanders, mentioning the numbers of incidents and arrests and outlining police activities in train to deal with the situation: a weekend, overtime night van; the resident beat system; the organization of football competitions for local youngsters; community liaison; the placement of a sergeant on permanent duty in a local black youth club. The report, which was sent to the DCC, also added that the incidents cited were similar to those that occur in every police district.

The head of the police community-relations department briefed the CC prior to the visit, suggesting that successive influxes of immigrants brought problems; that, since the interventions of a prominent MP, outside extremists had taken an interest in the area; that much black–white antagonism was an example of mindless youthful violence; that the attitudes of some officers had led to communication problems, problems upon which extremists capitalized.

Correspondence between the Home Office and the MP continued on the question of checks on police fascists, on the case of the arrested student Anti-Racist Committee organizer and other related matters. After the meeting between the MP and the police, the CC wrote to the Home Office saying it had been very useful, that the MP had been persuaded over the question of police extremists, had been surprised and impressed by the community-relations activity of the force and had not pursued the case of the arrested student organizer.

Analysing the Narrative: the Question of Policy

The source of policy consideration in connection with the original confrontation between black and white youths was clearly the incident itself and the ensuing national reports. The local division then 'reported' it to the DCC, the person responsible for force community relations, who then proceeded to attempt to allay the fears of local black representatives by consultation, by attendance at an open meeting organized by local critics and generally by countering accusations. The problem was 'defined initially' as basically one of communication: a failure to consult and to explain police actions. The principal 'discussants' in the process were the DCC and the CC. 'Inquiry' was conducted by the DCC, utilizing the services of the divisional commander, and the results were reported to the Home Office, which based its replies to inquiries on this police report. 'Decisions' were taken by the DCC in close consultation with the CC. These decisions, by confirming the original definition of the problem, limited *policy* initiatives to this area. Thus it was decided that there had been insufficient attention to communications and explanations; that the improvement of community relations required more consultation; that certain failings required attention; but that some success was evidenced by the arrest and charge of those responsible for incidents. The type of policy consideration, then, is *consolidating* rather than inaugural: a re-application of concepts already in existence, not the establishment of new ones. As the DCC himself put it, in commenting upon the incident, 'We changed *attitudes.*' 'Implementation' took the form of personally consulting with the CRC, attending locally organized meetings to answer critics and avoiding the Anti-Racist Committee. This re-emphasis on community-relations policy was accompanied by a certain redeployment of senior personnel and a restatement of the importance of resident beat-work, a restatement which had certain concrete effects: the restaffing of vacant resident beats, more involvement by RBOs with community projects and greater efforts to ensure RBOs remained on their beats.

The 'source' of policy consideration with respect to the intervention of the local MP was the report delivered by the MP to the party conference. The Home Secretary 'reported' the matter to the force, forwarding the evidence, and the DCC was responsible for 'defining' the matter. This he did in saying that the allegations were being dealt with and that a meeting should be arranged to disabuse the MP. 'Discussions' between the DCC and the CC led to the decision to invite the MP to a meeting, to the decision to establish an 'inquiry' instigated by the DCC and conducted by the local divisional commander to look into the allegations, and to a briefing of the CC by the head of the community-relations department. The 'initial definition' remained unaltered. 'Implementation' took the form of the planned meeting, which was apparently concluded to the satisfaction of all parties.

Both these policy matters, which effectively constituted a single policy matter, were impregnated throughout, as should be clear, by a strong community input. Concern by representatives of the local community, including the local MP, was paramount and influenced both initial and subsequent police actions. The problem throughout was defined, precisely, in terms of a failure to consult with community representatives; it was *the* issue. However, since the specific allegations made by the various community representatives involved were not admitted, but consistently rebutted, the influence of the community on specific *policy* with respect to racially motivated offences was nil, though certain *related* changes, as we have just outlined, were set in train. There was thus no policy commitment to give special attention to racially motivated attacks; rather there was an insistence that there was nothing special about such attacks, which, as criminal attacks, would be dealt with in the normal way.

The above example has attempted to illustrate a simple but important point: the absence of a policy on racially motivated offences despite widespread and persistent concern among ethnic minorities and their representatives over a number of years. This does not mean that community-relations policy has not been of concern to the force during this period; quite the reverse, since in certain respects it has been an issue of major importance. There would thus appear to be, as we suggested at the outset, a paradox. An issue of burning concern to particular minority groups, expressed through appropriate democratic channels, is taken very seriously by the force – but not in a way which leads to the inauguration of policy (that is, new policy) in the area causing the initial concern.

It needs to be emphasized that the absence of a policy on racially motivated offences does not mean the absence of either policy consideration or changes in the area of community policing. The force concern with community-relations policy has entailed its entry into the process of policy consideration with definite accompanying practical initiatives – as the examination of our example indicated. This point is central to the argument and therefore merits further elaboration.

We have already said that in talking about 'community policing' in this particular force we are effectively talking about the resident beat system. The work of these officers must be considered in relation to two areas of policework; on the one hand, RBOs are an integral part of the basic beat system of policing an area; on the other, they are effectively the 'operational' arm of the community-relations department. Both these areas have been the subject of much policy consideration in recent years and have seen many changes in policy and practice. For example, an internal Joint Branch Board working-party report on the operation of the new 'unit beat system' highlighted the importance of the selection and training of RBOs, and was followed by the Home Office study of 'urban workloads' (Comrie and Kings, 1975) which evaluated the effectiveness of the new system and its constituent roles.[4] Later still the Management Department produced evaluations both of the 'unit beat system' and, more specifically, of the workings of RBOs – the latter evaluation concluding, in somewhat contradictory fashion, that there was no objective means of evaluating RBO performance, yet that improvements in team co-operation, the dissemination of information and the selection of personnel were all needed. This concern with information was neither new, since it echoed the 1975 Home Office report, nor unrecognized, since force working parties had been established to look specifically into the role of collators both before and after amalgamation. More over, the latter working party paralleled an ACPO working party on the same theme of criminal intelligence. As an integral component of the 'unit beat system', then, the subject of RBO working has been part of widespread and constant policy consideration and accompanying changes: on the one hand, to keep beats staffed and resist the temptation to use the RBOs as a pool of reserve personnel (not necessarily successfully, as we saw earlier); and, on the other, to develop and sustain personally a range of community contracts. Less direct, but perhaps equally important, has been the sustained attempt to upgrade the status of the RBO post by insisting on its operational importance – an importance which has doubtless produced effects at the level of selecting candidates for the job and in terms of evaluating a successful period in post for promotion purposes. This insistence, at the level of force command, has been unswerving.

However, despite this constant implication of RBO work in the process of policy consideration, and despite definite changes – both evidence of genuine concern with the effectiveness of the unit beat system and with community relations – there has been *no policy with respect to how RBOs, or other officers for that matter, should deal with offences involving a racial motivation.* Indeed, the question of discrimination, which was at the heart of the ethnic-minority concern, has been hardly a substantive policy issue at all. This absence is crucial to an understanding of why, on the one hand, ethnic minorities consistently accuse the police of a lack of urgency in such matters;[5] and why, on the other, the police reply by insisting that complaints are being investigated and point to the range of activities instituted to improve community relations as evidence of the seriousness with which they take such matters. The truth is that the response, concerned as it is, fails to match the specific nature of the grievance. The reason has to do with the problem of formulating an *operational* policy, as distinct from questions of establishment and training, where, to be sure, RBO systems do command attention.

Essentially the same issue arose in the case of unit beat car speeds. In the operational field the overriding commitment is to a legal duty. Policy can only conform to such a superordinate responsibility, not subvert it. This means, in operational areas, either the permissiveness evident in our unit beat example, or the vacuum evident in this resident beat one.

Concluding Policy: the Hypotheses Compared

If we return to our original hypotheses we find that none of the ideas of policy as super-relevant ('machine'), irrelevant ('subculture'), shaped by the environment ('environmental'), or by class ('class-functionalist') captures the bipolar nature of policy that our detailed observations have revealed. The notion of policy as a universal, homogeneous entity (instructions, guidelines, or principles to inform practice) cannot therefore withstand a critical, concrete examination. Such an investigation produces, as we have seen, a conception of policy embracing two distinct forms (administrative versus operational), each possessing a distinctive discourse (rational-scientific versus common sense) and each producing a distinctive kind of practical outcome (predictable, calculable effects versus unpredictable, incalculable effects).

In terms of the idea of policy being concerned to produce calculable outcomes (a notion of policy which comes closest to the conventional notion employed by those who have never examined policy concretely), this means that only administrative policy issues qualify. Operational policy issues, characterized by a common-sense discourse, do not produce this kind of policy. Thus, in these areas it is meaningless or irrelevant to talk of a 'blockage' existing between policy and practice ('machine'-model hypothesis) or of a rank-and-file subculture subverting managerial policy ('subculture'-model hypothesis). In these areas, permissive or absent policies *allow* a diversity of practices; nothing is precluded because, in policy terms, nothing specific is demanded. Since neither 'blockage' nor 'subversion' accounts for our findings, can the hypothesis of 'environment' or 'class' shaping policy assist? In the case of environment, in so far as this suggests a relatively strong democratic input, what was striking throughout was the comparative absence of the democratic structure and, where present, as in the last example, its inability to override the effects of the legal structure. As for the hypothesis about class, the centrality of the legal structure precludes *any* social group from *unmediated* influence.[6]

Which brings us to our hypotheses about the importance of the three structures and the role of the legal structure as 'organizer'. Our hypotheses produced the possibility of different, task-related policy issues – administrative and operational – a possibility that an examination of the policy system and the process of policy consideration confirmed. This confirmation also revealed the different discourses – rational-scientific and occupational common sense – applicable to each, with their different practical outcomes (predictable versus unpredictable). Most importantly, our concrete examination revealed the inherent relationship between 'operational' and 'common sense', and the ultimate priority of the latter over the rational-scientific when both are being invoked in relation to an operational matter. This latter revelation demonstrates the centrality of the legal structure in understanding operational policy; the importance of the office of constable, vesting discretion in the office, thus allowing occupational 'common sense' to be dominant as against other considerations including those emanating from the democratic audience.

Finally it is necessary to mention the theoretical and conceptual bases of this analysis. In doing so we shall anticipate a central theme of Chapter 9, which is concerned to scrutinize the fundamental significance of our conceptual instruments, in particular the concept of structure. We need to emphasize the theoretical value of a structural analysis, one which delimits the notion of policy and places it within a specific context. In particular this analysis owes much to an appreciation of the discursive nature of policy consideration in which the would-be interpreter must examine how topics are defined, the scope of inquiry, the range of discussants, their use of the appropriate discourses (common sense and scientific management, in particular). By defining policy discursively, as a particular kind of statement, the analyst pinpoints its characteristic basis as a form of *signification*: in other words, as a way of giving meaning to the topic of policework.

A discursively based conception of the process of policy consideration highlighted the discrete steps in the whole movement from 'source' to 'implementation'. As a process of signification, policy consideration had to be understood in terms of the interpretive work associated with receiving a message from the source, constructing an initial definition and so on. It is in this process of interpretive work that a potential for 'resignifying' a given topic lies; hence we have had to look closely at the manner in which this process is performed, to discover whether given definitions are accepted, resisted, altered, or dispensed with, and so on. More important than particular 'resignifications' is the reproduction of those discursive understandings which we observed, especially of understandings based in the principal categories of common sense and scientific management. Part of this endeavour takes the form of a recreation of 'consent' among the lower ranks, a means of ensuring compliance. This is consistent with a force outlook in which it is also felt that *public* consent should be cultivated, as we have seen.

The political implications of an analysis of policy also deserve some mention since they bear on the possibilities for reform in police organizations. Policy might be one instrument for reform; but how viable might this prove? Our evidence implies that change might be achieved only by a 'repositioning' of the discourses so as to enable the production of operational policy that is legal, effective and likely to be perceived as equitable. But this in turn would depend on a change in the pattern of accountability which is itself discursively defined. However, these political implications, together with the theoretical implications of a structural discursive approach, must await a full discussion in Chapter 9.

Notes

1 We excluded seven (three SPG, two CID, two Management Department) as being irrelevant for our present purposes.

2 Anybody seriously doubting the equation of 'community' with ethnic minorities so far as police policy is concerned has only to examine the history of the establishment of community-relations (or public-liaison) departments in forces throughout the country. As the old Birmingham City Police succinctly put it in its evidence to the Parliamentary Select Committee on Police–Immigrant Relations (1971–2): 'Before coloured immigration affected us, no police force in Britain ever deemed it necessary to set up a department to promote relations with the indigenous community' (quoted in Judge, 1974, p. 201).

3 Indeed, as we suggested in Chapter 5, the situation is compounded by the fact that RBO contacts are concentrated on 'consensual' publics, which means that community 'hostilities' can arise apparently 'out of the blue': out of what are believed to be 'good' police–community relations. For existence of ethnic minority grievances, a concern by certain police officers for community policing and a police belief that police–community relations were generally cordial shortly before a major confrontation, see Gifford (1986, pp. 35–64).

4 In official parlance, the 'unit beat system' includes the 'unit' and the RBOs: a combination of foot and car patrols for each beat feeding information to a collator. Introduced as a Home-Office-sponsored experiment in the late 1960s, it quickly became (and remains) the standard system for organizing uniformed police duties (cf. Home Office, 1967). This differs slightly from our usage, which has been based on the fact that for all practical purposes they are separate systems, as our earlier analyses have attempted to demonstrate.

5 See, for example, Bethnal Green and Stepney Trades Council (1978) and *Race and Class* (1979). Later the Home Office, upon conducting its own research into the question of racial attacks, was forced to concede the same point; see Home Office (1981).

6 Lee's discussion of the complex relationships between social stigma and class, and his conclusion that 'class is not always the *governing* factor' (1981, p. 52, italics in original), endorses this position, though not necessarily the supporting argument.

PART V

Conclusions

CHAPTER NINE

From the Theory to
the Politics of Policework

The present chapter attempts to place under critical scrutiny the principal sociological concepts we have so far applied. It is hoped that, by a deeper examination of their significance in the context of particular sociological theories, we shall be able to define them more explicitly and usefully than has previously been possible. The first step along this road is our 'settling of accounts' with the work of Althusser, which requires us to put in context his use of the concept 'structure' and to develop our own version of 'structure' by reference to 'structuralism' more generally. Then we turn to the issues presented by important theoretical perspectives – those of Foucault and Gramsci – which confront the problem of structure by constructing a set of dynamic and historical conceptions of society; beat-work forms our means of exemplifying these conceptions and showing how they enable us to interpret in structural terms concrete changes in police practice within historical conjunctures. From conjuncture as a theoretical notion, we turn then to the current political conjuncture in the shape of the 'police debate'. It is our intention to examine the relevance of existing sociological models to the decisive questions of police reform, before bringing out the sociological inadequacies of various reform proposals, from the political left, the right and the centre. Finally we sketch the lineaments of an agenda for reform based on the conclusions of structural analysis.

Developing a Conception of Structure

At the outset we discussed a series of theoretical positions on the police which hinged around the broad distinction between sociological liberalism and class functionalism. The instruments of our criticism were drawn from the theoretical armoury of Althusser, the Marxist philosopher, whose key categories provided a guiding thread for our comments; thus the mingled 'idealism' and 'empiricism' of liberalism, readily shifting from abstractions about order and liberty to the substantive and profane disorderliness of police culture, were contrasted with the more dogmatic formulations of class functionalism, well representing the toils of 'economism'. These terms – idealism, empiricism, economism – witnessed the Althusserian borrowings of our thought. We further relied on his characteristic distinction between 'dominant' and 'determinant' structures in order to single out the more fundamental determining role of law in policework. Finally, our most crucial affiliation to Althusser is to be found in the general usage of 'structure' as a concept, with all that this implies in suggesting a unified mechanism to be 'read' in its effects (Althusser and Balibar, 1970).

Our employment of a concept of structure should not however be understood as a logical application of Althusser's thinking in the sense that the problematic of the work is constructed narrowly by reference to his *oeuvre*. It remains for us therefore to draw out the implications of a structural theory of policework. In part this requires a disavowal of Althusser and in consequence a sifting of the broader structuralist inheritance in order to place such a theory on a firmer foundation.

From the Marxist structuralist perspective associated with Althusser the forms of the state do not simply reflect the economic structure; instead they achieve an important degree of correspondence with that structure. This means that the state is shaped not by mechanical transmissions from an economic base but by a sequence of relatively autonomous developments on which the economic structure exercises a decisive (not omnipotent) influence. If this conception reveals the structural character of his thought, it should not lead us to overlook its more conservative and exclusive features.

The downfall of structuralist Marxism has not been due directly to any deficiency of rigour or theoretical acuity but to their indirect consequences – an extraordinary poverty of sociological imagination arising from a self-denying conceptual method. A *locus classicus* of this purism is to be found in Hirst (1975) in refuting the possibility of a Marxist theory of crime and deviance (before becoming one of Althusser's fiercest critics). The argument here was that crime could not be conceived within the given conceptual apparatus of Marxism; the study of crime was therefore at best an appendage to a social theory centred elsewhere in the concepts of mode of production and so on. Despite the centrality of law and crime to the definition of the modern state, these could not be brought within an adequate theoretical purview. With no basis for a theoretical understanding, the study of crime appeared to be adventitious to Marxism. Not surprisingly, if the structuralist hand *did* reach out to incorporate such social phenomena within its theoretical perspective the result was reductionist in the extreme (notwithstanding its origins in the desire to escape such a fate).

Althusser's most influential discussion of the state appears in an essay purportedly concerned with adding an extra dimension to the Marxist theory of the state by a recognition of the ideological functions performed by a portion of the state apparatuses (Althusser, 1972). He contrasts these latter with the repressive state apparatus, operating mainly by violence. Thus he allocates the police to the repressive sector, which appears to fall within the traditional theory he nonetheless endorses (despite his wish to supplement it). Hence:

> The State apparatus, which defines the State as a force of repressive execution and intervention 'in the interests of the ruling classes' in the class struggle conducted by the bourgeoisie and its allies against the proletariat, is quite certainly the State, and quite certainly defines its basic 'function'.
>
> (1972, p. 249)

Such formulations remain simplistic, functionalist, exclusive (of other structures and topics) and non-discursive, for example, in not relating the police to the law (which confusingly Althusser regards as both an ideological *and* a repressive apparatus). Our approach has been quite different in intention.

Our most important methodological protocol in the opening discussion concerned the need to be aware of diversity, to pursue differentiation where necessary and to resist the temptations of reductionism. Thus, whereas law might appear as an 'essence' – 'the-law-in-books' or, more radically, 'capitalist law' – we emphasized the benefits of a *composite* and *differentiated* conception, to which classes and groups might be found to have a range of relationships, depending on the type of legal discourse and the sector of law concerned. This approach did not, we hoped, lend itself to an inverse conception, in which law became simply a vehicle of pragmatic intentions, the unhappy opposite of an essentialist conception. But it encouraged us to look for a limited range of possibilities that constituted at any one time the horizon of law. We were examining law as a contemporary process rather than searching for a unitary essence.

Where then can we turn for a structuralist conception which

does reach out in inclusive, non-reductive fashion to grasp, as a combination, a series of structures? Our answer is to lay out certain core elements of a structuralist approach, which in our view constitute its strengths. No single thinker can provide a ready-made model; instead we can outline in the form of several theses a general position drawn from a number of sources.

(1) Social intercourse presupposes the constitutive significance of signs through which individual activity becomes a social 'possession'. Material activity and material events assume meaning to the extent that they are construed as signs. Thus the importance of language as an orienting point of reference is affirmed by many versions of structuralism (Levi-Strauss, 1963, p. 34). Individual utterances take on a social character through signifying structures which are based on the differences among and between linguistic elements. Utterances become meaningful to the extent that this social structure of signification is in place, allowing messages to be encoded and decoded by competent speakers. Statements drawn together as a unity constitute a discourse, of which law forms an obviously relevant example.

(2) The elements of discourse are seen as objective, forming the basis for group communication; while discourse can be a field of diversity and contest, it cannot be coherently sustained on a subjective foundation. It follows that the discourses sustaining police cultural forms must be regarded as objectively intelligible.

(3) The structured character of language allows the formation of levels of signification, in which some elements possessing a given signification become the vehicle for further forms of signification (Barthes, 1973, p. 115). Levels of signification imply the possibility of a non-reductive analysis of events (Leach, 1976, p. 41). An event can therefore be understood as having a series of discursive implications.

(4) Complex expressions can be produced by the application of simple generative rules. This insight permits structuralism to offer simple key terms as the basis for explaining elaborate discursive expressions, whether these form the basis for social or cultural institutions (Levi-Strauss, 1970, p. 10). Hence our choice of merely three structures as key terms for the concrete analysis of policework.

(5) Elements can be regarded as arbitrary, from the point of view of a given level of analysis. Just as particular word forms may be considered irrelevant to the analysis of linguistic signifi-

cation, so it is possible that a variety of social actions can qualify as, say, 'theft'; what matters are the common features that allow members of a society, and police officers in particular, to nominate actions in that way. Hence we can discern levels of common social activity that are more than randomly grouped events *and* less than literally identical events.[1] It does make sense then to talk for example about a systematic structure of law even if this displays discrepancies within and between its domains.

(6) The notion of a possible arbitrariness in the relation between levels reminds us more generally not to insist on a necessary relationship of signification, since in principle elements can be regrouped in order to create a further signification (Coward and Ellis, 1977, p. 22). How far this is done depends on the extent to which the relevant logical relations are critically reappraised at every appropriate point in the system. Thus we cannot propose an eternal structure of policework in which 'law', 'democracy' and 'work' circle one another for ever. Rather we suggest that these form a powerful signifying set which would require considerable significatory work to disentangle or rejig. But the politics of police accountability contributes precisely the critical significatory operation we have in mind here. The possibility of a structural transformation remains importantly open (cf. Jameson, 1974).

(7) Transformation takes the place of history in the structuralist interpretation of society. Given the nature of a structure, particular sequences can be seen as logical outcomes of a given 'repertoire' rather than as unique historical events. History therefore remains a subordinate descriptive moment in the analysis of structure, with structural transformations playing a key role, instead; by contrast the mundane progression of history speaks only of the properties of structure. In this particular sense we can refer to the 'historical present' of the structure (Levi-Strauss, 1963, p. 23).

Structuralism is not without its critics; a number of the most salient criticisms have been exemplarily summarized by Sumner (1979, pp. 106–13).[2] Thus the structuralist's apparent exclusion of history is condemned along with the search for the functional integration of elements and the abstraction implied by the analysis of structural differences. The charge of mere descriptiveness emerges from this allegation of abstractness and lack of historical specificity. In addition structuralism is accused of proposing closed systems incapable of being linked with one another in a logically adequate manner. Hence structuralism finally resorts to an absolute Logos as the transcendent structure in which everything is included. Out of this critique we can discern a general dissatisfaction with the purgation of concrete substance allegedly performed by a structuralist method. Yet it can be argued in reply that the concept of structure creates the first condition of a concrete understanding in separating out the terms through which concrete objects can be constructed in thought (cf. Carver, 1975, p. 73). Hence the accusations of an 'ahistorical' approach based on 'closed' systems fail to encompass this purpose. It is a methodological protocol that dictates the abstraction of a structural approach, not some epistemological assumption.[3] How a methodological alternative to structuralism is to be produced which retains its strengths and dispenses with any weaknesses still remains unclear.

Structure and History

In seeking to outline a core version of structuralism within which we can begin to place our fundamental concepts, we have distanced our position from Althusser's. In substantive terms this move helps to explain why we start our analysis with a concept of law, since law provides a central discursive framework for police activity; it defines the principal elements of the police task, distinguishes the police from other state institutions and produces the forms of police accountability. This is not to say that law may not 'represent' other social structures by means of signification; indeed, our rendering of structuralism provides for this. Rather, we mean that the discourse of law is the starting-point for making sense of *policework* (as distinct from a study of the manifold *conditions* underpinning policework within a given society, which we cannot here undertake). Furthermore we have argued that the structure of law organizes the positioning and significance of the other structures: work and democracy. It is now our intention to examine beat-work in a more general theoretical context. In order to approach this discussion, we have chosen first to refer to two exemplary social theorists whose importance in theoretical criminology makes their work an unavoidable point of reference: Gramsci and Foucault. Though these figures do not deliver a general schema for our analysis, they do offer, in different but related ways, insights which can assist a general interpretation of our work and hence in orienting our own theorization within the theoretical field of criminological studies as a whole. In particular, they appear to offer a way of thinking about significant transformations in the structures we have been concerned to delineate; they raise the question of relating history and structure, an issue that the critics of structuralism have not been slow to broach. Both thinkers represent dialogues with the heritage of Marx. In the case of Gramsci, this interchange is focused on the clarification of the political superstructure and its relation with 'civil society', in which the law is seen as an active instrument, among others, for the reorganization and development of society. In the process, the question of public consent is given close attention. The relation of the state and civil society is clearly an important topic in thinking theoretically about policework.

While Gramsci's thought stands within the tradition of Marx, that of Foucault remains external in significant respects, deriving sustenance from Nietzsche in reformulating the question of power (Smart, 1983). Thus Foucault affirms the importance of systematic modes of subordination, especially at the micro-level, and particularly those forms of domination outside or supplementary to the formal juridical apparatus. A particularly sharp delineation of power in action (and the resistances these evoke) emerges from this highly concrete approach.

Though Foucault's radical notion of power seems to consist of a systematic inversion of the conceptual and methodological protocols of classical Marxism – for example, his attention to the techniques and procedures of power exercised in local institutions rather than the centralized power of the state (Foucault, 1981, p. 94) – it is none the less possible to regard Gramsci and Foucault as united in their attempts to produce non-reductive accounts of power. This is a perceptive connection made by Mouffe (1979, p. 201) in producing an important non-reductionist reading of Gramsci's conception of hegemony, and one we wish to utilize concretely here.[4]

The importance of Gramsci lies in his theoretical concentration on questions of power viewed from a perspective emphasizing complex and shifting strategic movements and balances of forces, ranging widely across the social terrain. Social 'hegemony' is thus constituted in broader terms than a confrontation of fundamental classes – as class functionalism would have it – and encompasses instead all kinds of associations and interests, thus incorporating an attention to many forms of social struggle. In particular, for our purposes, the state is conceived not simply as a repressive but as a positive educative force promoting new forms of 'civilization'. Rationalization and innovation are aspects of state activity conducted according to this policy of acculturation, in which the law is pressed into service: 'The law is the repressive and negative aspect

of the entire positive, civilizing activity undertaken by the State'
(Gramsci, 1971, p. 247).

By incorporating the substratum of the society within this
ethical framework, the hegemony of dominant social forces can be
sustained. Thus the positive significance of the state and its
agencies is affirmed. In addition the rationalization of these
agencies themselves is given theoretical attention, emphasizing the
transformations possible within the state.

FOUCAULT: LEGALITY AND THE NORM

Foucault's work has been wide ranging, addressing, variously, 'the
question of the relations "between experiences . . . knowledge . . .
and power"[5] . . . the formation of the modern subject . . . the forms
in which power is exercised over life; and the associated matter of
the government and self-government of individuals and populations' (Smart, 1985, p. 121). It also remains controversial, with
supporters and critics divided over whether such concrete analyses
of power produce a needed alternative to the reductionist tendencies of global theorizing, or an important moment to be
incorporated within a more general framework such as that offered
by Marxism.[6] For our purposes, Foucault's methodological commitment to the unprejudiced examination of the specific mechanisms, techniques and procedures through which power is exercised
in particular institutions gave warrant to our detailed empirical
examination of policework (albeit an institution of the central
state). Theoretically, his attention to forms of power, and
especially his conception of 'a historical shift . . . from the pre-
dominance of sovereignty–law–repression to the development and
diffusion of more subtle and economical forms of power' (Smart,
1985, p. 127), produced a highly relevant distinction for us. The
key technique of these new forms of power is discipline, which has
as its object not repression but normalization. This key distinction, between 'legality' and 'discipline', offers the possibility of
interpreting the important differences between unit and resident
beat-work. 'Legality' here refers to the juridical structure with a
corpus of laws and texts forbidding some and permitting other
actions. Quite distinct are the instruments of discipline – 'hier-
archical observation', 'normalizing judgement' and 'the examination' – by which individuals are observed, differentiated,
classified and judged against a norm of conformity (Foucault,
1979, p. 170).

Where our analysis apparently departs from the letter of Foucault is in retaining hold of the idea of law as a core of the police
function. This must remain a clear commitment on our part

precisely because the police occupy the 'legal-repressive' space in modern society that was characteristic *in general* of the older state whose obsolescence Foucault seems to proclaim. Indeed, Foucault argues that the Norm joins with Law in the construction of power in modern society (1979, p. 184). We do not mean that 'legal repression' represents the whole of police practice – far from it, as we have indicated, some laws *are* based on 'legal normalization' or administrative regulation. But 'upholding the law' comes to assume a greater importance in society precisely to the degree that the techniques of disciplinary power are restricted by public policy or are seen to fail to come to terms with certain kinds of open resistance. At this point policework renews its lineage, going back to its pre-bourgeois origins in the royal office of constable and deploying a traditional negativity against 'violence' or 'subversion'. The panoply of dramatic intervention, the display of authority and force: all these derive from the continuing repertoire of traditional legality which retains a certain strategic significance alongside the manifold disciplinary mechanisms of the contemporary state. And precisely by means of this legality, of being associated with 'the law', repression has been legitimated, just as the norm legitimates administrative regulation.[7]

The unit therefore carries the paradox of this historical development. While its internal relations are relatively 'disciplined' (in the Foucauldian sense), its external relations with the public sometimes reveal a weariness with the sober task of regulation, and a tendency to welcome opportunities for the decisive act, the critical confrontation in which legality/repression can be reaffirmed in something like the historic sense associated with the older origins of policing. The public, accordingly, becomes the instrument and object of these processes, routinely generating only pockets of combative non-conformity and resistance within a social ethos generally presided over by the various disciplines of employment, social security, social hygiene and so on. This analysis, which centres on immediate tendencies in the organization of unit work, should therefore be accompanied by a cognate examination which takes into view the general relations and functions of social control within a capitalist social order. It is on the margins of the capitalist social order, for example, among blacks and youth, that sporadic expressions of disaffection pose a threat against which the unit mode of policing forms a potential shield, in a recoil from its mundane functions of routine surveillance and incident response.

The function of the resident beat officer appears less as a representative of the law than as a guardian of the norm, as a community worker rather than as a gendarme. Beat-work is rendered as a form of normalizing leadership by those deemed best able to judge an area's needs because of their extensive acquaintance. Law becomes one instrument, one method of dealing with infractions of the norm, norms being relative to the singularities and particularities of the locality. Rather than an abstract calculation of illegalities, normative measures – 'what is normal for the area' – enter the field of decision-making criteria.

Rather than imposing absolute standards or responding to a universal need, the practice of resident beat-work is closely tailored to a perception of a *local* need faithfully monitored by a *local* officer. The diversity of style observed among officers reflects the integrity of each diagnosis even if in reality the stylistic possibilities of individual officers remain limited and even predictable. The unique area, in principle, authorizes the 'unique style'; what matters is the perceived authenticity of the officer's relationship with an area, confirmed and enhanced by community feedback. Everything therefore depends on the proximity of the officer to the area's essential impulses, a proximity which legitmates a chosen path of intervention as 'right for the area'.[8] On the basis of extensive surveillance and intensive contact over a period of time, the failings and problems of an area can thus be diagnosed and rectified, it is suggested, without any crude and damaging mistakes. Even crime problems are felt to retreat in the face of an officer's local knowledge and tactful intervention; errant youth can be put on the right lines by the appropriate mixture of guidance and education.

The problem of incorporating a normalizing practice into policework is to be located in the primary status of law as an objective and guide for the police. Upholding the law not only forms a mandatory objective, it also legitimates the powers of the police and authorizes their operational independence. To complicate this picture by introducing an explicit normalizing element could detract from the claims of the police to a position of constitutional independence, since the admission of non-legal criteria of action opens up scope for bodies other than legal ones to aspire to power and influence. Indeed, it becomes possible for the communities themselves to challenge the basis of a normalizing leadership, if they can claim a prerogative of normative definition; after all, norms may be felt to be communal in origin. This is not to deny that the police can call on their 'democratic' tradition to support their independence, since one origin of the constable can be derived from the tradition of communal self-responsibility. Indeed, this tradition is just what one beat officer, in talking to local schoolchildren, refers to. However, such a reformulation sits uneasily alongside the predominant conception of the police force as a whole, in which the due application of law takes precedence. Perhaps this unease explains the shifting status of resident beat-work with its subordination to individual management priorities and to constables' stylistic preferences. Discretion and independence are reaffirmed in the face of the possible dissolution of policing into 'what the community wants'. We have also noted the strong pull of well-established styles of policing drawn from the repertoire of an 'old bureaucracy'.

GRAMSCI: BUREAUCRACY AND CONSENT

From a point of view consistent with Gramsci, unit beat policing represents an attempted rationalization of the activities conducted within the 'superstructure', an elimination of the waste associated with proliferating employment within the revenue-supported state sector. It belongs to the historical trend identified by Gramsci which he termed 'Americanism', in which work is constructed into ever more rationalized units so as to achieve the most effective result (Gramsci, 1971, pp. 277–318). The provision of expensive technology was aimed at an expansion of police services and of individual productivity, measured by calls, reports, detected crimes and so on. Unit beat policing was therefore a movement attempting to reform 'unproductive' patrolling, to sharpen the sluggish responses of the older system to emergencies and to replace them with a rapid and extensive service, integrated under the supervision of radio control. Like industrial mechanization, unit beat policing was intended to serve the goal of enhanced productivity and responsiveness and likewise it brought in new forms of internal supervision based on a close scrutiny of motivation and an appreciation of personal welfare.

The 'machinery' of the unit specified the elements of an organizational form which appears highly rationalized. Hence a system of command, a hierarchy of competences and a routinization of work, on a technically refined basis (cf. Weber, 1968). Thus in unit work we find the Inspectors and sergeants formally assigned within a hierarchy of both competence and command; below these are ranged the hierarchies of first-response and panda drivers, and the ranks of foot patrollers and station assistants. A system of work allocation provides each with an appropriate type or zone of responsibility, shifting upwards from the foot patrollers' supervision of stationary vehicles to the pursuit of suspects in vehicles and finally to the Inspectors' investigation of fatal accidents. Routinization is formally assured by the system of paper reporting and radio command which determines the due dispensation of activity and time corresponding to standard requirements. All work is putatively assisted by management study, training supervisory advice and so on, reflecting throughout the organization the impact of technical virtuosity and refinement. Unit work in this context purports to represent a paragon of rationalization.

Yet even within a 'high-crime' area we find unit work subject to a fluctuation of input which as we have seen draws radically into question the real pertinence of bureaucratic organizational forms. In the absence of a stream of *appropriate* work, the formal mechanisms of work allocation, advice, supervision and so on break down, since they are predicated on a continuous 'production line' of activity which throws up a regular series of marks or indicators allowing checks and corrections to be made. The 'stop-start' character of the input conditions the periodic interruption of such checks. This does not mean that a wholesale deviation grips the system, rather that those who operate it keep moving, 'go through the motions', perform trivial tasks, or simply wait for the system to channel suitably relevant work on which they can at last deploy favoured competences. As constables performing legal work on the other hand they can aspire to exert the authority otherwise denied by the mundane or irrelevant incidents which form the texture of normal policework. It is the problem of relevance, and in particular *legal* relevance, that brings into question the whole function of rationalization.

Since legality is interpreted by constables according to commonsense norms, rationalization here necessarily reaches its limit. In order to assess the effect of this on the production of 'civilized' individuals, the generation of consent within 'civil society', we have to consider the relation of the unit with 'democracy'. This works in two ways. In the case of irrelevant contacts the democratic public is marginalized and passed over; in the case of legally relevant encounters the interests of rationalization tend to dictate a superficial form of contact, pressing forward to the next incident, while occupational norms of pragmatism encourage manipulativeness. The end result is unlikely to be a contribution to a positive 'civilizing' mission. A Gramscian perspective would thus emphasize the counter-pressure on a purportedly rationalized system, a pressure which demands that consent be regenerated. It is here that RBO work enters the field as a 'consent-producing' formation, supplementing the old, semi-rationalized bureaucracy with a 'new' one.

THE CONVERGENCE OF HISTORY AND STRUCTURE
At this point a Gramscian perspective can begin to be usefully welded to a Foucauldian one. If Foucault's genealogical analyses

of techniques of power have detailed the nature of significant differences between legal repression and disciplinary normalization, the latter more characteristic of the past two hundred years consequent upon the profound transformations that took place during the seventeenth and eighteenth centuries, Gramsci's notion of the centrality of consent provides a concept for understanding the motor of transformations between these different forms of power. It is the renewed search for consent, consequent upon a breakdown of legitimacy, that determines when the emphasis shifts from the uncertain rationality of the unit to the development of 'out-reach', 'community development' and all the other strategies associated with the interventionist search for public acceptance typical of the RBOs – from Law to the Norm.

Thus we have reviewed some of the significant results of the study in the light of theoretical contributions from two important thinkers, each committed to a non-reductive understanding of the way a social order is sustained and regenerated, each pinpointing dynamic processes of positive subordinations, each therefore proposing a history of strategic movements in forms of social hegemony and control. Our fundamental purpose here is not to arbitrate between their separate claims as theorists but to show how a study informed by their insights can approach the manifestation of structure in history. We have previously tried to show how elements of structure are identifiable within concrete forms of policework. Now, using historical conceptions of social control, we can indicate the sequence in which the elements may appear, bound up in particular forms of policework that have a definite historical location. Hence, just how 'community policing' emerges from a scene dominated by a unit beat policing system can be understood if we attend to the structural combination of elements that constitutes policework and notice the way in which elements of the 'old' system are regrouped in the 'new' (though both remain, as we have seen, in operation). Since the 'old' was based on the organizational premises of responsiveness, speed and mobility, it enlarged the scope of contact with the public while reducing its intensity, causing contradictions in the 'message' transmitted to the public. The result was a pressure on the structure to produce a 'new' and more consistent 'message', by intensifying public contact; in consequence, the democratic structure is highlighted while the work structure and the legal structure are selectively reshaped for the task of 'normalization' – an occupational reflection of the democratic structure. As Reiss (1971, p. 1) remarked, the police mediate between the law and the community; changing forms of policework provide this mediation. We have tried to demonstrate the presence of structures offering repertoires of policework that can be selectively called upon in particular historical conjunctures. A historical understanding of conjuctures in policework, which Foucault and Gramsci can help us to grasp, complements our knowledge of structures and enables us to approach the task of understanding the present political conjuncture framed by the 'police debate'.

The Translation of Theory into Politics

In order to tease out the relationship between the theory and politics of policework, we intend to proceed via a number of steps. First, we shall spell out the broad political implications of the various approaches which have guided our discussion throughout, ending with our own. Next, we shall concretize the whole discussion by setting it firmly within present concerns about policing, concerns which have produced an ongoing debate about what kind of police force, with what kind of powers, is needed to do what kind of job. This will entail outlining those aspects of the debate that touch upon matters with which we have been concerned, and then subjecting the various 'positions' within the debate to critical scrutiny for their sociological adequacy. We end by pointing towards a politics of policework adequate to the sociological complexities we hope by now to have established as a necessary starting-point for any worthwhile programme of police reform.

The Political Implications of the Various Approaches

THE 'MACHINE' MODEL
The idea that the law or the organization, idealistically conceived, determines rank-and-file behaviour leads to a politics of endlessly tightening formal processes – legal or organizational – and to constantly blaming a lack of success on 'poor leadership', 'lack of professionalism', or, classically, a 'problem of communication between the ranks'. Unaware of ways in which the formal structures of the law and organization may be less than efficacious as determinants, since inattentive to them as concrete, material realities, and with no notion of possible other structures operating as determinants, it is committed to a cycle of reform which is as weak on insight as it is sharp on moral prescription.

THE 'SUBCULTURAL' MODEL
For the subculturalists the political problem is normative. Since legal and organizational prescriptions, however tightened, are

always ultimately fragile, the real question becomes one of how to alter the value system of the rank and file so that it accords with that of management. The negative route is clearly via punishments, but since that can build up resentment it can also strengthen resistance to those very changes being promoted. Therefore, the favoured mode is to concentrate on reforming the motivational structure through the reward system. Essentially, the politics of this approach are about how to create a new morality of an informed and humane 'professionalism'. Besides the reward system, training has a key role in such a politics, as does leadership (which bears on the practice of deployment). Whilst few would object to the desire to create a greater liberalism in the police through better leadership, improved training and a system which rewarded humane crime prevention above crime arrests, we must remain doubtful of the efficacy of reform initiatives which fail to recognize the centrality of the fundamental structure, namely, law. This recurrent failure to recognize the importance of law explains why calls for a 'new professionalism' are recurrently advanced. Reiner's (1985b) echo of Skolnick's (1975) similar call many years previously is symptomatic in this regard.

THE 'ENVIRONMENTAL' MODEL
The idea that the environment shapes police behaviour leads to a politics of restructuring the environment. In principle, there is little to object to in this – but it remains too general, notwithstanding the importance of work like that of Sherman (1978; 1983), for example, in beginning to spell out the conditions under which changes in the external environment can affect the internal capacity to reform. Indicative though such work is, until it can begin to conceptualize the environment other than in terms of empirical effects, the influence of reform initiatives are liable, ultimately, to remain as imprecise as the old notion of environment these replace, and less permanent than desired.

CLASS FUNCTIONALISM
Since law is ultimately bourgeois law or at least enforced to the advantage of the bourgeoisie, then reform efforts are always defeasible, this side of socialism. Consequently the strategic political struggle is for socialism. Under socialism, law will play a radically different role and so would the police, and in some versions they will 'wither away'. The politics of police reform within such a scenario are merely tactical and essentially subordinate to the revolutionary strategic objective. However, the relationship between tactics and strategy tends to be based on a

'politics of exposure'. Thus, the tactic of engaging in a politics of reform is in order to *expose* the inability of the system to reform itself, rather than to see such reforms as essential *steps* in the achievement of a given end. The result, ironically, is a vested interest in the failure rather than the success of reform initiatives, since the latter merely incorporate more successfully. One consequence, inevitably, is a highly opportunistic relationship with the question of reform.

OUR FRAMEWORK

The approach we propose entails a concern for the details of law – constitutional, substantive and procedural – so that the use of discretion is circumscribed and rendered more rational and responsive. In broad terms this means political campaigning to tighten up on questions of police power and accountability. Principles of justice to guide the exercise of discretion need to be established in all areas where the law itself can offer no guidance (and which currently is supplied by police 'common sense' or a version of the 'public interest'), something which would apply even after any legal change, but even more urgently now. These discussions ought, for democratic reasons, to involve as wide an audience as possible. The practical adoption of these principles would then need to be supported through appropriate training, policy change, reward systems and so on, at which point the formal proposals, if not the substance of the principles to be adopted, mirror those proposed by the subculturalists.

Later we shall concretely expand on some of these general remarks about our framework. But first we must render the whole discussion more specific by looking at the current debate about policing, and the sociological adequacy of the various positions within it.

The 'Police Debate'

It is probably true that issues arising from policing are currently more numerous and more contentious than at any time since the passage of the 1829 Police Act and the immediately succeeding period. These issues, in so far as they bear on our present concerns, fall into one of five linked and overlapping categories, namely, police powers, the control of the police, styles of policing and public relations, training, and police–black relations.

POLICE POWERS

The question of what powers police should possess has surfaced periodically, usually as a consequence of an incident highlighting the abuse of existing powers. The most pertinent for our study have arisen on the streets in the handling of public-order and minor offences by uniform patrol officers.[9] In this area, the increasing youthfulness of uniform street patrol officers (a consequence, apparently, of the persistent postwar shortfall in establishment, wastage and the growth of specialist squads denuding the streets of experienced officers) has often been blamed, whereas the enforcement of law requires mature judgement and patience.[10]

As a consequence of these and other abuses, a Royal Commission was established to look at the question of police powers (see Royal Commission on Criminal Procedure, 1981). It saw its role, very conventionally, to decide on the precise balance needed, in the contemporary period, between police *powers* and their *control*. Many argued that the resulting proposals, which culminated in the Police and Criminal Evidence Act (PACE) 1984, accepted the case for more police powers but not for more vigorous control of their usage (cf. Hillyard, 1981; Baldwin and Kinsey, 1982, pp. 191–216; Greater London Council, 1985). For our purposes the form of this debate foreshadows our second category: the control of the police or 'police accountability'.

THE CONTROL OF THE POLICE/ACCOUNTABILITY

Since the police are subject to a number of controls, the question of accountability can be posed in a number of ways. In the recent period this question has arisen at two distinctive levels: that of the individual incident and that of general police policy or strategy.

At the former level, the question has been the vexed one of complaints. The reason for dissatisfaction undoubtedly is that despite the changes in this area introduced in 1964 and 1976, and most recently in PACE 1984, the police, contrary to all the rules of natural justice, still predominantly investigate one another (cf. Walter, 1981). It remains to be seen whether the introduction of the new Police Complaints Authority with powers to supervise the investigation of serious complaints will provide a sufficient level of independence to satisfy the public.

At the level of general police policy, the question has become, 'Who should control it?' Whilst it is arguable that dissatisfaction with the complaints procedure – and failure to achieve acceptable changes – led to a more thoroughgoing review of police accountability, it is also true that numerous large-scale incidents resulting in violent police–public controntations, most dramatically the inner-city riots, have forced many to rethink the question. Specifically, we can point to, as instances in this rethink: Labour MP Jack Straw's two Private Member's Bills attempting to give Police

Authorities control over 'general policing policies' in their area (introduced on 14 November 1979 and 11 March 1980); the Association of Metropolitan Authorities (AMA) discussion documents attempting to clarify the existing powers and practices of police authorities (cf. AMA 1982; 1985); disagreements between Police Authorities and their Chief Constables, for example, Greater Manchester, Merseyside, South Yorkshire (cf. Simey, 1985); the Labour Party commitment to elected Police Authorities charged with responsibility for determining police policy within their areas (Labour Party, 1983); the establishment by the Greater London Council (now abolished) of a Police Committee with a brief to struggle for democratic control over London's police (cf. Greater London Council, 1983); the establishment by Manchester City Council of a similar police committee; the high priority given to the question by the NCCL in recent years (cf. Spencer, 1985); the concern shown by the Labour Campaign for Criminal Justice (cf. Downes and Ward, 1986); and the entry of a 'critical' right into the debate (cf. Warren and Tredinnick, 1982; Regan, 1983).

Once again, it remains to be seen whether the government's own response to this issue, the requirement contained in PACE 1984 that each Police Authority establishes consultative arrangements in its force area, is anything other than cosmetic. From our viewpoint, as will be seen, it fails to engage decisively with the critical structure of the law guiding operational policework, and thus the prospects for significant change must be, at best, very uncertain (but see Morgan and Maggs, 1984; Morgan, 1985).

The questions of who controls and who should control police policy are necessarily linked to the question of what kind of policing – which leads to our third category: styles of policing and public relations.

STYLES OF POLICING AND PUBLIC RELATIONS
The question of controlling policy is linked to the question of style of policing. Present dissatisfaction with arrangements for police accountability has something to do with the felt inability to influence the style of policing adopted.

Debate about styles of policing has tended to contrast the favoured 'proactive' community policing with the out-of-favour 'reactive' car-based unit beat system. This dichotomous contrast is not without its ironic features, given the origins of the unit beat system in the desire to maximize public contact in a situation of chronic staffing shortage (cf. Home Office, 1967) and the potentially intrusive dimension to proactive policing. There can be little doubt however that getting police officers back on the beat –

the popular idea of 'community policing' – is seen by many as the means by which they can be brought 'closer to the communities they serve' (Labour Party, 1983, p. 27).[11]

If the object of control is seen to be a new style of community policing (or the resurrection of a very traditional one), one means of achieving the necessary attitudinal reorientation is thought to be training.

TRAINING

Without officers capable and prepared to operate within the bounds of their legal powers and according to the policies laid down by the force – without, that is, officers appropriately trained – the questions of powers, control and style are to some extent redundant. Thus it is that, at any time when policework comes under sustained discussion and scrutiny, the question of training emerges. The recent report by the Police Training Council working party (1983) on community and race-relations training for the police, the row over racism amongst recruits at Hendon and Lord Scarman's critical remarks on training in his report on the Brixton disorders (Scarman, 1982)[12] all highlight one salient concern in this area: the question of dealing with ethnic minorities.

POLICE–BLACK RELATIONS

This question of racism in dealing with ethnic minorities clearly links up with all the others – the questions of power, account-ability, styles of policing and training. Indeed, police–black relations have probably been the most controversial single issue in policing of the last fifteen years or so precisely because the issues that have emerged – for example, 'sus'/'stop and search' and the harassment of black youth (Roberts, 1982), the under-protection of the Asian community subjected to racial attack (Home Office, 1981) – both raise, in the starkest form, questions about the central issues of policing. And such questions, especially in connection with police–black relations, were all central to an understanding of probably the most important recent stimulus to the discussion on policing, that is, the riots of 1981 and their official response, the Scarman Report (see Benyon, 1984). The question for us is, how do all these *political* issues relate to an adequate *sociology* of policework?

To answer this, we intend to show how the various political positions in the debate fail to take account of the structural complexities we have demonstrated, before pointing towards the direction a worthwhile politics of police reform must take.

Political Standpoints and the Sociology of Policework

In broad terms, we can identify three political responses to the issues of policing we have identified: the classical liberal response represented by the Scarman Report; the response of the political right now embodied in controversial sections of the new Police Act; and the response of the left seen in the GLC initiative and the Labour Party proposals on policing.

The Scarman Report has been seen, rightly, as the classic liberal critique because of its attempts to 'balance', politically, a number of conflicting elements: more consultation with the community over policy, yet without making the police less accountable to law; more community policing, yet with the SPG still kept intact 'for emergency use' (cf. Hall, 1982). This political balancing act rests implicitly on an assumption that it is possible for the structures conditioning policework – law, democracy and work – to be similarly integrated. Thus the structure of legal accountability is not to be dismantled but complemented by an increase in the effectiveness of the weak democratic structure (the proposal which led to the new statutory requirement to establish consultative arrangements to ensure that consultation over policing policies takes place locally). The proposed improvements in training are similarly designed to strengthen the effectiveness of the work structure – or, perhaps, to put it another way, to make occupational common sense correspond more closely with 'organizational' requirements. The whole package, to reiterate, is designed to lead to a balanced set of 'structural' influences. What is not addressed is the crucial question of the coherence of a policy package which strengthens the democratic and work structures, yet leaves the legal structure of discretion intact.

The response of the right, recently seen in the new Police Act, is less liberal than the Scarman document. This is precisely because it fails, as the preceding Royal Commission would have wished, to 'balance out' new powers for the police with new controls on their use (and abuse). Nearly all its critics point to this failure. In fact, in our terms, it is even more conservative in its implications because the new powers it proposes for police are highly 'permissive' (cf. the definition of a 'serious arrestable offence' and the articles by Jones, 1981, and Reiner, 1981). The net result is that the legal structure – in so far as the degree of discretion has been expanded – has an expanded capacity to override the other structures precisely because of the ambiguity of the law to be appealed to (in the case of censure from 'the public' or 'management' or colleagues). This does not mean, as the Act's advocates simply see it, that the law *in general* has been strengthened. On the contrary, the increase in the amount of permissive legal powers for police *decreases* the controlling power of law, democracy and organizational policy. It is this aspect which renders the safeguards, of whatever kind, very uncertain as forms of control since it enables collegiate or occupational common sense to fill the vacuum. If this is what the government intends, it has not publicly said so; it is certainly the most likely outcome, given our analysis.

The response of the left, epitomized most concretely in the Straw Bill's proposals to give police authorities responsibility for general policing policies, certainly intends to strengthen the influence of the community on police policy, but in such a way that the Chief Constable's responsibility for particular acts of law enforcement is unimpaired. Whilst we can understand, in political terms, the attempt to have one's cake (increased democratic control) and eat it too (unaltered constabulary accountability to law), the result, were such a change enacted, would doubtless be a degree of confusion about the boundaries of respective responsibilities (cf. Jefferson and Grimshaw, 1984b, pp. 148–54).

Another way of understanding this political failure to resolve the respective responsibilities of legal and democratic authorities is as a consequence of an inadequate sociological understanding: a failure to see that the democratic or the legal structure cannot be altered in isolation. Structures always operate as an interrelated set, as we have stressed and exemplified throughout this study.

None of these critiques then, be they of the left, right, or centre, produces an effective framework for the reform of policework, precisely because none is aware of how the structures interact to produce current policing practices. This is true of even the recent document by the Greater London Council Police Committee (1983). Whilst it may claim to have removed some of the ambiguities of the Straw Bills in making police officers local government officers (p. 77) and giving police authorities responsibility for upholding the law, that is, operational policy, it too fails to remove the ambiguity surrounding a Chief Constable's power in the new situation, since 'police authorities would have no control over decisions relating to the cases of individuals' (p. 50). Our criticisms of the implications of proposals which place Police Authorities in exactly the same dilemma as present Chief Constables, as the GLC proposed, and our own alternative proposals, being based on the sociological understanding being offered here, do attempt to avoid these pitfalls (cf. Jefferson and Grimshaw, 1982; 1984b).

Sociology for an Adequate Politics of Policework

Under the present system, as we have argued (and demonstrated), to understand the nature of organized policework is to understand the relationship between its structural determinants – law, work and democracy – under different conditions. It is, moreover, to understand that the structure which assigns the others their place, the fundamentally determining structure, is law. We understand law to include common law, statutes and their interpretation by the courts and other working institutions of the law.

This notion that the law is the fundamental structure is not the same as conceiving the police to be concerned with crime control at the expense of other objectives, though it is sometimes conceived as such. As we saw with the RBOs, little of the time is spent in law-enforcement matters. *But* the condition of this freedom to pursue other matters was, we argued, precisely the relative absence of the legal structure as a constant empirical constraint. This absence proceeded from the decisions of organizational superiors about RBO work; their authority is based ultimately on the delegated responsibility of the Chief Constable, awarded to him by the 1964 Police Act. Drawing an analogy with language, even though these structures do not always manifest themselves empirically in a given particular slice of language, such absent structures constitute conditions of existence of any particular combination of (present) linguistic components (cf. Coward and Ellis, 1977, pp. 12–24). Law, too, can be *structurally* 'present in its (empirical) absence'.

Given the centrality of the legal structure, it is essential to start there. Indeed, failure to do so, as we saw with the 'subculturalists', is to provide an accurate descriptive empirical catalogue of happenings and influences without in any way being able to explain what makes it all possible. Worse still, if empirical influences are mistaken for structural determinations, the chance of an adequate understanding gets lost for fair.

At the level of the constable, the fundamental general feature of the office is the notion of constabulary independence. The crucial implication of this is to ensure that policework is conducted within a discretionary framework since its meaning is that particular acts of law enforcement are the responsibility of individual constables exercising their own (independent) judgement as to when the law has been broken. This requirement to judge, without undue influence, is in constitutional terms the guarantor of police impartiality.

This inherently discretionary framework is expanded under

certain conditions, for example, when the law concerned lacks objective criteria to guide a constable's judgement, such as public-order law, or those areas of case law where judges have effectively expanded the legal basis of police action. The contributory factors to the expansion of police discretion, whilst important in understanding particular police actions, should not obscure their *general* foundation in the *independence* of the office of constable.

The problem this poses for the constable on the street amounts to this: how to exercise impartial law enforcement in the individual case (that is, how to treat like offenders equally) when many offences dealt with are absolute and require no public complaint (for example, traffic offences) yet their sheer prevalence requires that some principles of selection operate, and many others (such as public-order offences) become offences only as a result of subjective, police-initiated definitional work *necessarily* involving principles of selection? In current practice this problem is left unresolved, as we demonstrated in the case of the unit. The use of discretion comes under scrutiny only when unacceptable empirical results flow from situations where it has been used. The guiding notion seems to be the pragmatic one of avoiding untoward events in the future.

The failure to resolve the problem is what enables occupational common sense to provide the principles of selection. One important consequence of this, as again we saw with the unit, was dealing with minor offences on the basis of the *attitude* of the offender with all the potential for amplifying differences between 'pro-police' and 'anti-police' sections of the community such a practice contains. Clearly what is needed is a suitable principle to guide the police use of discretion in individual cases, a principle to ensure the equal treatment of like offenders.

The problem this general independence or legal discretion (which is *not*, we must emphasize, a function of police officers *choosing to ignore* a legal mandate as a result of colleague influence, as the subculturalists would have it) poses at the level of Chief Constable is twofold. On the one hand, the independence of the office of constable renders problematic the relationship between a Chief Constable and his officers. It is this problematic relationship – a consequence of the legal structure operating here – which lies behind our finding with respect to policy, namely, that effective *operational policy* (authoritative statements signifying settled practices of law enforcement) cannot exist. The universality of constabulary independence makes operational policy effectively redundant, as we saw.

All critiques ignore this and its effect on the issue which most directly affects the public: operational policy. We tried to draw this out and exemplify it in the chapters on policy in arguing how, in operational matters, the process of policy consideration never resulted in the *making* of unambiguous policy, and the consequent reliance on other more indirect instruments of managerial control – deployment, supervision, training and so on.

On the other hand, since the CC has an obligation to uphold the law in his area, yet due to finite knowledge, time and resources cannot possibly do so absolutely, a process of *selective* law enforcement is inevitable. This has profound implications for the debate on accountability. In particular it raises two fundamental questions: how can a CC simultaneously discharge his obligation to impartial (or unselective) law enforcement if the reality of his position entails partial (or selective) enforcement? And by what criteria of *justice* can such selective enforcement be justified? This, of course, is the equivalent question, at the level of general law enforcement, to that posed for the constable on the street at the level of particular enforcement. And if the latter entailed the question of particular judgement, the former, in so far as it is concerned to ensure that all groups of citizens (men and women, young and old, black and white) receive equal treatment (as offenders or victims), entails the idea of *public justice*. Thus the question of judgement at the level of the CC touches on the political question: how can citizens have their interests in the process of law enforcement upheld? As possible offenders they may require protection from undue police attention; as victims they may need appropriate support from the police in terms of crime prevention and detection. In the absence of legal guidance, some source of alternative guidance must be provided to the police, and the political process offers this.

The political right ignores the unavoidable political dimension of this need to guide CC discretion by reducing it to a matter of 'professional' judgement, which must fall to the police as practitioners – which simply endorses the status quo and the occupational 'common-sense' judgements that effectively end up guiding such discretion, as we have seen. The left recognizes the political dimension but is ultimately unwilling to give up the ideal of impartial law enforcement for the CC (in 'cases of individuals': Greater London Council, 1983, p. 50). The result is confusion since the left's proposals saddle a CC with two masters, the 'law' and a democratic authority, but without addressing the critical question of the relationship between these two very different forms of authority, with their two very different discourses (law and democratic opinion). Beyond that, however, the left signally fails to come to terms with the issue of public justice: the *criteria* by which the discretion is to be exercised, as opposed to the *authority* which is to direct it. Only the creation of an elected supervisory institution bound not just to uphold the law but also to declare principles of public justice underlying its policies could overcome this confusion.

Let us, then, end by briefly spelling out what it implies to take seriously these political questions, which stem let it be remembered directly from our sociological analysis. In the first instance, it must be stressed that unless the issue of legal discretion, stemming from the notion of legal accountability, is properly addressed, other reforms may or may not prove valuable but are unlikely to be *predictable or decisive*. In this regard we must take serious issue with Reiner's contention that 'elected control of police policy-making is neither necessary nor sufficient for accomplishing the goal of a police force whose operations are "democratic" ' (1985b, p. 180). 'Sufficient' they may not be, and certainly that is true of the rather confused and incomplete current proposals, but, assuming such confusions and omissions are dealt with, *'necessary'* they certainly are, for only from such a base can democratically agreed principles of public justice be established, and only from such a base can effective operational policies be produced and enforced. *From such a standpoint*, the standpoint of a reformed legal structure, it would be possible to look at the prospects of *other* internal reforms, affecting both the work structure and the democratic structure, with some degree of optimism.

Since such a change is not on the immediate political horizon, what might be accomplished given a desire for change on the part of open-minded police chiefs – a desire which, however strongly held, can work only, let it not be forgotten, through the very uncertain instruments of deployment, supervision, training and so on? Three areas in particular need to be addressed, corresponding to the three structures identified: law, work and democracy.

In relation to the law, questions of public justice need to be thought through. Thinking about such questions in relation to the unit, for example, involves addressing the question of the basis of selective action. With absolute offences, which do not require public complaint, the element of selection could be simply removed by making public complaints the explicit foundation of police attention, with the absence of complaints being a reason for not taking action. In other legal areas involving public complaint, such as disorderly disputes requiring sensitive judgement, the avoidance of partiality based on attitudes, reputation or character can probably be achieved only by encouraging sustained and recurrent contact with complainants – a sort of legal casework – a practice which would help prevent the insidious and recurrent 'minor complaint' disappearing into the routine case-load (for example, vandalism against ethnic-minority households). If intimate knowledge in the individual case results from sustained contact, such knowledge in relation to the pattern of attention to offences generally can come only through monitoring. Such monitoring is the necessary pre-condition for ensuring that particular groups or communities do not suffer the fate of either 'over-' or 'under-attention' with respect to police activity.

In relation to the work structure, what is required in the first instance is to develop conceptions of rational effectiveness relevant to operational areas. At present, as we have seen, 'rational-scientific' criteria are confined to technical and administrative questions, common sense providing the basis for other operationally related matters. Such conceptions, in providing a clear and definite purpose to operational roles, would provide a purpose against which individuals could measure themselves, and be measured, as to their effectiveness. Once again, monitoring provides a key instrument in the development of such conceptions.

Monitoring unit work, for example, might allow some rational assessment of the complex pattern of incidents for which the call system at present demands the most cursory attention. It might also enable some reasonable schedule of priorities to be produced for call response, in order to avoid unnecessary deployment of resources (for example, for faulty burglar alarms), or to dispel panic. The deceleration of response could then permit casework to be performed with a greater likelihood of success; patrol visits could then be more often made on the basis of appointments. This might mean a closer resemblance between unit officers and RBOs in their respective modes of operation, releasing the first-response vehicles for more wide-ranging deployments on a divisional basis if necessary. Casework approaches would help to expand the role of the unit constable in a more responsible way and perhaps thereby improve the prospects of adequate supervision. Such questions as the appropriateness of panda drivers' patrolling on foot and the attraction of catching speeding motorists would fall into a wider perspective if it was clear that the driver's job was linked to a developing case-load approached in a measured style. Some reorganization of the shift system, improving communications between members of different shifts where required and reducing unnecessary coverage, would permit the organization to move beyond the present level of service which is more appropriate to 'one-off' emergencies.

In relation, finally, to the democratic structure, the key term is 'public acceptability'. The success of the police in terms of the democratic structure is marked by the degree to which their public transactions prove acceptable to its plurality of publics, each drawing on a common sense which may be divergent or coincident with the police's own. Such acceptability can be assessed in various ways; what is crucial is that acceptability includes *all* sections of the public. Thinking about public acceptability and the RBOs, it is clear that much in the present RBO working conduces towards a high degree of public acceptability. Indeed, in the absence of legal performance measures of public justice and organizationally pro- duced measures of rational effectiveness, to be accepted by the public as evidenced in a RBO's local 'community reputation' is probably a primary motivation. Yet, given the breadth of the mandate, the resulting reputation can be acquired by any number of possible routes: ability to lecture to schools; ability to organize a five-a-side competition; willingness to take youths on camping holidays; and so on. Moreover, this 'reputation', as we saw earlier, tends to be acquired as a result of contact with a fairly narrow range of sources, namely, 'respectables' and representatives. Reform would entail here a more definite mandate and hence a far more definite conception of what sort of 'community reputation' would be acceptable to the organization, and a much broader community sample providing the basis of the reputation. In other words, it should prove possible, once criteria of public justice and rational effectiveness have been developed and implemented, to test the community response to the performance of these known and specified RBO tasks, and, in particular, to see how acceptable the performance of these are to the relatively powerless minorities in particular: youth, 'problem families' and so on.

In Conclusion

Unit work is determined by the texture of a variety of legal demands differing in form, all of which depend on the discretion afforded to the constable in law. The Inspector is likely to have to deal with a heterogeneous group allotted to different roles and with differing supervisory needs and has to cope with complex con- tingencies in the operation of the supervisory system in its various modes. On the other hand, an Inspector is capable of influencing a group style of work; much more problematic is the possibility of managing work according to priorities when there is so much of an organizational emphasis on immediate reactive response. This emphasis also fragments public contact into fleeting and immediate responses to individual consumers. Justice, effectiveness and public acceptability cannot emerge as real questions of substance when the processes described combine and take command. Before these issues can be incorporated in decisions about organizational roles, training and advice in the future, there needs to be a fundamental review of unit work in the present forums of policy consideration in the force and elsewhere.

The work of the RBOs is characterized by its flexible character. This flexibility is a consequence of the organizational arrangements which minimize the amount of time spent on legal work, combined with the organizational failure to develop specific alternative objectives which supervisors could use as the basis for evaluating performance. In this situation of the relative absence of legal and supervisory constraints, the community can begin to exert its influence. This influence is assisted by the regular, reciprocal public contacts routine RBO working achieves; however, its restriction to 'respectable' publics sidelines the crucial question – acceptability to the deviant and powerless minorities which bear the brunt of the imposition of police legal powers.

Justice, effectiveness and an inclusive notion of public acceptability remain uninfluential categories since currently beyond the scope of consideration. Only in so far as these categories are made the subject of discussion within the present forums of policy consideration, and subsequently incorporated in decisions about organizational roles, training and advice in future, is there any chance of some limited change in this area, even if more substantial change must necessarily await those changes that would allow the incorporation of such (needed) decisions within direct policy consideration. In the mid-1980s, in the wake of Brixton, Handsworth and Broadwater Farm, some changes are sorely needed, in order to address issues of public justice in law enforcement, and to open up these questions to democratic debate and direction. In the hope of providing useful background material for that important debate, we end this book.

Notes

1 On the question of arbitrariness, see Levi-Strauss (1963, p. 93), and Leach (1976, p. 19).

2 Wilden (1980) critically shows the links between structuralist thinkers.
3 See Levi-Strauss (1963, p. 333) for a defence of the formal conception of an 'order of orders'.
4 Foucault (1981, p. 94) invokes a characteristic conception of hegemony as the resultant of a number of effects sustained by a series of confrontations in the lower (rather than higher) regions of the social body.
5 Quoted from M. Foucault, 'omnes et singulatim', in McMurrin (1981, p. 239).
6 For a critical Marxist discussion, see Fine (1979); for a view emphasizing the merits of Foucault against the claims of Marxism, see Smart (1983).
7 His discussion of the police admits the nuances of legal-juridical duty and disciplinary intervention; see Foucault (1979, p. 213–15).
8 As we have noted at the end of the relevant section, no objective link between style and area was apparent; the issue is one of an *acceptable* style.
9 For a rapid listing of general causes of concern, see Jefferson and Grimshaw (1982, p. 82).
10 For an interesting empirical demonstration of the contradiction between the ideological commitment of the police to the importance of the 'bobby on the beat' and the practice of giving this the lowest priority in terms of manpower, skill and experience, see Jones (1980).
11 See also Brown and Howes (1975), Moore and Brown (1981) and Alderson (1979; 1984). For more critical accounts which see community policing initiatives in terms of greater surveillance and control, see, for example, Bridges (1981–2), and Gordon (1984). For an overview of the literature, from a pragmatic standpoint, see Weatheritt (1983).
12 Scarman's remarks led to an inquiry conducted by a Police Training Council Special Working Party. Its proposals were 'immediately accepted' by the Home Secretary (*Guardian*, 29 July 1983). See reports of HM Chief Inspector of Constabulary, 1983 and 1984.

Interview Schedules

Interview Schedule: Main Topics and Questions

(1) *Background*

- Family; educational; occupational.
- Present personal status.

(2) *Recruitment and force history*

- Reasons for joining police force? Differences from what you expected?
- Cadet? Helpfulness of being a cadet?
- Relatives in police force?
- Roles experienced since joining?
- Preferences, i.e. which roles would you like to experience; particular geographical areas?
- Exams/boards sat/passed?

(3) *Training*

- Training influences? Most useful/least useful aspects of training? Does being a cadet make a difference? Significant influences on you during training?

(4) *Role*

- How did you become an occupier of this position?
- Briefly what does it comprise?
- What differences from your previous experiences did you find when you got into present position?
- Did you have to adjust to a new way of doing things?
- How did you learn your present job?
- Who was the biggest influence on you as you learnt to do it?
- What typical mistakes did you make at first?

- When did you discover that you had mastered the job?
- Could you define what you understand by being able to perform the job competently and well?
- Do all your peers do the job in the same way?
- What differences are there?
- Why do you think these differences may occur?
- Do you have disagreements with colleagues?
- What is the most important aspect of your job, the thing you have in mind most of the time?
- What is the least important aspect of it?
- What is the most important/least important aspect of policing generally, to your mind?
- What part of your job do you really concentrate on?
- What do you particularly like to do, i.e. what is the most satisfying part of your work?
- What is the most frustrating part of your job?
- Do you find any conflicts in practice between different functions you are expected to perform?
- What part of your job gives you the most problems?
- What part of policework generally gives the police most problems?
- How has the job changed in your experience? For better? For worse?
- What changes would you like to see to make your job easier/more satisfying?
- Would you like to do more job functions?
- What difference would it make to you if there were more peers?
- Do court outcomes influence arrest procedures?
- Is the role affected by the area/community being policed?
- Describe the area/community you police and your relationship to it.

(5) *Supervision*

- Who is the most important senior officer for you?
- Does he treat you and your peers the same/differently?
- What do you think is his highest priority?
- How does he impinge on your time?
- Do you ask for advice?
- What does he do about mistakes?
- How does he reward?
- Have you had disagreements?
- When you've got a problem, who do you go to?
- Can you go above him?

- Would it make a difference if somebody else was in charge?
- Do you prefer to be left to get on with the job or would you welcome more assistance from senior officers?
- Have you ever got together with your peers and got something changed in the way you do your job? Or got a change stopped when it was wrong?
- What changes in discipline have you noticed since you started?
- Have these been for the better or for the worse?
- In terms of discipline, who is the ideal senior officer?

(6) *Promotion*

- What are the prospects of promotion in your present position?
- Are there any obstacles to your promotion?
- What do you have to do to get promoted?
- What is your attitude to promotion?
- What is your best 'asset' on promotion?
- Are you satisfied with career prospects in the police?

(7) *Conditions*

- What is the best aspect of police employment?
- What is worse?
- Are you satisfied with staff representatives?
- Do you think you can influence policy regarding the position you occupy?
- How if at all could you do this?

Senior Officers' Interview Schedule: Main Topics and Questions

(1) *Background*

- Family; educational; occupational.
- Present personal status.

(2) *Recruitment and force history*

- Reasons for joining police force? Differences from what you expected?
- Cadet? Helpfulness of being a cadet?
- Relatives in police force?

- Roles experienced since joining?
- Preferences, i.e. which roles would you still like to experience?

(3) *Role*

- How did you become an occupier of this position?
- Briefly what does it comprise? Priorities? Routine/non-routine? Functions? Decision-making (initiation; supervision; implementation)?
- What difference from your previous job function did you find when you got into your present position (especially in terms of decision-making functions)?
- Did you have to adjust to a new way of doing things?
- How did you learn your present job? Informal influences? Formal influences? In-service training? Bramshill?
- Who or what was the biggest influence on you as you learnt to do your present job?
- What typical mistakes did you make at first, or what would you do differently with hindsight?
- When did you discover that you could perform your job with a degree of competence?
- Could you define what you understand by being able to perform your job competently and well?
- Do all your peers (i.e. colleagues of same rank doing same job) do the job in the same way?
- What differences are there?
- Why do you think these differences may occur?
- Do you have disagreements with your peers and subordinate officers?
- How resolved?
- Which part of your job do you really concentrate on?
- What do you particularly like to do, i.e. what is the most satisfying part of your work? Of policework generally?
- Most frustrating? Pressures: most demanding? Of policework generally?
- What part of your job gives you most problems?
- What part of policework generally gives the police most problems?
- Do you find any conflicts in practice between different functions you are expected to perform?
- How has the job changed in your experience? For better? For worse?
- What changes would you like to see to make your job easier/more satisfying?

- Would you like to do more job functions?
- Do court outcomes influence arrest/process decisions?
- Do different areas require different policing?
- Describe the area you police and your relationship to it. Preferences for particular areas?
- Most important/least important aspect of policing generally?

(4) *Supervision*

- Who is the most senior officer for you?
- Does he treat you and your peers the same/differently?
- What do you think is his highest priority? Does it coincide with yours?
- Do you ask for advice? Do you get asked for advice? How does he impinge on your time?
- What does he do about mistakes? About inefficiency?
- How do you judge inefficiency?
- How does he reward? How do you?
- Have you had disagreements with more senior officers?
- Do channels exist for communicating your dissatisfaction in the event of disagreements?
- If you disagree with your immediate senior officer, can you still influence policy? How?
- Who do you go to with problems?
- Can you go above him?
- Would it make a difference if somebody else was in charge?
- Would you welcome more or less assistance from more senior officers?
- Have you ever managed to change anything you thought was wrong?
- How?
- Role of the staff associations?
- Changes in discipline since you started? For better or worse?
- What have you done or could you do about these changes?
- The ideal senior officer?

(5) *Promotion*

- What are your present prospects of promotion?
- Obstacles? Hardest promotion barrier?
- What do you have to do to get promoted?

- Attitude to promotion, especially 'early' promotion?
- What is your best 'asset' on promotion?
- Are you satisfied with career prospects in the police?
- Ambitions?

REFERENCES

Alderson, J. (1979), *Policing Freedom* (Plymouth: MacDonald & Evans).
Alderson, J. (1984), *Law and Disorder* (London: Hamish Hamilton).
Althusser, L. (1969), *For Max* (Harmondsworth: Penguin).
Althusser, L. (1972), 'Ideology and ideological state apparatuses', in B. R. Cosin (ed.), *Education: Structure and Society* (Harmondsworth: Penguin/Open University), pp. 242–80.
Althusser, L., and Balibar, E. (1970), *Reading Capital* (London: New Left Books).
Association of Metropolitan Authorities (1982), *Policies for the Police Service* (London: AMA).
Association of Metropolitan Authorities (1985), *AMA Three Years on: Policies for the Police Service* (London: AMA).
Baker, E. R., and Dodge, F. B. (1977), *Police Promotion Handbooks no. 3 General Police Duties* (London: Butterworths).
Baldwin, R., and Kinsey, R. (1982), *Police Powers and Politics* (London: Quartet).
Banton, M. (1964), *The Policeman in the Community* (London: Tavistock).
Barthes, R. (1973), *Mythologies* (St Albans: Paladin).
Baxter, J., and Koffman, L. (eds.) (1985), *Police: The Constitution and the Community* (Abingdon: Professional Books).
Benyon, J. (ed.) (1984), *Scarman and After* (Oxford: Pergamon).
Bethnal Green and Stepney Trades Council (1978), *Blood on the Streets* (London: Bethnal Green and Stepney Trades Council).
Binney, V., Harkell, G., and Nixon, J. (1981), *Leaving Violent Men: A Study of Refuges and Housing for Battered Women* (England: Women's Aid Federation).
Bittner, E. (1970), *The Functions of the Police in Modern Society* (Maryland: National Institute of Mental Health Center for Studies of Crime and Delinquency).
Black, D. J. (1970), 'Production of crime rates', *American Sociological Review*, vol. 35, no. 4, pp. 733–48.
Blumer, H. (1969), *Symbolic Interactionism* (Englewood Cliffs, NJ: Prentice-Hall).
Bouma, D. (1969), *Kids and Cops: A Study in Mutual Hostility* (Michigan: Eerdmans).
Box, S. (1981), *Deviance, Reality and Society*, 2nd edn (London: Holt, Rinehart & Winston).
Bridges, L. (1981–2), 'Keeping the lid on: British urban social policy, 1975–81', *Race and Class*, vol. XXIII, nos. 2–3, pp. 171–85.

Brogden, M. (1982), *The Police: Autonomy and Consent* (London: Academic Press).

Brown, D. and Iles, S. (1985), *Community Constables: A Study of a Policing Initiative*, Home Office Research and Planning Unit Paper No. 30 (London: HMSO).

Brown, J., and Howes, G. (eds.) (1975), *The Police and the Community* (Westmead: Saxon House).

Brown, R. (1979), 'Bureaucracy: the career of a concept.', in E. Kamenka and M. Krygier (eds), *Bureaucracy: The Career of a Concept* (London: Edward Arnold), pp. 135–55.

Bunyan, T. (1976), *The History and Practice of the Political Police in Britain* (London: Julian Friedmann).

Bunyard, R. S. (1978), *Police: Organisation and Command* (Plymouth: Macdonald & Evans).

Cain, M. (1971), 'On the beat: interactions and relations in rural and urban police forces', in S. Cohen (ed.), *Images of Deviance* (Harmondsworth: Pelican).

Cain, M. (1973), *Society and the Policeman's Role* (London: Routledge & Kegan Paul).

Cain, M. (1979), 'Trends in the sociology of police work', *International Journal of the Sociology of Law*, vol. 7, no. 2, pp. 143–67.

Carver, T. (ed.), (1975), *Karl Marx: Texts on Method* (Oxford: Blackwell).

Center for Research on Criminal Justice (1977), *The Iron Fist and the Velvet Glove: An Analysis of the US Police*, 2nd edn (Berkeley, Calif.: Center for Research on Criminal Justice).

Chambliss, W. J., and Seidman, R. B. (1971), *Law, Order and Power* (Reading, Mass.: Addison-Wesley).

Chatterton, M. (1979), 'The supervision of patrol work under the fixed points system', in S. Holdaway (ed.) (1979), pp. 83–101.

Chatterton, M. (1983), 'Police work and assault charges', in M. Punch (ed.) (1983), pp. 194–222.

Clarke, R. V., and Hough, J. M. (1984), *Crime and Police Effectiveness*, Home Office Research Study No. 79 (London: HMSO).

Comrie, Chief Supt, and Kings, E. J. (1975), *A Study of Urban Workloads*, Police Research Services Unit, Home Office, Final Report 11/75. (London: HMSO).

Coward, R., and Ellis, J. (1977), *Language and Materialism: Developments in Semiology and the Theory of the Subject* (London: Routledge & Kegan Paul).

Cranfield Papers (1978), *The Proceedings of the 1978 Cranfield Conference on the Prevention of Crime in Europe* (London: Peel Press).

Critchley, T. A. (1978), *A History of Police in England and Wales*, 2nd edn (London: Constable).

Cumming, E., Cumming, I., and Edel, L. (1965), 'Policeman as philosopher, guide and friend', *Social Problems*, vol. 17, pp. 276–86.

Downes, D. and Ward, T. (1986), *Democratic Policing: Towards a*

Labour Party Policy on Police Accountability (London: Labour Campaign for Criminal Justice).

Ekblom, P., and Heal, K. (1982), *The Police Response to Calls from the Public*, Home Office Research and Planning Unit Paper No. 9 (London: HMSO).

Emsley, C. (1983), *Policing and its Context, 1750–1870* (London: Macmillan).

Ericson, R. V. (1982), *Reproducing Order: A Study of Police Patrol Work* (University of Toronto Press).

Etzioni, A. (1964), *Modern Organizations* (Englewood Cliffs, NJ: Prentice-Hall).

Faragher, T. (1985), 'The police response to violence against women in the home', in J. Pahl (ed.) (1985), pp. 110–24.

Fine, B. (1979), 'Struggles against discipline: the theory and politics of Michel Foucault', *Capital and Class*, 9, pp. 75–96.

Fine, B., and Millar, R. (eds.) (1985), *Policing the Miners' Strike* (London: Lawrence & Wishart).

Foucault, M. (1979), *Discipline and Punish: The Birth of the Prison* (Harmondsworth: Penguin).

Foucault, M. (1981), *The History of Sexuality Vol. I: An Introduction* (Harmondsworth: Penguin).

Friedrich, R. J. (1978), 'The impact of organizational, individual and situational factors on police behaviour', PhD dissertation, Department of Political Science, University of Michigan.

Gifford, Lord (1986), *Report of the Independent Inquiry into Disturbances of October 1985 at the Broadwater Farm Estate, Tottenham* (London: Borough of Haringey).

Gill, O. (1977), *Luke Street: Housing Policy, Conflict and the Creation of the Delinquent Area* (London: Macmillan).

Glaser, B., and Strauss, A. (1967), *The Discovery of Grounded Theory* (London: Weidenfeld & Nicolson).

Gordon, P. (1984), 'Community policing: towards the local police state?', *Critical Social Policy*, vol. 4, no. 1, pp. 39–58.

Gramsci, A. (1971), *Selections from the Prison Notebooks* (London: Lawrence & Wishart).

Greater London Council (1983), *A New Police Authority for London: A Consultation Paper on Democratic Control of the Police in London*, GLC Police Committee Discussion Paper No. 1 (London: GLC).

Greater London Council (1985), *The Police Act 1984: A Critical Guide*, GLC Police Committee Discussion Paper No. 3 (London: GLC).

Hall, J. (1953), 'Police and law in a democratic society', *Indiana Law Journal*, vol. 28, no. 2, pp. 133–77.

Hall, S. (1982), 'The lessons of Lord Scarman', *Critical Social Policy*, vol. 2, no. 2, pp. 66–72.

Hall, S. (1985), 'Cold comfort farm', *New Socialist*, no. 32, November, pp. 10–12.

Harvard Business Review (1979), *On Human Relations* (London: Heinemann).

Hillyard, P. (1981), 'From Belfast to Britain: some critical comments on the Royal Commission on Criminal Procedure', in Politics and Power (eds.) (1981), pp. 83–97.

Hindess, B. (1980), 'Democracy and the limitations of parliamentary democracy in Britain', in Politics and Power (eds.) (1980), pp. 103–24.

Hirst, P. Q. (1975), 'Marx and Engels on law, crime and morality', in I. Taylor, P. Walton and J. Young (eds.), Critical Criminology (London: Routledge & Kegan Paul), pp. 203–32.

Hirst, P. Q. (1979), On Law and Ideology (London: Macmillan).

Holdaway, S. (1977), 'Changes in urban policing', British Journal of Sociology, vol. 28, no. 2, pp. 119–37.

Holdaway, S. (ed.) (1979), The British Police (London: Edward Arnold).

Holdaway, S. (1983), Inside the British Police: A Force at Work (Oxford: Blackwell).

Home Office (1967), Police Manpower, Equipment and Efficiency (London: HMSO).

Home Office (1981), Racial Attacks (London: HMSO).

Hough, J. M. (1980), Uniformed Police Work and Management Technology, Home Office Research Unit Paper No. 1 (London: HMSO).

James D. (1979), 'Police–black relations: the professional solution', in Holdaway, (ed.) (1979), pp. 66–82.

Jameson, F. (1974), 'The vanishing mediator: narrative structure in Max Weber', Working Papers in Cultural Studies (Centre for Contemporary Cultural Studies, Birmingham University), Spring, 5, pp. 111–49.

Jefferson, T. (1986), 'Policing the miners: law, politics and accountability', in M. Brenton and C. Ungerson (eds.), Year Book of Social Policy in Britain 1986 (London: Routledge & Kegan Paul), pp. 265–86.

Jefferson, T., and Grimshaw, R. (1981), 'The Organisation and control of policework', unpublished report to the Home Office (Centre for Criminological and Socio-Legal Studies, University of Sheffield).

Jefferson, T., and Grimshaw, R. (1982), 'Law, democracy and justice: the question of police accountability', in D. Cowell, T. Jones and J. Young (eds.), Policing the Riots (London: Junction Books), pp. 82–117.

Jefferson, T., and Grimshaw, R. (1984a), 'The problem of law enforcement policy in England and Wales: the case of community policing and racial attacks', International Journal of the Sociology of Law, vol. 12, no. 2, pp. 117–35.

Jefferson, T., and Grimshaw, R. (1984b), Controlling the Constable: Police Accountability in England and Wales (London: Muller/Cobden Trust).

Johnson, R. (1979), 'Three problematics: elements of a theory of working class culture', in J. Clarke, C. Critcher and R. Johnson (eds.), Working Class Culture: Studies in History and Theory (London: Hutchinson), pp. 201–37.

Jones, J. M. (1980), Organizational Aspects of Police Behaviour (Farnborough: Gower).

Jones, P. (1981), 'Police powers and political accountability: the Royal

Commission on Criminal Procedure', in Politics and Power (eds.) (1981), pp. 53–81.

Judge, A. (1974), 'The police and the coloured communities: a police view', New Community, vol. III, no. 3, pp. 199–204.

Labour Party (1983), Labour's Manifesto 1983 (London: Labour Party).

Leach, E. R. (1976), Culture and Communication: The Logic by which Symbols Are Connected (Cambridge University Press).

Lee, J. A. (1981), 'Some structural aspects of police deviance in relations with minority groups', in C. D. Shearing (ed.), Organizational Police Deviance (Toronto: Butterworths), pp. 49–82.

Leigh, L. H. (1975), Police Powers in England and Wales (London: Butterworths).

Levi-Strauss, C. (1963), Structural Anthropology (New York: Basic Books).

Levi-Strauss, C. (1970), The Raw and the Cooked: Introduction to a Science of Mythology: I (London: Cape).

Lidstone, K. W., Hogg, R., and Sutcliffe, F. (1980), Prosecutions by Private Individuals and Non-Police Agencies, Royal Commission on Criminal Procedure Research Study No. 10 (London: HMSO).

Lustgarten, L. (1986), The Governance of Police (London: Sweet & Maxwell).

McBarnet, D. J. (1978a), 'The police and the state: arrest, legality and the law', in G. Littlejohn, B. Smart, J. Wakeford and N. Yuval-Davis (eds.), Power and the State (London: Croom Helm), pp. 196–216.

McBarnet, D. J. (1978b), 'False dichotomies in criminal justice research', in J. Baldwin and A. K. Bottomley (eds.), Criminal Justice: Selected Readings (London: Martin Robertson), pp. 23–34.

McBarnet, D. J. (1981), Conviction: Law, the State and the Construction of Justice (London: Macmillan).

McMurrin, S. M. (ed.) (1981), The Tanner Lectures on Human Values, Vol. 2 (Cambridge University Press).

Macpherson, C. B. (1966), The Real World of Democracy (Oxford University Press).

Manning, P. K. (1971), 'The police: mandate, strategies and appearances', in J. D. Douglas (ed.), Crime and Justice in American Society (Indianapolis: Bobbs-Merrill).

Manning, P. K. (1979), 'The social control of police work', in Holdaway, (ed.) (1979), pp. 41–65.

Manning, P. K. (1980), 'Organization and environment: influences on policework', in R. V. Clarke, and J. M. Hough (eds.), The Effectiveness of Policing (Farnborough: Gower), pp. 98–123.

Manning, P. K. (1983), 'Organizational constraints and semiotics', in Punch, (ed.) (1983), pp. 169–93.

Manwaring-White, S. (1983), The Policing Revolution (Brighton: Harvester).

Marshall, G. (1965), Police and Government (London: Methuen).

Mawby, R. (1979), Policing the City (Westmead: Saxon House).

Mayo, E. (1945), *The Social Problems of an Industrial Civilisation* (Boston, Mass.: Harvard University Press).

Moore, C., and Brown, J. (1981), *Community versus Crime* (London: Bedford Square Press).

Morgan, R. (1985), *Setting the PACE: Police Community Consultation Arrangements in England and Wales* (University of Bath Press).

Morgan, R., and Maggs, C. (1984), *Following Scarman: A Survey of Formal Police/Community Consultation Arrangements in Provincial Police Authorities in England and Wales* (University of Bath Press).

Mouffe, C. (1979a) 'Hegemony and ideology in Gramsci' in C. Mouffe, (ed.) (1979b), pp. 168–204.

Mouffe, C. (ed.) (1979b), *Gramsci and Marxist Theory* (London: Routledge & Kegan Paul).

Newman, Sir Kenneth (1978), 'Prevention *in extremis* – the preventive role of the police in Northern Ireland', in Cranfield Papers, (1978), pp. 193–205.

Pahl, J. (ed.) (1985), *Private Violence and Public Policy: The Needs of Battered Women and the Response of the Public Services* (London: Routledge & Kegan Paul).

Parker, S. (1985), 'The legal background', in Pahl, (ed.) (1985), pp. 97–109.

Piliavin, T., and Briar, S. (1964), 'Police encounters with juveniles', *American Journal of Sociology*, 70, pp 206–14.

Police Training Council (1983), *Report of the Working Party on Community and Race Relations Training for the Police* (London: HMSO).

Politics and Power (eds) (1980), *Politics and Power 1: New Perspectives on Socialist Politics* (London: Routledge & Kegan Paul).

Politics and Power (eds) (1981), *Politics and Power 4: Law, Politics and Justice* (London: Routledge & Kegan Paul).

Pounder, C., and Anderson, S. (n.d.), *The Police Use of Computers*, Occasional Publication No. 1 (Edinburgh: Technical Authors' Group (Scotland)).

Punch, M. (1979a), *Policing the Inner City: A Study of Amsterdam's Warmoesstraat* (London: Macmillan).

Punch, M. (1979b), 'The secret social service', in Holdaway, (ed.) (1979), pp. 102–17.

Punch, M. (1981), 'Management and control of organizations: occupational deviance, responsibility and accountability', Inaugural Lecture, Nijenrode (Leiden: Stenfert Kroese).

Punch, M. (ed.) (1983), *Control in the Police Organization* (Cambridge, Mass.: MIT).

Race and Class (1979), *Police against Black People* (London: Institute of Race Relations).

Raisbeck, B. L. (1976), 'The legal framework', in M. Borland (ed.), *Violence in the Family* (Manchester University Press), pp. 88–106.

Rees, T., Stevens, P., and Willis, C. (1979), 'Race, crime and arrests', *Home Office Research Bulletin*, no. 8 (London: HMSO).

Regan, D. (1983), *Are the Police under Control?*, Research Reports Paper 1 (London: Social Affairs Unit).

Reiner, R. (1981), 'The politics of police powers', in Politics and Power, (eds.) (1981), pp. 27–52.

Reiner, R. (1983), 'The politicization of the police in Britain', in Punch, (ed.) (1983), pp. 126–48.

Reiner, R. (1985a), 'Police and race relations', in Baxter and Koffman, (eds.) (1985), pp. 149–87.

Reiner, R. (1985b), *The Politics of the Police* (Brighton: Wheatsheaf).

Reiss, A. J. (1971), *The Police and the Public* (New Haven, Conn.: Yale University Press).

Reiss, A. J., and Bordua, D. J. (1967), 'Environment and organization: a perspective on the police', in D. Bordua (ed.), *The Police: Six Sociological Essays* (New York: Wiley), pp. 25–55.

Reuss-Ianni, E., and Ianni, F. A. J. (1983), 'Street cops and management cops: the two cultures of policing', in Punch, (ed.) (1983), pp. 251–74.

Roberts, B. (1982), 'The debate on "sus"', in E. Cashmore and B. Troyna (eds.), *Black Youth in Crisis* (London: Allen & Unwin), pp. 100–28.

Rosenberg, D. (1971), 'The sociology of the police and sociological liberalism', unpublished ms., Oxford Polytechnic.

Royal Commission on Criminal Procedure (1981), *Report*, Cmnd 8092 (London: HMSO).

Royal Commission on the Police (1962), *Final Report*, Cmnd 1728 (London: HMSO).

Scarman, Lord (1982), *The Scarman Report: The Brixton Disorders 10–12 April 1981* (Harmondsworth: Penguin); originally published in 1981 as Cmnd 8427 by HMSO.

Scott, E. J., and Percy, S. L. (1983), 'Gatekeeping police services: police operators and dispatches', in R. R. Bennett (ed.), *Police at Work: Policy Issues and Analysis* (Beverly Hills, Calif.: Sage), pp. 127–44.

Sherman, L. W. (1978), *Scandal and Reform: Controlling Police Corruption* (Berkeley: University of California Press).

Sherman, L. W. (1983), 'Reducing police gun use: critical events, administrative policy, and organizational change', in Punch (ed.) (1983), pp. 98–125.

Simey, M. (1985), *Government by Consent: The Principle and Practice of Accountability in Local Government* (London: Bedford Square Press).

Sivanandan, A. (1985), 'Britain's gulags', *New Socialist*, no. 32, November, pp. 13–15.

Skolnick, J. (1975), *Justice Without Trial*, 2nd edn (New York: Wiley).

Smart, B. (1983), *Foucault, Marxism and Critique* (London: Routledge & Kegan Paul).

Smart, B. (1985), *Michel Foucault* (Chichester: Ellis Horwood).

Smith, D. J. (1983), *Police and People in London, Vol. III: A Survey of Police Officers* (London: Policy Studies Institute).

Smith, D. J., and Gray, J. (1983), *Police and People in London, Vol. IV: The Police in Action* (London: Policy Studies Institute).

Spencer, S. (1985), *Called to Account: The Case for Police Accountability in England and Wales* (London: National Council for Civil Liberties).

State Research (1980), 'Policing the eighties: the iron fist', *State Research Bulletin*, vol. 3, no. 19, August/September, pp. 146–68.

Sumner, C. (1979), *Reading Ideologies: An Investigation into the Marxist Theory of Ideology and Law* (London: Academic Press).

Taylor, F. W. (1911), *Scientific Management* (New York: Harper).

Tifft, L. L. (1978), 'Control systems, social bases of power and power exercise in police organisations', in P. K. Manning and J. Van Maanen (eds.), *Policing: A View from the Street* (Santa Monica, Calif.: Goodyear), pp. 90–105.

Van Maanen, J. (1983), 'The boss: first-line supervision in an American police agency', in Punch (ed.) (1983), pp. 275–317.

Walter, T. (1981), 'Complaints against the police', *Poly Law Review*, vol. 6, no. 2, spring, pp. 77–83.

Warren, K., and Tredinnick, D. (1982), *Protecting the Police* (London: Conservative Political Centre).

Weatheritt, M. (1983), 'Community policing: does it work and how do we know? A review of research', in T. Bennett (ed.), *The Future of Policing*, Cropwood Papers 15 (Cambridge: Institute of Criminology), pp. 127–42.

Weber, M. (1968), 'Bureaucracy', in *Economy and Society*, Vol. 3, edited by G. Roth and C. Wittich (New York: Bedminster), pp. 956–1005.

Westley, W. (1970), *Violence and the Police: A Sociological Study of Law, Custom and Morality* (Massachusetts: MIT).

Wilden, A. (1980), *System and Structure: Essays in Communication and Exchange* (London: Tavistock).

Wilson, J. Q. (1968), *Varieties of Police Behaviour: The Management of Law and Order in Eight Communities* (Cambridge, Mass.: Harvard University Press).

Wycoff, M. (1982), 'Evaluating the crime-effectiveness of municipal police', in J. R. Greene (ed.), *Managing Police Work: Issues and Analysis* (Beverly Hills, Calif.: Sage), pp. 15–36.

INDEX OF NAMES

INDEX OF SUBJECTS